# Rock and Roll vs. Modern Life

# Rock and Roll vs. Modern Life

Seth Kim-Cohen

BLOOMSBURY ACADEMIC

NEW YORK • LONDON • OXFORD • NEW DELHI • SYDNEY

BLOOMSBURY ACADEMIC
Bloomsbury Publishing Inc
1385 Broadway, New York, NY 10018, USA
50 Bedford Square, London, WC1B 3DP, UK
29 Earlsfort Terrace, Dublin 2, Ireland

BLOOMSBURY, BLOOMSBURY ACADEMIC and the Diana logo are trademarks of
Bloomsbury Publishing Plc

First published in the United States of America 2023

ISBN: HB: 979-8-7651-0131-5
PB: 979-8-7651-0132-2
ePDF: 979-8-7651-0133-9
eBook: 979-8-7651-0130-8

Typeset by Deanta Global Publishing Services, Chennai, India

**For Noa**
*and your super bears*

*Sometimes I feel like a human movie, y'know, like, people are watching a movie and sometimes what they forget is that they are also the movie that I'm watching.*

—Patti Smith

# Contents

| | | |
|---|---|---|
| 1 | That's Peanut Butter! | 1 |
| 2 | Counter, Culture, Counterculture | 19 |
| 3 | We Shall Raise the Flag of Nothingness | 35 |
| 4 | The Politics and Ethics of Ecstasy | 55 |
| 5 | Funk Lessons | 69 |
| 6 | Gnostics of the North, *or* Music to Recolonize Your Anxious Capitalist Dreams by | 93 |
| 7 | All the Needles Are on Red | 111 |
| 8 | The Wee Hours of Etc. | 129 |
| 9 | The Feeling You've Been Cheated | 153 |
| 10 | Video Killed the Radio Star | 175 |
| | *Acknowledgments* | 197 |
| | *Works Cited* | 200 |
| | *Index* | 207 |

# That's Peanut Butter!

I am a camera. You are a camera. All of us, cameras. We've learned to be cameras from watching our world on screens. Our TV sets and movies, our computer monitors and phones, animated bus-stop billboards, and the great glass curtains of the infinite metropolis, framing or reflecting the world from inside or out. We are granted access to all that the world is from the objective stance of the camera's perspective. Look there's a seagull. Now a passenger train, a bullet, a baseball bat, a bottle of beer. We are hungry eyes expecting to be fed. The screens oblige. They feed us not just image after image, but the image of images. We come to see the world as the camera sees it: flat and forever familiar, made bright and thin like cellophane, and smooth and flickering, always on the verge of forever going away. This is the modern world.

Images of these images are legion: *The Truman Show. The Matrix. Synecdoche, New York.* We love to be reminded of our own screenishness. Guy Debord and Jean Baudrillard wrote of "the spectacle" and of "simulacra." The contemporary imagination imagines reality in pixels. We're watching ourselves watching ourselves living our thin, flickering lives. Cameras all.

Or camera-actors. Perhaps, once upon a time, what Shakespeare said was true, that all the world's a stage and all the men and women merely players. But cameras changed all that. Now we are camera-actors, playing not beneath the proscenium and across the fourth wall, but into and through the aperture of the lens. We play to an invisible audience, represented on our side of the divide by a technological avatar: the ground convex glass, the telescoping Swiss cylinder, the blinking red light. We forge our identities in the crucible of these reflections. Platforms happily (and profitably) oblige: Instagram, Facebook, Tik Tok—or whatever platform you're using now, maybe only months after I've written this. Refresh the browser. New screen.

Picture this: the camera dutifully trained on the spectacle. A man contorts. All sinew and sweat, he's dolled himself up suitably for the camera: silver gloves extend halfway up his forearms, a dog collar snugly around his neck. He glowers, he shrugs, he mugs. He's playing to the cameras and the cameras reciprocate, following his every gyration, zooming in tandem with his provocations. Behind him, a band roars out chords and Detroit-piston-driven beats, providing an excuse for his scowling grunts and exhortations. It is 1970. We're in southwest Ohio for the Cincinnati Pop Festival. Well, that's not exactly right. We're cameras, remember. We're watching footage of the Cincinnati Pop Festival on our screens. The whole twelve-hour mess has been edited down to ninety minutes for broadcast by local station, WLWT, and packaged as one of the first televised rock festival broadcasts. On television it is called *Midsummer Rock*. The evening news crew—square and smiling, besuited and bemused—talks us through it. The broadcast's host, Jack Lescoulie, acts as naïve witness, translating the goings-on for the uninitiated:

> One of the things that amazes me is that they do not go about this in a show business way. For instance, when somebody says "here's an act," and they announce the act, they may very well tune up for 10 or 15 minutes before they ever play the first number that they're going to play. And the kids don't seem to mind this at all. They watch it all and listen to the tune-up and listen to them check speakers . . . and I think we've got some action coming up now. We'll leave [reporter] Bob Waller for the moment and go to the stage and listen to Iggy and the Stooges. (Jack Lescoulie, host of *Midsummer Rock*, WLWT https://www .youtube.com/watch?v=Pf-sDjS8YR8, accessed 200104)

The broadcast cuts to the stage. We are the camera, positioned behind Ron Asheton. Over and beyond the neck of his guitar, Iggy Pop's plasticene torso is expelled upward and out of his low-ride jeans. Iggy bends forward at ninety degrees, taunting and taming the audience. At 10:43:54 of the video's time code, our perspective shifts. We are in front of Iggy now, seeing him as the audience does. Behind him is a giant, c. 1970, TV camera, trained on Iggy from our previous vantage point framed by Asheton's guitar neck. We are a camera looking at a camera, the space between mediated by a man grunt-singing about his own double predicament, caught in the crossfire of the cameras' twinned gazes, "She got a TV eye on me."

If we are the TV eye, then "she" is modernism, modernity, the modern world . . . take your pick. The point is not to name this phenomenon, nor to engage the etymological or categorical debates about these related terms. Instead, what we're after here is the tension between what the TV eye wants and what Iggy wants.

Even more to the point, we're trying to distinguish two opposing conceptions of the world: one which assumes there is a frame that can be meaningfully imposed on experience in order to render it intelligible, and one which rejects the frame's restrictions and conceives of experience as an amorphous, sloshing fluidity that can't help but leak its own substance; to overflow and soak whatever's nearby while also sponging up the secretions of its surroundings.

At the 10:44:38 mark, using the mic stand as a rickety bannister, Iggy descends into the audience. Host Jack Lescoulie reports, "There goes Iggy, right into the crowd." Iggy bellows, "oh!" and Lescoulie inexplicably announces, "We've lost audio on him. This seems like a good chance to get a message in." Iggy shrieks—quite audibly—as the picture fades. On YouTube, we're spared the advertisement that would have followed when this aired in southwest Ohio in 1970. But the tension we're after is already on stark display. The TV eye must see. It must see something.

When the broadcast resumes, the Stooges are partway through the song "1970." Lescoulie informs us that "since we broke away for our message, Iggy has been in the crowd and out again three different times." At 10:46:17, Iggy dips in again. At 10:46:40 the frame and its rejection come head-to-head: "We seem to have lost him and we're trying to get a light on him now." Twenty seconds later a patch of the crowd is suddenly illuminated and Lescoulie proclaims, "there they are!" unconsciously switching from singular to plural. This amounts to an inadvertent acknowledgment of defeat. The TV eye depends on a focal point, a singularity, an "it," upon which it can center its frame. When Iggy goes into the audience, he denies the camera this center. The frame fails if it has nothing to frame. Lescoulie lets us in on this logic when he tells us that "we're trying to get a light on him now." The jig is up. The "we" trying to get the light on Iggy is, of course, most specifically, the WLWT television crew. But more broadly, it is television as a medium. It is the linear vision of the camera as inherited from the discovery of Renaissance perspective. It is the logic of marketing, which must always have a focal point, an object, at its center. And it is the endowment of a way of thinking that sheds light on topics, that focuses on ideas: a legacy passed down to the camera via the lucent metonyms of the Enlightenment. Of course, the Enlightenment is another name for what we have already called modernism, modernity, and the modern world. So this light that we are trying to get on Iggy is the framing light of modernism itself.

Iggy and Lescoulie face off. Rock and roll versus modernism. Needless to say, each is an avatar for his side. Knowingly or not, Lescoulie represents the framing, illuminated, explanatory demands of modernism. The camera must see something, framed and properly lit. The TV anchor (the term is apt: solid, centering, stabilizing) supplements the camera's plain-fact transmissions like a UN translator decoding the remarks of the LaTVian delegation. Iggy, on the other hand, writhes implacably against the camera's retention; against lights and explanations. Even his bounded body, the object of the camera's attention, melts into the air as he evacuates the frame of the stage to merge with the crowd. It is at this point that Lescoulie's clear sense of what he is watching begins to blur. He slips when he announces: "there they are!" because this isn't supposed to be about *them*. It's *him* the camera's interested in. The performer—whether Iggy or, earlier in the day, Mountain's Leslie West or Traffic's Stevie Winwood—is the focal point, the singularity, the "it," that establishes the center of this framed experience.

The frame itself, however, is multiple: the WLWT cameras, the living room TV set, the news crew exegesis, the ninety-minute packaging of this all-day event. Indeed, the framing is made literal by the broadcast, which, before and after cutting away for commercials, imposes a kind of art nouveau-hippie-Aztec frame upon the screen to help us realize that what we are watching can, in fact, be contained by the boxed medium of television. Fear not, mothers and fathers, these convulsing long-haired demons of the changing times are safely contained like the comforting familiarity of the products of modern life: deodorants and ball point pens, soft drinks, and sedans (Figure 1.1).

**Figure 1.1** The title frame for the *Midsummer Rock* broadcast of the Cincinnati Pop Festival on WLWT.

Yet, when Iggy wades into the crowd like a cranberry farmer into his bog, the camera—that is, each of us—doesn't know what to do. The Stooges (Scott and Ron Asheton, Dave Alexander) are like ornaments, like columns on the façade of a Greek temple. When Iggy disappears into the crowd, the temple vanishes and with it all the gods. To whom do we pray?

Alright cameras, let's zoom out a bit. By 1970, there was already some sense that the paradigms were shifting. The Civil Rights Movement refused the frames that had repressed African Americans and sustained the fictional narratives that excused such repression. Popular pushback against the war in Southeast Asia announced a new relationship between the governed and the government. Mass media found itself pulled in competing directions. In 1968, even Walter Cronkite was forced to admit that something was amiss. Campuses erupted in dissent. Cities burned. Hatred and a uniquely Americanized form of violence took the lives of a president, a preacher, and more than one Panther. In popular culture, Dylan and the Beatles had made it clear that style and substance were being revised before our eyes and ears.

During the second half of the 1960s, modernism's frames became porous. They no longer held their objects as securely as they once had. Commentators on both sides of the divide sensed the breach. Possibly the most astute of these was the art critic, Michael Fried, who in 1967 published the essay "Art and Objecthood," in *Artforum*. Fried's aesthetics developed in the prodigious shade of the critic, Clement Greenberg. Like Greenberg, Fried was, in 1967, an avowed modernist, something like a zealot holding close to a set of fundamental beliefs about art. Both critics saw their task, and the task of art, as a constituent part of modernity and modernity as a coextensive with the Enlightenment project. Just as science had divided its realm into component parts, which together constitute the whole of the natural world, so too should art understand itself as a composed of distinguishable practices and forms, which together constitute the whole of the aesthetic world. If biology can be distinguished from chemistry and both from physics, each framed in order to better understand the phenomena of their discipline, then the art critic and the artist should be able to distinguish painting from sculpture and both from theater. In doing so, each discipline would be "entrench[ed] more firmly in its area of competence" (Greenberg 5). Greenberg explicitly connected this line of thinking to that of an Enlightenment philosopher, Immanuel Kant, declaring Kant "the first real Modernist" (Greenberg 5).

It would be difficult to overstate the importance of Fried's "Art and Objecthood." Nonetheless, if you don't know the essay, you will be convinced that overstating is exactly what I'm doing. Since its publication more than fifty years ago, symposia have been convened, journal issues edited, panel discussions organized, all to readjudicate the essay's claims. Nearly every recognized critic of postwar American art has weighed in. To this day, the essay appears on art history syllabi with the frequency and insistence of insects at a porch light, fritzing against (and for) the enlightenment of modernism. You would be hard-pressed to think of another piece of art criticism that has remained as actively foregrounded in the aesthetic imagination for this half-century-plus. What's more, in many ways, it deserves this prominence. It is an astonishing act of tea leaf reading.

Essentially, from a small set of geometric sculptural forms made by young artists including Donald Judd, Robert Morris, and Tony Smith, Fried arrives at the conclusion that modernism as a project, as a worldview, and as a coherent aesthetic program, is under attack. If this new work—known now as "minimalism"—is taken seriously and allowed to encroach on the serious discourse and exhibition of art in the late 1960s, then calamity awaits. This is not, in Fried's view, a simple matter of taste, but an eschatological struggle. For Fried, as for Greenberg, modernist art represents a reprieve from the tyranny of objects. In their view, the modern world has become little more than a network of things: soup cans and transistor radios, Chevrolets and mohair sweaters, propping up our relations to ourselves and to each other. Works by Judd, Morris, and Smith are too closely aligned—formally, ontologically—with such literal objects. They fail to do what art ought to do—to transcend everyday existence; to deliver an experience above, beyond, and different from, the one delivered by the furnishings and furniture, the appliances and tchotchkes of our workaday world. For this reason, Fried refers to these artists as "literalists" and their work as "literalism."

Sometime in the 1950s, Tony Smith packed three of his Cooper Union art students into his car and took what I suppose we must call a "joy ride" down the unfinished New Jersey Turnpike.

> It was a dark night and there were no lights or shoulder markers, lines, railings or anything at all except the dark pavement moving through the landscape of the flats, rimmed by hills in the distance, but punctuated by stacks, towers, fumes and colored lights. (Smith)

This was Smith's "road to Damascus" moment (but for the fact that he was on the road to Paramus). On the turnpike, Smith experienced something that art had never provided. "The experience on the road was something mapped out but not socially recognized. I thought to myself, it ought to be clear that's the end of art" (Smith). Careening down the dark road, Smith's experience is unbounded, uncontained in an object, dislocated. Formalism is no use to you here. Rather it is the entirety of the situation that delivers Smith's experience. As he writes, "There is no way you can frame it, you just have to experience it" (Smith). For Michael Fried, this unframeability is precisely the problem. As he writes, "What Smith's remarks seem to suggest is that the more effective . . . the setting is made, the more superfluous the works themselves become" (Fried 20). Without an object, the borders of which can be definitively ascertained, this experience liquefies. One can assert that it then assumes the shape of its container. But this merely kicks the problem of borders down the road, from object to subject. The intractable problem, as Fried sees it, is that Smith's experience cannot be properly contained. It does not depend on the work, but on a complex of shifting, indistinct forces and factors. As such the work cannot be stabilized in formal or ontological terms. Its boundaries shift in space. Its identity and meaning shift in time. Such experience is irredeemably relational, dependent on considerations outside itself. As with Gertrude Stein's assessment of Oakland, for Tony Smith on the Turnpike, there is no there there. There's no it in it.

Although he doesn't pursue this line of thinking, Fried's argument bears some resemblance to Marx's critique of the commodity as "a definite social relation between men, that assumes, in their eyes, the fantastic form of a relation between things" (Marx 48). Fried also worries, maybe for different reasons, that mere objects might become stand-ins for other relations: those between people, yes, but more importantly for Fried, between a singular subject and a variety of experience that transcends the everyday. When standing before a great work of modernist art, Fried says, one escapes the quotidian demands of the telephone and the coffee cup and enters into a relation with the wholeness of experience. Such an encounter eschews even the pestiness of the ticking clock, existing in what Fried refers to as "presentness."

To confirm the implications of Fried's position, one need look no further than the epigraph that introduces the essay. Excerpted from Perry Miller's biography of the eighteenth-century Puritan theologian, Jonathan Edwards, the epigraph describes "a meditation [Edwards] seldom allowed to reach print" (Miller, quoted in Fried 12). Edwards suggests that every moment of our lives, each of us is privy to the moment of biblical creation because the world is constantly being recreated before our senses, "it is certain with me that the world exists anew every moment; that the existence of things every moment ceases and is every moment renewed." Edwards concludes from this that "we every moment see the same proof of a God as we should have seen if we had seen Him create the world at first." (Edwards, quoted in Miller, and subsequently in Fried 12) This instantaneous creation of the universe, delivered in what theologians and philosophers have called "the blink of an eye," escapes the earthbound experience of everyday objects in laborious time, delivering a kind of transcendence that Fried names in the essay's final sentence: "Presentness is grace" (Fried 23).

It is this presentness, this transcendence, that Fried prizes in encounters with modernist art. And it is this same experience—an experience that Fried licenses us to call "religious"—that is attacked by the work of the minimalists. Their work, says Fried, invites a kind of participation that he terms "theatrical." What he means by this is that the work "performs"; that it does what it is meant to do, delivers its inherent aesthetic message, only if there is someone there to see it. Minimalist works are, in a sense, like theatrical productions. If the show is about to begin and the players peek out from behind the curtain to see that not a single seat is filled, that not one soul has shown up for tonight's performance, the actors do not take the stage anyway and deliver their lines. Instead, they take off their costumes, remove their greasepaint, and head home (or to the bar). Without an audience the work does not happen.

According to Fried, the same cannot be said of the modernist work. A painting by Mark Rothko or Jules Olitski does not depend upon what Fried calls the "beholder." A great abstract expressionist painting can be put away in storage, in a climate-controlled room in the basement of the museum. The lights can be turned off, the door locked. And still the great modernist painting would continue to be great. It would continue to deliver. Because, as Greenberg's and Fried's aesthetic would have it, what is great about the great modernist painting is inherent to the painting. It is there, on the canvas. Its greatness is a product of form, of accounting for the shape of the canvas and solving the problems it presents with technique and formal mastery. In the end, both critics insist that the work be "convincing"; that the beholder finds themself "convinced" by what they encounter on the canvas and in the work.

Picture yourself in a room with Robert Morris's *Untitled* (Mirrored Cubes), first made in 1965 and then reconstructed in 1971. This is an ideal work for a camera like you. As you enter, you pick up movement on one of the cube's surfaces. Almost immediately, you realize that what you're seeing is your own legs. You move closer. As you do, you see less of yourself, but in greater detail. You shift to your left and one leg appears in the surface of the mirror perpendicular to the first surface. You play with these angles and the perspective of your lens, swaying left to right, modulating the contents of the cube's surfaces. Just then you realize that you're selling yourself, or the work (probably both), short. There are four cubes. The variations multiply endlessly. You can catch bits of yourself in multiple mirrors, flickering your legs across these cooly kaleidoscoping screens of reflective glass. You can dolly in or out, affecting angles and the mise-en scène. It should have occurred to you instantly!—you can stand between cubes, producing an infinite regress: reflection of reflection of reflection of reflection. Visual eternity. Someone else enters the room and your visual universe becomes a multiverse.

Fun, perhaps, but Fried is having none of it. "Literalist sensibility is theatrical because, to begin with, it is concerned with the actual circumstances in which the beholder encounters literalist work. [. . .] the experience of literalist art is of an object *in a situation*—one which, virtually by definition, *includes the beholder*" (Fried 15).

So what's the big deal? you might ask. Aren't we already concerned with the circumstances and the situations in which we encounter art? And shouldn't we be? Is it even possible to disregard circumstance and situation? Well, that's the crux of our biscuit, of Fried's and Iggy's. It is precisely here, on this very point, that rock and roll and modernism make contact; where they come together only to part ways.

Let's pan on our tripods back to Iggy in Cincinnati. Just after Jack Lescoulie announces "we're trying to get a light on him," inadvertently providing a kind of advertising slogan for the demands of Enlightenment-modernism, Iggy, swallowed up by the crowd, sings the reprise from "1970": "I feel alright, I feel alright." A woman's voice, close enough to be picked up by Iggy's mic, responds, "Are you alright?" The performance—singular, sanctified, amplified, illuminated, and framed—is breached. The retaining walls of convention, media, and capital, collapse at a casual touch: "Are you alright?"—a contravention that Fried would never abide. Try asking Barnett Newman's *Vir Heroicus Sublimis* (*Man, heroic and sublime*) "are you alright?" Your voice, your entreaty, your concern, would be devoured instantly by the modernist abyss, the monolithic, the imperturbable, the self-sufficient, the singular's deep disdain for everything but itself.

But no one said it would be easy to repudiate our camericity. A few seconds later, as Lescoulie proclaims, "there they are," this same woman's voice pleads with Iggy "Please, lemme take a picture." She is unable or unwilling to relinquish her role as viewer, audience, beholder. More to the point, she is unwilling to allow Iggy to relinquish his role as the beheld. Simultaneously, this unknown woman—merely an incorporeal voice—acts as both a camera, forming-by-framing the object of modernist desire, and a node or a switch point in the amorphous mass of a post-camera network, the desires of which are fugitive and unframeable.

"A friend and I were getting stoned and watching the TV eye's broadcast of the Cincinnati Pop Festival the other night." When WLWT originally aired its broadcast of *Midsummer Rock*, one of its contemporary viewers happened to be the most astute rock critic of the moment. Lester Bangs's judgment was summary: "Most of the show was boring" (Bangs 1987, 34). But Bangs perks up at the halfway mark when the Stooges hit the stage. And vis-à-vis their performance and that of Alice Cooper, Bangs spins a theory of rock and roll's necessity.

> What we need are more rock "stars" willing to make fools of themselves, absolutely jump off the deep end and make the audience embarrassed for them if necessary, so long as they have not one shred of dignity or mythic corona left. Because then the whole damn pompous edifice of this supremely ridiculous rock 'n' roll industry, set up to grab bucks by conning youth and encouraging fantasies of a puissant "youth culture," would collapse, and with it would collapse the careers of the hyped talentless nonentities who breed off of it. (Bangs 1987, 34)

Bangs puts his finger on the same button we're trying to push here. He does so in real time, without the benefit of hindsight. His response is agitated and intended to agitate, indicting the apparatus of his modern world, c. 1970. What he calls the "rock 'n' roll industry" is a synecdoche for late capitalism, the society of the spectacle, the modern world. Bangs is a true believer in the ability of rock and roll to provide a picture of, a blueprint for, a better world. He doesn't see this working through a positive-vibes 1960s, self-realization agenda, nor through entrepreneurial 1980s, bootstrap directives. Rather, Bang imagines something like psychoanalysis or exorcism: a clear-eyed confrontation with individual and collective demons. Our sickness manifests in our fantasies and jokes. Art, too mannered, too formal, can't do the dirty work that the disease demands. The chore requires desperation and depravity in kind. And rock and roll, unschooled and adolescent, rushes in where Fried's modernism fears to tread.

> Some of the most powerful esthetic experiences of our time [. . .] set their audiences up just this way, externalizing and magnifying their secret core of sickness which is reflected in the geeks they mock and the lurid fantasies they

consume, just as our deepest fears and prejudices script the jokes we tell each other. This is where the Stooges work. They mean to put you on that stage, which is why they are super-modern, though nothing near to Art. (Bangs 52)

Bangs calls the Stooges not modern but supermodern. I take Bangs to mean super—not as in "to a great or extreme degree." The Stooges are not exemplars of the modern. I take Bangs to mean "above; over; beyond"—existing beyond the border of the modern, spatially above it, temporally after it, categorically distinct. So here we have micro- and macro-versions of the same fundamental friction. Just as Iggy subverts the frame that the camera seeks to impose upon diffuse and dispersed experience, the supermodern bleeds out beyond the borders of the modern, beyond what the category is capable of framing.

This friction is endemic to the late 1960s and 1970s. It plays out not only in visual art, literature, and film but also in basic conceptions of the relation between government and the governed, between a kind of unencumbered human experience and that same experience quantified and framed as motivated by, and producing, economic activity. We see this friction in the clashes of cultures as the sheltering logic of colonization recedes, revealing bald exploitation and unfounded presumptions of racial, ethnic, technological, and historical superiority. Throughout Asia, Latin America, and Africa, the colonized don't merely fight back against their colonial oppressors, but simultaneously dismantle the self-serving frames that had legitimized centuries of brutality and plunder. In the United States, this same dismantling is directed at the subjugation of African Americans and at the infrastructural racism whose initial foundations were laid by the savage abduction and enslavement of generations of Africans. Much of what had underpinned the local and global orders of the postwar decades began to buckle under the pressure of these new supermodern intensities.

It is in this context that Bangs recognizes Iggy as an archetype of the supermodern. Oddly, as Bangs's account of the Cincinnati Pop Festival unspools it becomes apparent that the signal moment of the event, the moment in which the modern is grasped like a branch and snapped across the knee of the supermodern, does not even involve Iggy. Instead, it is Alice Cooper who exemplifies all the attributes that Bangs wants to celebrate. But as a figure, Cooper can't hold the position that Bangs is constructing. He is too schticky, too B-movie, too aware of the tongue in his cheek. Bangs transmogrifies Cooper's act that night into Iggy's corpus; into his body and into his body of work, allowing the act to make greater sense, to land (in Bangs's retelling at least) with a thump that travels seismographically well beyond the confines of Cincinnati's Crosley Field and ripples through the rest of the 1970s.

This mythical crack—once only a legend set down upon the hallowed pages of *Creem* by a rock and roll scribe, a true believer—can now be seen at one's leisure on YouTube. Let us once again remove our lens caps to focus in on Alice Cooper, with campy black eye makeup, shiny reptile-skin pants, and matching shawl, at the stage's edge. He honors the footlights' age-old barrier, only pretending to threaten to cross it. As the band (also named Alice Cooper) chugs ham-fistedly through the song "Black Juju," Cooper (the singer) crouches, clutching the chain of a pocket watch. The watch pulses from side to side as Cooper shushes his band and the audience. The faux-modal, counterfeit psychedelia of the song settles into a jejune ticktock supplied by the higher register of the piano. Cooper launches into a sideshow hypnotism routine. Deliberately, he annunciates, "Bodies need rest / We all need rest / Sleep, easy sleep."

And then, at 10:59:41 of the video's time code, it happens. It's difficult at first to understand what we've witnessed. The stage is dark, the video quality is decidedly 1970 and transferred across analogue media more than once. Our attention, lulled by Cooper's entreaties, and perhaps more effectively by the band's tedious performance, is startled by an errant, dull, two-beat *thhh-wupp* . . . Cooper falls back from the balls of his toes to his haunches and looks down to surmise the source of the offence.

> Some accomplished marksman in the mob lobbed a whole cake (or maybe it was a pie-yeah, let's say it was a pie just for the sake of the fantasy I'm about to promulgate) which hit him square in the face. So there he was: Alice Cooper, rock star, crouched frontstage in the middle of his act with a faceful of pie and cream with clots dripping from his ears and chin. (Bangs 35)

At first, Cooper merely continues, "rest . . ." the watch still swinging on its chain. He scoops up a handful of cream from the stage and muddles it between palm and thumb like a luckless gambler contemplating what could be his last roll of the dice. Again he shushes the band and the crowd. "Sleep . . . sleep" he implores, and he fake snores. The whole enterprise rises to the level of a kid's bedroom fantasy of what a vaudeville production is supposed to look like. The band starts to accelerate, the ticktock now supplied by guitar harmonics. "But come back in the morning," declares Cooper, leaving the phrase to hang un-requited. An organ and unsteady slide guitar strain to give the sonic clutter some form. Cooper finishes the thought (I guess), "come back hard." The organ jumps awkwardly to a higher octave, establishing a two-chord pattern. Cooper bounces in his crouch and the song explodes as he shrieks, "Wake up! Wake up! Wake up! Wake up!" The band kicks into a vaguely metal descending riff and Cooper, for the first time in almost six minutes, rises to his feet. He scoops up another handful of cream and at 11:01:39, he extends his arm out over the audience and slaps the wad of cream into his face. He then repeats this gesture over and over again, scooping up more cream as needed. And this provides the material for the fantasy that Bangs promised to promulgate. Cooper's response to the pie in the face is not to storm off the stage in indignation, but to incorporate the pie into his act, to bring it quite literally into his corpus, into his body and the body of his work. There is a fundamental distinction between this incorporation and the distance that Fried prescribes between the modernist art work and the beholder. For Bangs, Cooper's gesture represents a de-hierarchization and the invention of a cultural form that is fundamentally participatory, even democratic.

> With Alice Cooper you have the prerogative to express your reaction to his show in a creative way. Most rock stars have their audiences so cowed it's nauseating. What blessed justice it would be if all rock stars had to contend with what A.C. elicits, if it became a common practice and method of passing judgment for audiences to regularly fling pies in the faces of performers whom they thought were coming on with a load of bullshit. Because the top rockers have a mythic aura around them, the "superstar," and that's a basically unhealthy state of things, in fact it's the very virus that's fucking up rock, a subspecies of the virus [. . .] which infests "our" culture from popstars to politics (imagine throwing a pie in the face of Eldridge Cleaver! Joan Baez!), and which the Stooges uncategorically oppose as an advance platoon in the nearing war to clear conned narcoleptic mindscreens of the earth. (Bangs 1987, 36)

While it's Cooper who takes the pie in the face and who accepts it as both the welcomed voice of his audience (the people) and an impromptu prop, it is the Stooges who get credit for opposing the virus that infects our culture. It is the Stooges who wage war against the "conned narcoleptic mindscreens." For Bangs, it's impossible to disregard circumstance and situation, as Fried implored. It's not simply that Cooper or the Stooges are making the happenings part of their work, or making their work a happening. It's that, as the old adage would have it, "shit happens." Or to put it in a way that a modernist like Fried might understand, "circumstances happen." While *Vir Heroicus Sublimis* is unlikely to take a pie in the face while it hangs austerely in the David Geffen galleries on the fourth floor of the Museum of Modern Art in New York, you may encounter it beside a pair of vociferous lovers quarrelling or while a hot dog scarfed hurriedly on your way uptown begins to make its presence known in your lower GI. What's a beholder to do?

Bangs's esteem for the Stooges is produced not only by Iggy's willingness to share the seats of his power—his spotlight, his microphone—but also because a Stooges performance is a site of contestation. "The Stooge act is wide open. Do your worst, People, falsify Iggy and the Stooges, get your kicks and biffs. It's your night!" (Bangs 1987, 38). This vision is, fundamentally, utopian; democratic at least, or a kind of unkempt offspring of an anarchic socialism in which the performer is the boss, turning over the means of production to the workers, the audience, the people. Alice Cooper offers a less radical vision,

> an outrageous blitz of shifting sexual identities and "perversions" that's just the old *épater la bourgeoisie* riff again, and for all the talk of Artaud and audiences convulsed with certain unstable souls in frothing fits, it still and f'rever will remain that A.C. is putting on a show in the hoary DC manner, and with fewer and fewer people game for sprained sexual sensibilities, since nobody gives a fuck anymore, a seemingly futuristic band like this must fall back on its music, which is too bad, because there's not much happening there outside the context of the act, as their records bear out. (Bangs 1987, 38–9)

To accommodate circumstance and situation is not to turn a blind eye (or a deaf ear) to the work. The Stooges are Bangs's paragon because amidst, and regardless of, the circumstances and situation, they deliver ballast. At the eye of the circumstantial storm, Iggy provides, not so much a point of focus—that would merely perpetuate the old cameric modernism—but a magnetic pole, attractive and repellant. At 10:47:30 of the *Midsummer Rock* video, Iggy hoists himself onto the shoulders of the crowd around him. He rises like a dimestore Jesus, walking on the water of the people. He strikes a pose, right leg forward, silver-gloved right hand outstretched and pointing forward, as if impelling his troops to the walls of the castle. The image is now so iconic that you can purchase a statuette of it for a mere $210 (+$40 shipping) (Figure 1.2).

By the time Iggy assumes the statuette's position, someone in the crowd below him is already holding a large jar aloft, seemingly offering it as part of this communal-sacrificial moment. Iggy crouches down on the audience's shoulders and delivers two impassioned, tremulous middle fingers. Then he reaches down for the jar. He stands back up, extracts a handful of the jar's contents, and smears it across his bare chest before flinging the remainder exuberantly into the audience. Modernism can't resist the compulsion to append a frame to these

**Figure 1.2** Wax Face Toys' Iggy Pop statuette.

fugitive goings-on—de-staged, spontaneous, inexplicable. But the only frame Lescoulie can offer is utterly insufficient. "That's peanut butter!" he explains, as if this could possibly explain it. The statuette too falls prey to this urge to fix the transience of this wildering moment in the stasis of black resin; to render it inert: ("from Latin, *in-* [expressing negation] + *ars, art-* 'skill, art'") ("Inert," New Oxford American Dictionary).

For Fried (as for Greenberg before him), modernist art—Abstract Expressionism, paradigmatically—represents the most advanced stage in the evolutionary development of visual art. Greenberg asserts that painters have always disguised the fact that their craft consists of nothing more than applying pigment to a surface. They do so through what Greenberg calls pictorial illusionism. "Realistic, illusionist art had dissembled the medium, using art to conceal art. Modernism used art to call attention to art" (Greenberg 6). Abstract Expressionism, finally, reveals a painting (and painting as a medium) for what it is, the negotiation of formal issues via the application of paint to canvas. The modernist critics celebrate the arrival of art at its point of greatest advance, its culmination, its long-sought zenith.

Bangs frequently positions rock and roll as art's Other. He says of the Stooges "that their music is as important as the product of any rock group working today, although you better never call it art or you may wind up with a deluxe pie in the face" (1987, 32). The Stooges generate their effects as a by-product of their crude, unschooled, impulsiveness. (Although, this too, is an illusion as a listen to the *Fun House* sessions boxset—Iggy testing the rhythmic placement and the precise guttural setting of each "ugh" and "yeah"—will demonstrate.) The Stooges embrace the rudiments of their medium. Bangs calls their music "monotonous and simplistic on purpose" and says that "within the seemingly circumscribed confines of this fuzz-feedback territory the Stooges work deftly with musical ideas that may not be highly sophisticated (God forbid) but are certainly advanced" (Bangs 1987, 39).

With the Stooges, rock and roll arrives, not at a point of developmental apotheosis, but at a recognition and reclamation of its founding self-understandings; understandings that reject specialization and technique, the dilettantism and connoisseurship that build barriers between artist and their art on the one hand, and the audience, the beholder, the people, on the other.

> It comes out of an illiterate chaos gradually taking shape as a uniquely personal style, emerges from a tradition of American music that runs from the wooly rags of backwoods string bands up to the magic promise eternally made and occasionally fulfilled by rock: that a band can start out bone-primitive, untutored and uncertain, and evolve into a powerful and eloquent ensemble. [. . .] rock is mainly about beginnings, about youth and uncertainty and growing through and out of them. And asserting yourself way before you know what the fuck you're doing. [. . .] It can't grow up—when it does, it turns into something else which may be just as valid but is still very different from the original. (Bangs 1987, 45–6)

Of course, there's a healthy dose of naïve romance in his account. But Bangs's generally pessimistic worldview always reserves a little pocket of optimism when it comes to rock and roll. Writing about the Shaggs, eleven years after the Stooges article, Bangs proclaims that the three sisters from rural New Hampshire, crafted into a band by their father,

> are true one world humanists with an eye to our social future whose only hope is a redefined communism based on the open-hearted sharing of whatever you got with all sentient beings. Their and my religion is compassion, true Christianity with no guilt factors and no vested interest, perhaps a barter economy, but

certainly the elimination of capitalism, rape, and special-interest group hatred. (Bangs 1981)

Fried and Bangs may look and listen in very different directions for the sources of their remedies, but they share a common yearning: that art (or rock and roll) can do something that religion, politics, and capitalism have all failed to do. Each believes that art can transcend the experiences, the structures, and the values that, by the mid-1960s, had entrapped the inhabitants of the modern world in a cube of mirrors turned inside out. Cameras with nothing to look at but ourselves and our objects, each sold back to themselves and to each other in a recursive loop of buying/being bought, selling/being sold: not so much entrepreneurs of ourselves (as the champions of neoliberal ideology would have it), but *extractors* of ourselves, mining bits and/or pieces of our lives, sacrificing deposits and ore, for the smooth functioning of the smoothly framed, featureless marketplace of desacralized democracy.

# 2

# Counter, Culture, Counterculture

Norman Mailer wasn't always an ass. Or maybe he was. What do I know? Watching his pitiful fight with Rip Torn on the set of Mailer's film *Maidstone*, it's not hard to feel sorry for him. In the movie, which Mailer wrote and directed, Mailer plays a version of himself, Norman Kingsley (Kingsley is Mailer's middle name), a film director who is also running for president of the United States. *Maidstone* was made between 1968 and 1970. In 1969, during production, Mailer actually ran for mayor of New York City. The film's plot involves a shadowy group known as "PAX, C," which decides that Kingsley must be assassinated, leading to the film's final scene, which is more famous than the film itself. It has been excerpted and is something of a YouTube cult classic ("Rip Torn vs Norman Mailer") (Figure 2.1).

In an unscripted moment that apparently came as a surprise to Mailer, actor Rip Torn attacks Mailer, striking him in the head with a hammer. After the blow, Torn continues to stalk Mailer, hammer still in hand, while Mailer retreats, his arms extended to keep Torn at bay. Torn explains that he doesn't want to kill Mailer, but that he must kill Kingsley. As Torn cocks to swing the hammer a second time, the two men fall to the ground in a clumsy, thrashing embrace. Ali-Frazier this ain't. Mailer's teeth lunge for Torn's ear. The two men settle like Jell-o in a shallow bowl. They negotiate a momentary truce until Mailer elbows Torn and they're back at it. Two crew members pry them apart as Mailer's wife, Beverly Bentley, smacks Torn repeatedly in the head, Mailer's young kids shrieking in the background. Both men get back to their feet. Blood tracks a rivulet from Mailer's hairline and along his jawline. Slowly expanding seepage from Torn's partially severed ear advances across his cheek and neck. In the aftermath, at various moments, Torn can be heard saying, "I had to do that. You know that. [. . .] The picture doesn't make sense without this" ("Rip Torn vs Norman Mailer").

The fight is an allegory. Mailer becomes the victim of his own myth. As he exaggerates the facts of his life, inflating each aspect to the size and shape of fantasy,

**Figure 2.1** Norman Mailer and Rip Torn (with hammer), on the set of *Maidstone*.

Torn takes it upon himself to puncture the illusion. Mailer emerges diminished. He has lost control of his camera, literally and figuratively. Buffeted by the swirling winds of the late 1960s he can't master the frame he's damned to construct. Along with well-deserved derision, the pathetic wreckage of this love/hate, boy-on-boy scrap, elicits a kind of sympathy. The wannabe hero is an unavoidably tragic figure.

In 1961, James Baldwin paints a similar picture of Mailer, at once pitiful and sympathetic. Inimitably, Baldwin humanizes Mailer while also generalizing him as a symptom of a particular patrimonial inheritance of what we would now recognize as White Privilege. With Mailer in mind, Baldwin writes, "the thing that most white people imagine that they can salvage from the storm of life is really, in sum, their innocence" (Baldwin 270). A Black man, on the other hand, must jettison his innocence. For the White man, innocence has been walled off within. The demands of working and earning and leading and knowing look on innocence as a weakness lurking within his masculinity; an affordance that the entitlements of machismo cannot abide. Once a White man has secured his domain, he can go back to salvage his innocence. But for the Black man, innocence is a luxury that opens the door to very real violence. The Black man must live alertly, vigilantly; invulnerable to the gullibility and susceptibility of innocence. He has no innocence to salvage, because he was never allotted any in the first place.

Baldwin's essay, "The Black Boy Looks at the White Boy," originally published in *Esquire*, is a response to Mailer's essay, "The White Negro," published in *Dissent* in 1957. Baldwin is at pains to establish his respect, even his love, for

Mailer before taking up the task of painstakingly dismantling Mailer's claims. "The White Negro" (like *Maidstone* a decade later) focuses Mailer's camera on himself as he is and as he would like to be. As Baldwin points out, "it is not always easy—in fact, it is always extremely hard—to maintain a kind of watchful, mocking, distance between oneself as one appears to be and oneself as one actually is" (Baldwin 271). Baldwin does Mailer the service of offering precisely this watchful, mocking, distance.

Mailer's essay begins in the deep end of its title and sinks. The basic premise is this: Mailer is feeling claustrophobic. The walls of his suburban house are closing in. The straitjacket of fatherhood and husbandhood is pinching in the armpits and crotch. The expectations of breadwinning and career-making, of domestic and public responsibility, are yapping in his ear while he's awake, in his conscience while he sleeps. To construct meaning from the odds and ends that constitute a life has become a matter either of following the rote assembly instructions and ending up with the same trite answers as everybody else, or of confronting the existential doom of the atomic bomb that had ended the War in the Pacific and now stands prepared to end everything else. Mailer: "our psyche was subjected itself to the intolerable anxiety that death being causeless, life was causeless as well, and time deprived of cause and effect had come to a stop" (Mailer 20). Three years before Daniel Bell published *The End of Ideology*, Mailer reaches another kind of end. The bomb ticking in our collective cupboard. White American society retreats into a shell of commodified consensus. If meaning is now out of the question, then comfort will suffice. And comfort demands a strict adherence to the rules of the game as written out and refereed by market logic; by one's ability to sell what one has to sell in order to buy what the current dictates of comfort require. As Mailer sees it, there is no wiggle room, no space for deviance or experimentation, certainly not for dissent.

> One could hardly maintain the courage to be individual, to speak with one's own voice, for the years in which one could complacently accept oneself as part of an elite by being a radical were forever gone. A man knew that when he dissented, he gave a note upon his life which could be called in any year of overt crisis. No wonder then that these have been the years of conformity and depression. A stench of fear has come out of every pore of American life, and we suffer from a collective failure of nerve. (Mailer 21)

Mailer surveys this bleak scene, desperate to dream up a plan of escape. Middle-American values, middle-class life won't cut it, he decides. He has no choice but to head for the periphery. Only there, on the border, at the fringe, in the underground, can the freedom Mailer feels he's been promised be found. The only true break would be "to live with death as immediate danger, to divorce oneself from society, to exist without roots, to set out on that uncharted journey into the rebellious imperatives of the self" (Mailer 21). It is here, in this necessity, on this journey, that the concept of "hip" is born. The escapee is the hipster. Those left behind, squares.

We track Mailer's hyperbole, his doomsday laments, his plights and gripes as bad as Achilles. Perhaps we're even a little seduced by the angelheadedness of it all, by the ever-blooming assurance of wide-open physical and mental spaces, by the covenant of American freedom. But—imagine James Baldwin moistening his fingers to turn the page—Mailer takes an inexplicable turn into historical dementia and unaccountable racist fantasy.

> It is no accident that the source of Hip is the Negro for he has been living on the margin between totalitarianism and democracy for two centuries. (Mailer 22)

Perversely, Mailer constructs a kind of imaginary privilege for Black men living in America in 1957. When Baldwin says that the Black man has no innocence to lose, he identifies this as a dire state of being: debilitating in principle, sadistic in practice. But for Mailer, it is freedom. Rushing headlong into all the tropes of "primitivism," Mailer's delusions allow him to flip American racial oppression on its head, allowing the Black man to walk out (or be forced out) into the full light of living, while the White man is left shackled: not to the whipping post, but to the white picket fence and the mortgage that paid for it (conferred, of course, by a bank that, as a matter of institutional policy, denies that same mortgage to non-Whites).

> the Negro (all exceptions admitted) could rarely afford the sophisticated inhibitions of civilization, and so he kept for his survival the art of the primitive, he lived in the enormous present, he subsisted for his Saturday night kicks, relinquishing the pleasures of the mind for the more obligatory pleasures of the body, and in his music he gave voice to the character and quality of his existence, to his rage and the infinite variations of joy, lust, languor, growl, cramp, pinch, scream and despair of his orgasm. For jazz is orgasm, it is the music of orgasm, good orgasm and bad [. . .] it was indeed a communication by art because it said, "I feel this, and now you do too." (Mailer 23)

We can now see how this relates to the friction between the Stooges' rock and roll and Michael Fried's modernism. Music is the note passed from cell to cell, announcing the time, the date, the method of the prison break. It is a note passed from Black America to White America, pointing Mailer and his hip, White brothers in the direction of the "obligatory pleasures of the body." But in 1957, jazz—not yet rock and roll—was the music of bodily pleasure, of liberation, of rebellion. Think of the scene in *The Wild One* (1953). Marlon Brando and his biker gang rampage into the small town of Wrightsville, California. At the local café, they pump quarters into the jukebox. Brando's character leans against the jukebox—too hip, too much of a lone wolf, to dance. He drums on the jukebox glass to the saxophone-led jazz. A girl dancing with one of the bikers catches a glimpse of another biker's jacket and inquires, "Hey somebody tell me what that means, B.R.M.C.?" The biker she's dancing with explains, "Black Rebels Motorcycle Club." "Isn't that cute," says the girl. She taps Brando on the arm and asks, "hey, Johnny, what are you rebelling against?" The camera cuts to a close-up of Brando's dispassionate face. "Whaddya got?" he asks. Had this representation of rebellion for rebellion's sake been shot a decade later, the music would surely have been rock and roll.

Or picture the film noir, *D.O.A.* (1950). The plot involves a man, Frank Bigelow (Edmond O'Brien), who has been poisoned and has only a few days to solve his own murder before the poison kills him. One would be hard-pressed to find a better filmic representation of Mailer's claims for jazz than the scene set at a dive bar at San Francisco's Fisherman's Warf. A quintet of Black musicians tear through some high-tempo bebop. The camera picks out pianist Ray LaRue, his right hand winging a melody, as he leans forward and grins at us with a knowing lasciviousness. The scene depicts the conversion of the almost entirely White audience. They bounce and rock in time with the band, periodically exhorting in Hollywoodized hipster patois: "cool, cool, really cool!" or "blow it, blow up a storm!" Saxophonist James Streeter launches into a frenetic solo and the camera zooms in on his physical strain, his cheeks and eyes bulging, sweat beading on his forehead. As Al "Cake" Wichard hurtles into a drum solo, a White patron, reeling in his seat, hollers, "stick with it! Go on, go on, go on, get it! get it!" The musicians and the editing generate a fevered pitch.

This is not Bigelow's demimonde. He moves from his table to the bar to escape the tumult and orders a bourbon and water, no ice. When he asks the bartender about a woman sitting at the opposite end of the bar, he is told, "oh, she's one of the chicks that hangs around here, she's jive crazy." When Bigelow says, "come again?" the bartender looks up from his pour, surprised. "Oh, you ain't hip, pal. Jive crazy means that she goes for this stuff." Another man sways into the scene, momentarily laying his head on Bigelow's shoulder. "What's the matter with him?" asks Bigelow. "He's flipped, the music's driving him crazy," explains the bartender, who then leans in assertively to this habitué of the hipster scene, "Come down, Jack," the bartender implores. The man wags a finger at the bartender and replies, "Don't bother me, man, I'm being enlightened."

For a brief period, from roughly the mid-1940s to the early 1960s, jazz represented the freedom Mailer describes: the rejection of middle-class norms and mores; a shift from the life of the mind to the life of the body; the adventurous pursuit of undefined experiences; uncodified and unaccounted for in the ledgers of the postwar lifestyle consensus. But something changed. (Had it not, perhaps this book would be titled "Jazz vs. Modern Life.") Rock and roll was both a catalyst and a beneficiary of this change. In 1955, every number-one song on the Billboard rhythm and blues chart was performed by a Black artist. In 1956, Elvis Presley cracked the chart, landing the number-one spot for one lonely week with "Don't Be Cruel." The following year, he held the top spot for ten weeks, while Paul Anka, Jimmie Rodgers, and Jerry Lee Lewis, accounted for another six. By 1965—although the Billboard chart categories had changed, making it difficult to compare apples and apples—the singles' chart was dominated by White artists making music almost entirely indebted to the Black music of the discontinued R&B chart. The Beatles, of course, but also Petula Clark, the Righteous Brothers, Gary Lewis and the Playboys, Herman's Hermits, Sonny and Cher, the Beach Boys, the Rolling Stones, the Dave Clark Five, and the Byrds with a cover of Bob Dylan's "Mr. Tambourine Man."

That's not to say that Black artists disappeared. Motown made a particularly strong showing in 1965. The Supremes had four number-one hits, the Four Tops had two, and the Temptations one. But over the course of one decade, rhythm and blues, re-christened rock and roll, had been wrested from the hands of its African American inventors and early innovators including Muddy Waters, Chuck Berry, Little Richard, and Bo Diddley, all of whom recorded for Chicago's Chess Records. Once it had been matured and market-tested by Black artists, record companies, radio stations, and promoters embraced rock and roll as a White youth music. With the emergence of White performers such as Elvis Presley, Jerry Lee Lewis, Carl Perkins, and Johnny Cash (all recording in Memphis for Sun Records), rock and roll was seen as safe for a new set of consumers. In tandem with the rock and roll record, the (White) "teenager" was born as a burgeoning demographic with unique tastes in fashion and entertainment. Rock and roll thus becomes one of the few significant cultural forms to emerge simultaneously with a market prepared to buy and sell it. One cannot speak of a pre-commercial moment in the development of rock and roll. Rock and roll is a commodity from the jump. And, as with so many markets, so much of American capitalism, its establishment and viability as a commodity depends fundamentally on racial distinctions.

Designating a founding moment, artist, or document of rock and roll may be a fool's errand, but as Lester Bangs has established, rock and roll is the kingdom of the fool. A confluence of factors arrive together to allow rock and roll to emerge as the dominant cultural form of the 1960s and 1970s. Electricity is essential. Foolishly, perhaps, I've nominated Muddy Waters's 1948 recording of "I Feel Like Going Home" as the record that launched a thousand franchises (think of the Rolling Stones, named after a Muddy Waters song).[1] Previous versions of the song performed by Son House, Robert Johnson, and Waters himself had carried different titles: "My Black Mama," "Walkin' Blues," and "Country Blues." When Waters recorded it in 1948 for Aristocrat Records (soon to be renamed after Leonard and Phil Chess, Polish-Jewish immigrants who had purchased the label), he changed the title yet again. But he also took advantage of the affordances of electric instruments, amplification, microphones, and a mixing console that allows individual instruments to be mic'd separately and balanced in what we now call post-production. That Waters found himself recording for Aristocrat—indeed, that the Chess brothers had forayed into the recording business at all—was due largely to electricity too. At Chicago's Macomba Lounge, Waters had been forced to adapt his Delta blues for a bigger room, a bigger audience. He had to make the music just as present for the people at the back of the room as for those up front. For the guitar to meet the drums on their own terms, amplification is required. But then the vocals too need a boost. So a sound system is required and microphones. When the Chess brothers witnessed the excitement prompted by Waters's electric sound, they saw the commercial possibilities and decided to buy in.

At the same time, electricity is central to the expansion of radio. Between 1940 and 1950, the number of AM radio stations in the United States grew from 847 to 2,144. With the addition of FM, there were more than 4,300 stations by 1960 (US Dept. of Commerce 796). Beyond the recording studio, the record industry depended on electricity for manufacturing. And, of course, you'd need electricity to listen to your radio and your record player at home. Rock and roll is wholly dependent on electricity for both its production and its reception. But

---

[1] See my *In The Blink of an Ear: Toward a Non-Cochlear Sonic Art.* Bloomsbury, 2009, pp. 23–28.

as we can see, electricity collaborates with the exploitation of racial categories and cultural forms, both merging with technological developments and new markets to facilitate the rapid rise of rock and roll on the American cultural landscape.

It is much more than foolish, then, to endow jazz or rock and roll with a mystical-energetics primed to fling open the jail cell doors to free the modern male (middle class, at worst, and invariably White). Norman Mailer, thick with his own ego and allowed by his power, his privilege, his fame, and his wealth, imagines himself still deprived of some "natural" entitlement; as if the universe owed men like him, after a decade or two of exertion, a moment of tranquility. What Mailer wants—what he thinks he deserves—is not so different from what Michael Fried wants: an experience of singularity, of clarity, of presentness. In short, these modern males practically demand transcendence. Fried escapes the damnation of the quotidian through a moment of perceptual grace. Mailer, on the other hand, yearns to inhabit the divestment of the Other while maintaining his entitlements, his prestige, his security.

> There was a new breed of adventurers, urban adventurers who drifted out at night looking for action with a black man's code to fit their facts. The hipster had absorbed the existentialist synapses of the Negro, and for practical purposes could be considered a white Negro. (Mailer 23)

He and his hipster pals toss their privilege into an overnight bag and hit the road for some kicks, knowing that when they've gotten their fill or reached the perimeter of their comfort, they can safely return to the refuge of America where their Whiteness is their amulet.

Baldwin is heartbroken by Mailer's betrayal—not only of their friendship but of Mailer's own talent. He can't imagine why Mailer would voluntarily sink to the level of Kerouac and the Beats. "It seemed very clear to me that [the Beats] glorification of the orgasm was but a way of avoiding all of the terrors of life and love. But Norman knew better, had to know better" (Baldwin 277). As Baldwin sees it, Mailer—in his novels and in real life—has a genuine feel for the responsibilities and the sacrifices of love; duties that can't be discharged in the instant of an orgasm. The Beats' pursuit of momentary diversions and pleasures rejects the obligations of tending, rearing, and caring. Baldwin sees— and condemns—in Mailer's adoption of their perspective, a disavowal of the veracity of the profane in favor of the figment of the sacred. As Baldwin sees it, this makes Mailer a truly dangerous man.

For, exactly because he knew better, and in exactly the same way that no one can become more lewdly vicious than an imitation libertine, Norman felt compelled to carry their mystique further than they had, to be more "hip," or more "beat," to dominate, in fact, their dreaming field; and since this mystique depended on a total rejection of life, and insisted on the fulfillment of an infantile dream of love, the mystique could only be extended into violence. No one is more dangerous than he who imagines himself pure in heart: for his purity, by definition, is unassailable. (Baldwin 277)

This purity that Baldwin identifies as so dangerous is the site of the contestation between rock and roll and modern life. This purity only exists in the non-place of transcendence, somewhere else, somewhere beyond. That's where one can be pure. When one is right here, feet on the ground, in one's own skin, such purity is impossible.

Fried wants frame and form and order, while Mailer wants flight and freedom and orgasm. Both fantasies are fantasies of elsewhereness, unbeholden to the exigencies of circumstance and situation. At its core, Mailer's fantasy—like Fried's—is constructed from a set of frames. Without an unassailable understanding of who he is and who the "Negro" is, Mailer cannot proffer his nostrum. Only by this crossing, from one's own frame, burdened with privilege and privileged with burdens, to the impoverished frame evacuated of all obligation and expectation, can the White Mailer circumvent his own encumbered life and abscond into a purity that he ludicrously imagines to be the province of the Black man.

What distinguishes Iggy's fugitivity from that of Fried and Mailer is the question of circumstance and situation. If what Iggy's after is also a kind of transcendence, it is not a transcendence of elsewhereness and purity. Rather it is made or discovered in the inevitably ordinary stuff of being commonly alive. There is nothing pure about it, because it is wholly dependent on the circumstance and the situations from which it is mined. It takes work. It takes dedication. It is not the result of magic, but of effort; not of faith, but insistence.

This recognition of circumstances and situations is symptomatic of an alteration in the ways in which the frames of society were understood and felt in the 1960s. No longer would strict yet arbitrary categorization blithely determine the identity or meaning of individuals, institutions, objects, or ideals. Such categorizations are matters, not of nature, but of culture and convention. For that reason, culture and convention became terrains of contestation. If the distinction between colonizer and colonized, between White and Black, between justified and unjustified violence is not to be found in anything "natural," but strictly in the customs of convention, then challenging these conventions has to be central to change.

In an article published in *The Progressive* in May 1960, Martin Luther King Jr. writes, "many Negroes recognize the necessity of creating discord to alter established community patterns" (King 450). King praises the efforts of Black students staging sit-ins across the South. He explicitly dispels the notion that these demonstrations are spontaneous, drawing attention to "clearly perceivable causes and precedents" (King 447). Among these he mentions the 1954 Supreme Court decision in Brown vs. Board of Education, which found that the doctrine of "separate but equal" was not sufficient to redress the inherent inequities of American institutions. King connects the struggle of African Americans to those of anti-colonial efforts around the globe.

> Many related, interacting social forces must be understood if we are to understand history as it is being made. The arresting upsurge of Africa and Asia is remote neither in time nor in space to the Negro of the South. Indeed, the determination of Negro Americans to win freedom from all forms of oppression springs from the same deep longing that motivates oppressed peoples all over the world. (King 448)

One of the sit-ins referenced by King occurred on February 1, 1960. Four African American freshmen at North Carolina A&T installed themselves at the Greensboro Woolworth's lunch counter. The "Greensboro Four"—Ezell Blair Jr., David Richmond, Franklin McCain, and Joseph McNeil—returned to Woolworths for six consecutive days until a bomb threat closed the store. Sit-ins spread to other Southern cities and continued at businesses in Greensboro through late July when the Woolworth's manager, faced with mounting financial losses, asked four Black employees to change out of their uniforms, to sit at the counter and order lunch. King asks why the movement targeted department store lunch counters.

> The answer lies in the fact that here the Negro has suffered indignities and injustices that cannot be justified or explained. Almost every Negro has experienced the tragic inconveniences of lunch counter segregation. He cannot understand why he is welcomed with open arms at most counters in the store, but is denied service at a certain counter because it happens to be selling food and drink. (King 449)

The lunch counter sit-ins attacked racism at the level of culture. They aimed to dismantle the frames that separated one counter from another, one customer from another. It is one of the characteristic geniuses of the Civil Rights Movement that it directed its efforts simultaneously at cultural attitudes and at legal and policy initiatives. Societal change could not simply be legislated. It had to emanate from and saturate the social fabric. If North Carolina judge J. Braxton Craven Jr. believed that "the key to this problem is to be found not in the law but in religion" (quoted in Pollitt 337), Minister King knew that institutions beyond the church would have to be part of the solution. Closing Woolworth's is only the beginning of the shift.

> It will spread to libraries, public parks, schools, and the like, and these too will have to be closed, thus depriving both white and Negro of necessary cultural and recreational institutions. This would be a step backward for the whole of society. Or finally, [segregationists] can accept the principle of equality. In this case they still have two alternative approaches. They may make the facilities equally bad for both white and Negro or equally good. Thus finally simply logic and justice in their own interests should direct them to the only acceptable solution—to accept equality and maintain it on the best level for both races. (King 450)

The same year as the Greensboro sit-ins and King's piece for *The Progressive*, Chubby Checker released his song "The Twist." It wasn't his originally. Hank Ballard and the Midnighters had recorded it a couple of years earlier, yielding a minor hit. Checker's version would go to number one in September 1960. The term "the twist" or "twisting" (a euphemism for sex and dance moves that emulated coital gyrations) had existed since the nineteenth century. Checker's antiseptic version spawned a wildly popular dance craze, which in turn propelled the ongoing success of the song (it returned to number one in January 1962, becoming the first song to ascend to the top spot as parts of two distinct campaigns).

Today, "The Twist" is quaint, anodyne, squeaky clean. In 1960, and again in 1962, that was part of its charm. Surprisingly—to twenty-first-century ears—when Eldridge Cleaver, minister of information of the Black Panther Party, published *Soul on Ice* in 1968, he identified something altogether more destructive in "The Twist," calling it "a nuclear explosion, sending its fallout of rhythm into the Minds and Bodies of the people [. . .] a guided missile, launched from the ghetto into the very heart of suburbia" (Cleaver 227–8). One could make similar claims for other songs of the era, but for Cleaver, "The Twist" smuggled distinct aspects of Black music, Black language, and, most importantly, Black dance, into White lives.

> It was Chubby Checker's mission, bearing the Twist as *good news*, to teach the whites, whom history had taught to forget, how to shake their asses again. It is a skill they surely must once have possessed but which they abandoned for puritanical dreams of escaping the corruption of the flesh, by leaving the terrors of the Body to the blacks. (Cleaver 223)

Cleaver's account resembles Norman Mailer's. Both bear witness to the birth of a new subculture in American society: the beatnik, the hipster. They connect this subculture to youth music—Jazz in Mailer's essay, rock and roll in Cleaver's. And both see this subculture as establishing itself on the boundary between White and Black, encamped there with the intention—conscious or not—of effacing the border, of opening it to the free interpolation of ideas and bodies and cultures.

> Like pioneers staking their claims in the no-man's land that lay along the racial Maginot Line, the beatniks, like Elvis Presley before them, dared to do in the light of day what America had long been doing in the sneak-thief anonymity of night—consorted on a human level with the blacks. (Cleaver 226)

Both Mailer and Cleaver diagnose a fundamental failing in White society. The twin impulses of Enlightenment clarity and Christian rectitude forced Whites to recoil from the irrational demands of sensuality and lust, to seek refuge in the frameable experience of reason and metered rhyme. This is not simple prudishness; not merely a kind of cultural embarrassment at the site of a lifted hemline. Rather it is driven by a compulsion to control. European society imagined itself as the proper source and symptom of propriety. It's not hard to extrapolate, to attribute to these same impulses, these same insecurities, the rise of capitalism in Europe. The boundless wilds of the land are parceled and particularized, recategorized as property: bounded, owned, attributed to a single point of responsibility. Even another man—his senses, his lusts, *his* reason, *his* rhymes, his strengths and weaknesses—can be owned and controlled.

The European mind (according, of course, to European minds) could be categorized and contained. Immanuel Kant (1724–1804) was thought by his contemporaries (among them Karl Leonhard Reinhold, who helped to establish Kant as the most important European philosopher of his time) to have solved the problem of epistemology—how it is that humans come to know what we know. Modeled on the systems of the physical sciences, Kant divided experience into its elementary particles: sensibility, intuitions, judgments, and understanding, all subsumed under categories. The operative metaphor is one of seeing clearly. The

Enlightenment moves us out of the darkness, lifts the curtain, and sheds light on the subject. If an advertising campaign were concocted for the Enlightenment (and, yes, the last 240 years of world history could easily be construed as just such a campaign) then perhaps Jack Lescoulie could be hired as head copy writer and his proclamation about Iggy Pop adopted (with one slight modification) as the campaign's insistent slogan:

## We're Trying to Get a Light on It Now

The problem, of course, is that light serves only one of our senses. The visuality of the Enlightenment's operative metaphor is only a metaphor. The act of knowing that it means to conjure is not simply a matter of seeing, but of hearing, touching, feeling, and more. Nor is it wholly spatial. Time plays a crucial role in how and what we know. The *augenblick*, the blink of an eye, is very slight. It must always be cross-referenced with knowledge acquired before and after that precious moment in which the eye is open. The grace that Fried found in presentness can only be apprehended as such if one compares it to other forms of experience. And comparison is always a temporal activity. Just as one cannot perceive an apple and an orange in precisely the same place, it is equally impossible to consider them at precisely the same time. One must toggle from here to there, from now to then.

I am a camera. You are a camera. All of us cameras. We are cameras because our vision is framed. Our mise-en-scène can be our world, allowing us to disregard the distractions, the mess, the complications, just outside the frame: left or right, before or after. Kant's conception of knowledge depends on a series of nesting frames, like conceptual Tupperware stacked in the fridge, each holding a distinct course of the epistemological feast that constitutes being human. His model depends on these containers, on their ability to contain. It depends on an even more foundational effect: that the container necessarily defines the contents it contains. The frame forms the content that it frames.

For Eldridge Cleaver, White culture lays claim to the conceptual containment of the mind, leaving the feral vagaries of the body to Black culture. Whites take possession of a life of the mind, and Blacks are relegated to a life of the body.

The separation of the black and white people in America along the color line had the effect, in terms of social imagery, of separating the Mind from the Body—the oppressor whites usurping sovereignty by monopolizing the Mind, abdicating the Body and becoming bodiless Omnipotent Administrators and Ultrafeminines; and the oppressed blacks, divested of sovereignty and therefore of Mind, manifesting the Body and becoming mindless Supermasculine Menials and Black Amazons. (Cleaver 222)

Again, the frames define their contents. The categories of Black and White impose sets of expectations on the bodies and minds grouped under one or the other. As James Baldwin notes,

To be a Negro, let alone a Negro artist, one had to make oneself up as one went along. This had to be done in the not-at-all-metaphorical teeth of the world's determination to destroy you. The world had prepared no place for you, and if the world had its way, no place would ever exist. Now, this is true for everyone, but, in the case of a Negro, this truth is absolutely naked: if he deludes himself about it, he will die. This is not the way this truth presents itself to white men, who believe the world is theirs and who, albeit unconsciously, expect the world to help them in the achievement of their identity. (Baldwin 279)

What Jack Lescoulie demands is a version of what Michael Fried demands, what Norman Mailer and, for that matter, Immanuel Kant demand. Each expects the world to help them in the achievement of their identity. Such identity depends on identification, knowing what something is and being able to distinguish it from other like and unlike things. It depends on framing, the clear establishment of categories with discernible borders. They expect to know what's what.

Cleaver describes the US Supreme Court decision in the case of Brown *v.* Board of Education, as striking a blow against the borders of the categories of Black and White. The decision determined that separate could never be equal. The determination of stable identities, the dividing of one from another, the establishment of borders to sunder Black schools from White schools, was not merely a symptom of the problem. It was the problem. For Cleaver, the suturing of Black and White also erased the divide between mind and body. Without the clear categorical distinctions afforded by the life of the mind, White society was forced to contend with new, unbounded experiences. Cleaver offers a metaphor that is strikingly reminiscent of Tony Smith's conversion story on the New Jersey Turnpike.

A radical break, a revolutionary leap [. . .] had taken place in the secret parts of this nation's soul. It was as if a driverless vehicle were speeding through the American night down an unlighted street toward a stone wall and was boarded on the fly by a stealthy ghost with a drooling leer on his face, who, at the last detour before chaos and disaster, careened the vehicle down a smooth highway that leads to the future and life. (Cleaver 224)

The future and life, however, cannot be delivered in their complex entirety by something as clinical as a Supreme Court decision. Life is lived amidst circumstances and situations. Only when those circumstances shift, does life change. When White children from Massapequa to Malibu start dancing the Twist, when rumors spread of Jackie O. twisting in the White House, then—as Cleaver sees it—we're getting somewhere.

# 3

# We Shall Raise the Flag of Nothingness

The humidity stacks up like bricks, heavy and smelling of neighborhood garlic and the Blommer cocoa processor west of the Loop. The minute you step out of the shower you start to sweat. Your clothes stick to your skin. Prior to July 30, 1971 (when the Union Stockyards closed for good), you might also pick up the faint but distinct note of abattoir miasma, an ever-present memento mori hanging where the city's air ought to hang.

Why the Democratic Party decided on Chicago for their nominating convention in 1968 is anybody's guess. Likely, Mayor Richard J. Daley, then in the thirteenth year of his twenty-one year reign, exerted his considerable political clout to bring the convention to the Windy City. In 1968, the Democratic Party was suffused in its own abattoir miasma. John Kennedy had been assassinated only five years earlier. Lyndon Johnson, Kennedy's successor, was mired in a pointless colonial bloodbath in Southeast Asia and in the mounting criticism of the involvement of the United States. When Johnson chose not to run for reelection and Robert Kennedy, John's younger brother, announced his candidacy, it seemed that he might salvage the party's standing and its electoral prospects. But when Bobby was murdered in Los Angeles, it started to seem that death was an inescapable feature of the Democrats' very soul. To hold the convention at the Chicago Amphitheater, directly adjacent to the Stockyards, in muggy August, was unlikely to contradict this impression.

As the convention began, the International Brotherhood of Electrical Workers went on strike. Delegates and news media were unable to communicate with their colleagues at downtown hotels. TV networks could not establish live feeds of the convention or of the protests that percolated and then boiled over on the streets of Chicago. Instead gophers ran video tape from the Amphitheater to the networks' Chicago affiliate studios—creating a significant delay between the unfolding events and their appearance on America's TV sets. The chant, "the whole world is watching," may have begun during the 1968 Chicago protests.

But the cameras—you, me, the whole world—that were watching were doing so on a time delay.

Abbie Hoffman and his Youth International Party (Yippie!) put a fine point on it. They dubbed the Democrats' gathering the "Festival of Death." As a corrective, just a mile or so up Lake Shore Drive in Lincoln Park, the Yippies staged their "Festival of Life," in conjunction with anti-war protests organized by the Students for a Democratic Society (SDS) and the National Mobilization Committee to End the War in Vietnam (the Mobe). Infamously, a report commissioned by the National Commission on the Causes and Prevention of Violence found that the protests were met with "unrestrained and indiscriminate police violence" (Walker 1968). The resulting melee, known colloquially as "the Battle of Michigan Avenue," saw the City of Chicago and its Police Department take a ruthlessly unforgiving stance toward the protestors. Mayor Daley refused demonstration permits to the SDS and Mobe organizers. Despite predictions that thousands of protestors would converge on Lincoln Park and Chicago's loop, the city refused to lift curfews and allow people to sleep in the parks. A final effort by the Mobe sought a permit to stage a rally at Soldier Field. The suit charged Mayor Daley and other officials with conspiring to deny prospective demonstrators their constitutional right of free speech and assembly. The suit was heard by Federal Judge, William Lynch, who, prior to his appointment to the Federal bench, had been a partner of Mayor Daley in private practice. He denied the motion. David Dellinger, national chairman of the Mobe, accused the authorities of using "police state tactics that threaten to make Chicago the Prague of the Western Hemisphere" (New York Times, "U.S. Judge William L. Lynch").

In connecting the events of Chicago to global struggles against authoritarianism and state-sanctioned violence, Dellinger reflected a burgeoning consciousness of the common cause of resistance to Cold War spheres of influence, the subjugation of the Global South, and capitalist exploitation of natural and human resources. Not only was the whole world watching the protestors in Chicago, but the protestors, in turn, were watching the whole world. All of us, cameras. The realization was dawning: frames placed around peoples and places, to contain them, to keep the inside in and the outside out, would not hold. Nor could these frames prevent the transfer of knowledge from one frame to another. In Prague, Chicago, Kinshasa, Paris, Mexico City, an awareness of shared conditions of oppression traversed the isolating frames of modernity. Circumstances and situations could not be bracketed out of one's experience. Whether aesthetic, political, or personal, experience is often pieced together of nothing but circumstance and situation. We might go farther and say that experience is *always* built of circumstance and situation; that the plaints of Fried or Mailer—against the nuisance of sharing the world with others, with objects, with responsibilities—amount to little more than fatuous delusions of self-regard.

Back in Chicago, as the Festival of Life rumbled into existence, Abbie Hoffman and the Yippies prepared for the arrival of tens of thousands of kids and a handful of bands, including Country Joe and the Fish; Blood, Sweat & Tears; Arlo Guthrie; Janis Ian; and the United States of America. (Al Cooper of Blood, Sweat & Tears and Joseph Byrd of the United States of America had each spoken at the only formal press conference to promote the Festival of Life.) A plot was chosen at the South end of Lincoln Park at Lake Shore Drive and North Avenue. A mini-city was established with services and amenities for the body and the soul, areas designated for "Grub Town," "Biker Park," "Free Store," "Church of the Free Spirit," and the "Yippie Pentagon." In the Northeast corner, a location was earmarked for the "Hog Farm." (The Yippies planned to nominate Pigasus, a pig acquired from a Northern Illinois farm, for president.) And just south of the farm was the "Music Area" (Figure 3.1). But not all went as planned. Apparently, no one had considered the issue of electricity for the bands' instruments and the p.a. system. This problem was solved in the most Chicago of ways, when a hot dog stand was converted into an electrical relay station, rerouting power to the stage. As it happens, getting power to the stage was not as significant an issue as it might have been. When word got out about potential violence in Chicago, most of the scheduled acts failed to show. Intrepid folk singer and activist Phil Ochs performed, followed by the MC5, a newly formed band who had driven down from Ann Arbor, Michigan.

The MC5 was managed by John Sinclair, an activist, poet, and raconteur. Under his influence, the band tapped into the late-1960s zeitgeist, adopting the image of militants. They posed for photographs against a backdrop of the American flag, wearing bandoliers and holding aloft musical instruments and rifles (Figure 3.2). In addition to managing the MC5, Sinclair founded the White Panther Party, as a sympathetic response to the Black Panthers, urging White people to join the cause of Black Power. The MC5 thus became the unofficial house band of the White Panthers. Sinclair—identified as "Minister of Information, White Panthers"—provided the liner notes for the MC5's debut, *Kick Out the Jams*.

> We are free men and we demand a free music, a free high energy source that will drive us wild into the streets of America yelling and screaming and tearing down

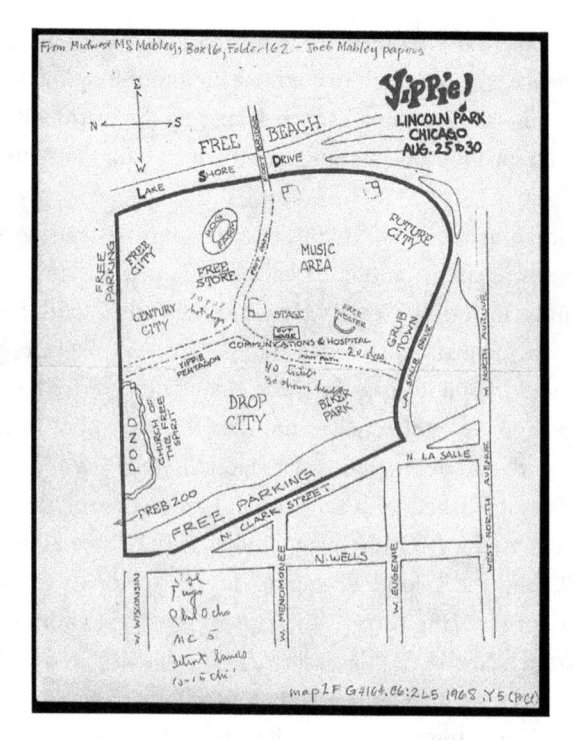

**Figure 3.1** Map of the Festival of Life in Lincoln Park, 1968 (Jack Mabley Papers, Collection of the Newberry Library, Chicago).

everything that would keep people slaves. The MC5 is that source. The MC5 is the revolution, in all its applications. (MC5)

It turns out that not only you and I are cameras. The US government is a camera too. The only footage of the MC5 playing at the Festival of Life is surveillance film shot by the FBI. The footage depicts the band on the back of a flatbed truck and a crowd sitting before them on the grass. We catch glimpses of Abbie Hoffman in a flattened cowboy hat and John Sinclair, stage left, keeping a watchful eye over his protégés. One might think that the Festival of Life and the ensuing confrontations in Chicago would have been the perfect forum for the MC5's politics. But the band was in Chicago to perform, not to put their revolutionary posturing to the test. As guitarist Wayne Kramer describes it, "The minute we stopped playing, we just threw our shit in the van and we drove right across the grass and over the median to get on the freeway to get our asses back to Detroit. That's when the tear gas started flying" (Thomas, *MC5: A True Testimonial*, 53:20–53:32). The MC5 were made for the camera. Their enduring success was in creating an

**Figure 3.2** Wayne Kramer of the MC5. Photo: Leni Sinclair (1969).

image of rock and roll revolution. But no revolution was forthcoming, neither in their politics nor in their music. Lester Bangs reviewed *Kick Out The Jams* for *Rolling Stone* in April, 1969, two months after its release. Bangs saw through the scrim. "Musically the group is intentionally crude and aggressively raw. Which can make for powerful music except when it is used to conceal a paucity of ideas, as it is here" (Bangs 1969).

The difference between revolution and retailing is all a matter of circumstance and situation. The precise measure is determined by the frame. If, as Fried would do, we frame the MC5 tightly, excluding all but the music, we encounter a blustery hard rock band similar to many of the day. Bangs cites the Seeds, Blue Cheer, the Kingsmen, and Question Mark and the Mysterians. If we construct the frame with a touch more room, allowing in the photographs and Sinclair's radical rhetoric, then we might take the MC5 to be the vanguard of a coming cultural insurrection. If we can hold the frame just so, neither too restrictive nor too permissive, we can see them as they wanted to be seen. And this, of course, is precisely what advertising and public relations aim to do: to construct a frame that includes only what the handlers, brand managers, and spin doctors want us to see. It's a Hollywood stage set, built for the benefit of our cameras. We are granted access only to the mise-en-scène, that which has been "placed"—as the

French would have it—in the scene for our delectation. If the frame is too narrow, we realize, with Bangs, that the MC5 offer nothing not already accounted for in the landscape of late 1960s rock and roll. If the frame is too broad, we see the MC5 scamper back into the van as the shit hits the fan. We understand, even if they and Sinclair didn't, that the guns and bandoliers are costumes, like Alice Cooper's b-stock Dracula and Kiss's greasepaint and platforms heels.

The MC5's most enduring signature, the source of their debut's title, is singer Rob Tyner's exhortation to "kick out the jams, motherfuckers!" The phrase was uttered at every show and was taken to be a rallying cri de coeur at the barricades. But the phrase is vague, just as applicable to a football game as a revolution. When the album was released, the band's label, Elektra, insisted on co-releasing a "clean" version with Tyner's "motherfuckers" replaced with "brothers and sisters." Still, Hudson's, the Detroit-based department store chain, refused to stock the album and the band decided that this was their Waterloo (or their Battle of Michigan Avenue). They took out a full-page ad in the Ann Arbor magazine, *Fifth Estate*, which repeated the uncensored phrase and urged readers to "kick in the doors if the store won't sell you the album on Elektra." They included the Elektra logo without the label's knowledge or permission. At the bottom of the page, the ad doubles down on the offending locution, in all caps, followed by an exclamation point: "FUCK HUDSON'S!"

Lester Bangs understood what the revolutionary jive was all about. "The difference here, the difference which will sell several hundred thousand copies of this album, is in the hype, the thick overlay of teenage-revolution and total-energy-thing which conceals these scrapyard vistas of clichés and ugly noise" (Bangs 1969).

For the MC5, the frame fixes the gaze on a single detail within the gestalt, demanding that the listener hear the otherwise undistinguished clunk of the band as something radical and new. For Michael Fried, the frame serves to exclude distractions from the *presentness* of transcendent aesthetic experience. For Abbie Hoffman, the frame is something else yet again. Hoffman understood that the media is agnostic regarding meaning. If as McLuhan claimed, "the media is the message," then the media doesn't need messages. It only needs images. The camera always wants the most striking image. But what the camera wants—what the camera operators (CBS, NBC, ABC) want—is not necessarily what they get. In Hoffman's *Revolution for the Hell of It*, published in 1969, he opens his account of Chicago '68 with the following epigraph:

*The medium is the mess.*

—Marshall McLu

Hoffman first made headlines in August of 1967, when, during a tour of the New York Stock Exchange, he and a group of accomplices dropped a wad of dollar bills from the observation catwalk onto the trading floor. Cameras were not allowed in the Stock Exchange, so there is no documentary evidence of Hoffman's antics that day. Instead, the news coverage presented a folk tale—fabulous in structure and allegorical in meaning. Hoffman called it "a perfect mythical event" (Hoffman 1980, 22). When a reporter asked, "How many are you?"

Hoffman replied, "hundreds . . . three . . . two. We don't exist! We don't even exist!" (Hoffman 1980, 101).

Hoffman came to the realization that a war fought with and for the cameras was more winnable than a war fought with the police. With little in the way of resources, planning, machinery, or manpower, battles could be staged and won, merely by being staged.

> The system cracked a little. Not a drop of blood had been spilled, not a bone broken, but on that day, with that gesture, an image war had begun. (Hoffman 1980, 102)

Hoffman's guerilla theater borrows from Artaud's theater of cruelty, from the West Coast Diggers and the San Francisco Mime Troupe, from East Coast provocateurs, The Up Against the Wall Motherfuckers. Hoffman adds the awareness of playing not just to those present, but through the camera to the viewer at home. By the very act of being broadcast via official channels, his antics become official, they become news, they become history, they become truth. Hoffman understood that the ground had been prepared by the radicality of innovations elsewhere in society. While Fried's beloved abstract expressionists may have had little to offer to Hoffman's scheme, they served a purpose by opening minds a little, by allowing the thought of the new and the unprecedented to exist in the minds of the masses and the media.

> No need to build a stage, it was all around us. Props would be simple and obvious. We would hurl ourselves across the canvas of society like streaks of splattered paint. Highly visual images would become news, and rumor-mongers would rush to spread the excited word. (Hoffman 1980, 102)

Jackson Pollock's gestures could serve as proofs of concept. If that Wyoming cowboy and his embodiment of a notion of the exceptionalism of the American purchase on freedom could garner multipage spreads in *Life* magazine, infiltrating newsstands and coffee tables from Plymouth to Petaluma, then surely a bunch of long-haired flower children, the very progeny of these American privileges, splattered on the streets—whether beatified by the bardo or bloodied by the cops—could capture the collective imagination. Hoffman borrowed from the language and methods of modern art, tweaking the meaning and the medium, widening the frame to his own specs. Allan Kaprow's "happenings" provided a model, a dozen things occurring at once: words, images, movements, costumes, lights, music. But Hoffman understood that happenings were "an extension of abstract art and as such were designed for the ruling class." Hoffman could use the template of the happening. By reframing it, he could make it intelligible not only when accompanied by a curator and program notes but by a TV dinner. "I thought we could improve on that. Perhaps the audience that appreciated *All in the Family* did not approve of our 'message' but they did understand it" (Hoffman 1980, 106).

The latest in a long history of purveyors of absurdist political street theater, Hoffman was an *agent preposteror*; a fly who invades the camera's point of view, revealing the mise-en-scène as a construction. What we see through the lens of the media is framed to reinforce a set of understandings. The screen purports to show us things *as they are*, in a natural state of inevitability. But the fly lets the director's cat out of the bag: this scene is anything but natural. First of all, there is a director. The director establishes the frame of the shot, the focal point. The frame excludes as much—more (much more)—than it includes. From a continuous field of space and interests it concocts distinctions, separating the foreground from the background, the principal players from the support, the signal from the noise. The fly disrupts the frame's naturalness and our own impartiality. As with the soup recently delivered by the waiter, the fantasy of purity is dispelled by the presence of the fly.

It is telling that Hoffman emerged the same year as Fried's "Art and Objecthood." The roil and restlessness of the social fabric of 1967 forced reckonings across culture. You had to take stock, decide what you wanted, and how it could be gotten. So even if Fried and Mailer and Iggy and Hoffman all want escape, they have different conceptions of what is being escaped, of how to break clear, why, and what comes next. Transcendence offers itself in versions both sacred and profane.

Still, it's hard in some ways to understand why Fried would focus so intently on minimalism. Why get one's back up about a set of mirrored cubes when

Fluxus and Kaprow's "happenings" are theatricalizing much more literally than Judd and Morris, when Iggy is hurling himself upon an Ann Arbor stage, when Hoffman is performing politics as farce? Clearly, Fried worries more about minimalism as a threat to the modernist art of the 1940s and 1950s than he does about the juvenile antics of the Fluxus crowd. In the art world inhabited by Fried, minimalism was being taken seriously, as a potential successor to Abstract Expressionism as the next important twentieth-century art movement. Iggy and the Stooges and Abbie Hoffman were probably not on Fried's radar, and even if they had been, they wouldn't have posed any direct threat to what Fried held most personally and professionally dear. But in retrospect, it is apparent that the heavier blow came from the performative politics of the Yippies and the living, changeable, temporal energetics of rock and roll. Fried is desperate to fix experience in a moment of suspension. The world should hold still for an instant to allow him with the time, the attention, the privilege, to soak up the bestowals of the great canvas. The frame delimits not only the space of the painting but the time of its reception and the conditions within which it is experienced. The work exists as a formal response to spatial challenges. The beholder "experiences . . . a kind of *instantaneousness*: as though if only one were infinitely more acute, a single infinitely brief instant would be long enough to see everything, to experience the work in all its depth and fullness" (Fried 22). As though circumstance and situation play no part. But, of course, they always do.

Two months after the New York Stock Exchange incident, Hoffman participated in the October March on the Pentagon organized by the Mobe. Having learned the power of outrageousness and rumor, Hoffman added an element of absurdist theater to the otherwise earnest march. "Rumors have power," he wrote in 1968. "Like myths, people become involved in them, adding, subtracting, multiplying. Get them involved. Let them participate. If it's spelled out to the letter there is no room for participation. Nobody participates in ideology" (Hoffman 19). For Hoffman, the New Left and the anti-war activists were playing by the rules of the establishment. They put on jackets and ties and made reasoned arguments against the war. But, as the Yippies saw it, the world was not reasonable. The jackets and ties were props pulling the wool over the world's eyes. The only way to confront the irrationality of the war, of American imperialism, of runaway capitalism was with a kind of ultra-irrationality. The Yippies sought to expose the status quo as a shell game with nothing but empty shells. In the run-up to the Washington march, Hoffman and his collaborators planned a smattering of nonsensical responses.

We will dye the Potomac red, burn the cherry trees, panhandle embassies, attack with water pistols, marbles, gum wrappers, bazookas, girls will run naked and piss on the Pentagon walls, sorcerers, swamis, witches, voodoo, warlocks, medicine men, and speed freaks will hurl their magic at the faded brown walls. Rock bands will bomb out with "Joshua fit the Battle of Jericho." We will dance and sing and chant the mighty OM. We will fuck on the grass and beat ourselves against the doors. Everyone will scream "VOTE FOR ME!" We shall raise the flag of nothingness over the Pentagon and a mighty cheer of liberation will echo through the land. (Hoffman 1989, 26–7)

Few, if any, of these things happened. But at the March on the Pentagon, Hoffman and a cohort of sundry Yippies circled the Pentagon and, employing a rite composed for the occasion by Ed Sanders (of satirical New York rock band, the Fugs), attempted to levitate the building in order to exorcise its demons. Among the rites performed, the levitators specified the "placing of love-articles & clothing onto the pentagon: beads, feathers, rock & roll records, books & the sacred Grope Relic" (Bloch).

The point was not whether or not they succeeded in lifting the building off the ground or whether or not such an action would function as an exorcism rite. The point was to play it straight, to look the camera directly in the eye, and to say with all certainty that this is what will happen. As with the Stock Exchange incident, the camera cannot film this activity. The camera is the wrong tool. And thus the camera becomes irrelevant, useless as a conveyor or verifier of truth. There exists no frame for the levitation of the Pentagon. Whatever this act is, it does not have a beginning or an end, an inside or an outside. It is pointless for the announcer to tell us that they're trying to get a light on it. The director, back at the studio, cannot control the goings-on by bellowing into the cameraman's headset, "pull back, Jim, part of it is out of frame." The whole damned thing is out of frame.

At a press conference announcing the Pentagon protest, Hoffman describes how the levitation will go down:

We're going to assemble a mass of holy men to surround the Pentagon. And they're going to surround it with chanting and love and drum beating. And the Pentagon is going to rise into the air on October 21st. And when it gets about 300 feet in the air, it's going to start to vibrate, slowly at first, and then a little quicker. And all the evil spirits are going to pour out. (Hoffman, "Exorcise the Pentagon")

As Hoffman speaks, his eyes drift upward as if taking in the sight of the military-industrial complex floating above him. He can see it and he invites us to follow the arc of his vision as it fixes on a point in the sky. This is the moment of levitation. Hoffman delivers the sole documentation of the levitation. The event is inaccessible to cameras, beyond the scope of their powers. The reality of the levitation exists solely in Hoffman's verbal description and by the evidentiary movement of his eyes following the building's ascent. This is a kind of performance, a happening. To make sense of it, one might turn, not to Pollock or Kaprow or even Fried's feared minimalism, but to the thought experiments and idea events of the burgeoning conceptual art movement emerging concurrently some 200 miles north, straight up I-95 in New York City.

Just eleven months prior to the levitation, in December of 1966, Mel Bochner organized a show at the gallery at the School of Visual Arts in New York. The exhibition's discursive title, *Working drawings and other visible things on paper not necessarily meant to be viewed as art,* announced its subversive intentions. These intentions were manifest in four identical binders set atop plinths in the otherwise empty gallery space. The binders contain contributions by artists including Donald Judd, Robert Smithson, Eva Hesse, Sol LeWitt, Robert Mangold, Dan Graham, and John Cage, alongside projects by engineers, mathematicians, and choreographers. As the title suggests, each project consists only of paper-based drawings, texts, and documents, photocopied and inserted into the binders. Bochner's show is often cited as the first bona fide exhibition of conceptual art.

Three months later, in February 1967, the Lannis Gallery, run by artists Joseph Kosuth and Christine Kozlov, presented the conceptual exhibition *Non-anthropomorphic art by four young artists: Joseph Kosuth, Christine Kozlov, Michael Rinaldi, Ernest Rossi.* Kozlov's work of this period is notable for its use of the materials of mass media and of mechanical reproduction. Her work includes reels of unplayable audio tape, 8-mm film locked inside its canister. Her *Information Drift* (1968) purports to be recordings of news reports of the shootings of Bobby Kennedy and Andy Warhol (the two events separated by less than forty-eight hours). The experience and meaning of Kozlov's tape works is contingent on information not *in* it, but *about* it, provided by the artist. This deference to description bears obvious similarities to the Pentagon levitation. Hoffman's description of the levitation would perhaps sit most comfortably beside the conceptual work that curator, Seth Siegelaub, began to organize in and around New York during this same period. Think, for instance, of Robert Barry's *All the things I know but of which I am not at the moment thinking—1:36 p.m. June 15, 1969,* which consists of the title, installed neatly on the gallery wall.

Ostensibly, the work takes place entirely in Barry's head. But, of course, he coveys it to our heads by means of the minimal gesture of describing it to us. Thus the work becomes its description and the description becomes the work. Each folds indiscernibly into the other. What's more, the act, the event, the happening, exists, so far as we, the beholders, are concerned, only in the act of description. The words on the wall are, for all intents and purposes, Barry's act.

The same year, Barry made (described? imagined?) his *Inert Gas Series/ Helium, Neon, Argon, Krypton, Xenon/From a Measured Volume to Indefinite Expansion.* In this series of five works, Barry presents unassuming photographs of locations around Los Angeles. Sometimes, but not always, the photographs include a canister or a flask, set matter-of-factly on the ground. Accompanying the photographs, Barry provides brief explanatory texts, such as this one for *Helium*: "Sometime during the Morning of March 5, 1969, 2 cubic feet of Helium will be released into the atmosphere." Siegelaub's observation about Barry's action could also be said of Hoffman's description of the levitation of the Pentagon, "He has done something and it's definitely changing the world, however infinitesimally. He has put something into the world but you just can't see it or measure it. Something real but imperceptible" (Siegelaub, MoMA).

Fine, you may be saying, but what has all of this—Abbie Hoffman, the Pentagon in midair, Robert Barry opening a canister of gas in Malibu—got to do with rock and roll in its existential battle with modern life? Well, to channel Lester Bangs, I'll tell ya why and how. As this story is usually told, modernism confronts a set of crises in the late 1960s and into the 1970s. For Michael Fried, this challenge is spearheaded by minimalism. But surely, conceptualism is at least, if not more, counter-modern. Rock and roll joins the fray, challenging the singularity that underpins what is modern about modern art: a singularity that obtains in the experience of the beholder. To the same degree as minimalism, conceptualism, Fluxus, land art, or body art, rock and roll asks us to reconsider the modernist narrative of aesthetic progress and the entrenchment of an insular fraternity of White, male, American artists, each secure in his singular stylistic contribution to the history of art.

In 1979, Jean-François Lyotard insists that modernism had exhausted the utility of what he calls "grand narratives," that is, overarching stories that claim to explain the world and how it works. Organizing myths such as those of Christianity, capitalism, democracy, or personal and societal development no longer provide satisfactory accounts of, or justifications for, the conditions of life in the late twentieth century. As this story is customarily told, certain factors and figures maintain key roles in the instigation and maintenance of the transition to what is sometimes (controversially) called "postmodernism." The civil rights and global anti-colonial movements, anti-war protests, the suddenly widening generation gap, the assassinations of Malcolm X, Dr. King, and the Kennedys, the ensuing unrest and violence in America's cities and on college campuses, the events of May 1968 in France, the Prague Spring. These and other events augured a new set of individual, social, economic, and political relations. Perhaps more saliently, the rationale of Western societies in the late twentieth century was now subject to much closer scrutiny. There was no longer any reason to accept modern life as given, justified, or unchangeable.

Not unrelated to these changes, audiences, critics, and artists no longer found the conventional art object to be sufficient to their aesthetic demands. A wide set of practices, fragmented and no longer able to provide a singular experience or explanation, invaded the space of modernism. Robert Rauschenberg and Jasper Johns detached painting from its internal, formal moorings, literally (in some cases) breaking the frame. Fluxus disregarded the sanctified mandates of propriety, principle, and privilege. Carolee Schneemann (on whom, more in the following), Judy Chicago, Mierle Laderman Ukeles, Adrian Piper (on whom, more in Chapter 5), Mary Kelly, and other women disavowed the authorized perspectives and personas of "legitimate" art, infiltrating the male spaces of the commercial gallery and the museum, bringing with them a new set of concerns and strategies.

Pity the 1960s art school student. Off to classes where teachers ten or twenty years your senior impart wisdom about brush stroke, composition, medium specificity. Later that night, hanging out with friends, passing a joint, debating the war, the records play: the Stooges, the Beatles, the Velvet Underground, Jefferson Airplane, Jimi Hendrix, Led Zeppelin. On the weekend, burning draft cards, a tense anti-war demo facing down the National Guard, or a show at the Fillmore. Maybe Iggy's in town, his claymation body heaving itself across/onto/off the stage. Broken bottles. Threats. Blood. Iggy berates a biker who gives no quarter. Iggy dives. Hair and leather whip cyclonically in the fray until Iggy emerges, a welt blooming beneath his eye, both elbows scraped clean of skin. He scrabbles back to center stage, reclaims the mic stand, and the Stooges launch into "1970,"

> Out of my mind on Saturday night
> 1970 rollin' in sight
> Radio burnin' up above

Beautiful baby, feed my love
All night till I blow away

It's Monday morning. Back at the studio, coffee cup on the paint-splotched stool. A half-finished canvas on the easel, right where it was on Friday afternoon. A hazy memory of thinking that it needed something there: perhaps an orange patch or a mustard yellow to offset the darker areas at the left. Starting to mix the color, while scanning the studio for an appropriate brush. A long, considered look at the canvas before approaching.

Hold on. How can our student, buffeted by the maelstrom of late 1960s society and culture go on dabbing pigment on canvas as if anything at all depends on it? It is impossible to imagine that scrupulous studio technique could be the key to the door of this moment. It is 1965 or 1968 or 1970. The Stooges rage out of their minds. Riot on the stage. Riot in the streets. Riot in the mind. Nothing holds still in its vessel. Everything spills. Pollock splatters his angst. Allan Kaprow pushes further out, citing Pollock's example, contorting the art work into a "happening." Abbie Hoffman, finding happenings too bourgeois, too contained and constrained, also conjures Pollock when he urges us to "hurl ourselves across the canvas of society like streaks of splattered paint." By now, though, calling it "art" is just unnecessary. The seeds of the revolution were planted by the Old Regime.

These seeds take the form of a fecund illogic in the modernist program. Pursuing the modernist project to its natural conclusions leads to distinctly counter-modern destinations. Greenberg and, more explicitly, Fried seek transcendence. Their chosen vehicle, though, is the staid, static, canvas, and the immobile sculpture, bounded by clear formal limits and by strict medial domains. Ultimately, the modernist work follows a line of evolution, continually improving upon the previous step, moving toward a denouement so convincing that it will speak declaratively for itself. The modernist proof will be in the modernist pudding.

Fried says of minimalism (which he insists on calling "literalism") that it "seeks to declare and occupy a position—one which can be formulated in words, and in fact has been formulated by some of its leading practitioners." It is this ability to formulate its positions in words which, "distinguishes it from modernist painting and sculpture" (Fried 12). The modernist work is self-evident, while the postmodern, the counter-modern, requires external explication to make sense of what it is doing and how. Yet, what have Fried and Greenberg been doing, if not formulating their modernist position in words? One could convincingly argue that modernist aesthetics only coalesces in the crucible of its theorization. (One could probably make this argument about any position, aesthetic, or otherwise.) Had it not been for Greenberg's brilliant, compelling interventions into the practices of Pollock, David Smith, de Kooning, and Barnett Newman, modern art might have been understood quite differently. Abstract Expressionism might not have risen to its place of prominence at all. Greenberg's methodical schema establishes the historical precedents (nearly the inevitability) of modernist painting and sculpture. At the same time, he makes a philosophical argument about how and why modernism complements the Enlightenment project, how it forms a more coherent system of composition and judgment than previous aesthetics. The arts, he insists, were obliged to respond to Enlightenment demands. Art needed to distinguish itself from other human endeavors and justify its contributions to social life, culture, and history.

> We know what has happened to an activity like religion that has not been able to avail itself of Kantian immanent criticism in order to justify itself. At first glance the arts might seem to have been in a situation like religion's. Having been denied by the Enlightenment all tasks they could take seriously, they looked as though they were going to be assimilated to entertainment pure and simple, and entertainment itself looked as though it was going to be assimilated, like religion, to therapy. The arts could save themselves from this leveling down only by demonstrating that the kind of experience they provided was valuable in its own right and not to be obtained from any other kind of activity. (Greenberg 5)

In nominating himself to provide this demonstration, Greenberg sanctified his own project as something more than the traditional task of the critic. His criticism could save art from the dustbin of post-Enlightenment history.

At the same time, Greenberg balances his efforts on a rickety political foundation that allows him to align his formalism with his vaguely leftist sympathies. In 1938, Greenberg was an editor at *Partisan Review*. He and his fellow editors sought the validation of the international Left. They wrote repeatedly to Leon Trotsky, then living in exile in Mexico, asking him to contribute to their journal. When Trotsky finally assented, he did so not as a contributor, but in the form of letters to the editor that would allow him to keep his critical distance from the *Partisan Review* project. In one letter, dated January 1938, Trotsky left little doubt about his assessment of the journal's politics, "It is my general impression that the editors of *Partisan Review* are capable, educated and intelligent people but they have nothing to say. They seek themes which are incapable of hurting anyone but which likewise are incapable of giving anybody a thing" (Trotsky). Nevertheless, he wrote again in June of that year.

> Art, like science, not only does not seek orders, but by its very essence, cannot tolerate them. Artistic creation has its laws—even when it consciously serves a social movement. [. . .] Art can become a strong ally of revolution only in so far as it remains faithful to itself. (Trotsky)

In this second letter, it is possible to discern what Greenberg might have taken to be a kind of permission from Trotsky, paragon and great hope of international socialism, to pursue art for art's sake. Greenberg could pursue his formalist analyses and valuations secure in his knowledge that formal, modernist art was doing its part in the revolution. Trotsky's declaration provided Greenberg with a committed ideological backstop.

By the 1960s, artists from myriad backgrounds began to suspect that the Greenbergian program was less airtight than had been reported. They found and sought experiences living outside modernism's hermeticism: out in the air, out in the streets (the New Jersey Turnpike?); manifest not in the fixed materiality of pigment, wood, or stone, but in the kinetic corporeality of the body, the fluidity of thought, the ephemerality of time. Pity the 1960s art school student. Except that Carolee Schneemann doesn't want your pity. Schneemann emerged as one of the earliest, most inspired, and radically innovative challengers of modernism's frames. Already, by the early 1960s, Schneemann's work had turned from emphasizing the formal output of a process (a painting, a sculpture) to stressing the process itself: time-based, dynamic, kinetic, or otherwise inconstant. Schneemann saw her work of this period as connected to the Abstract Expressionism of her schooling. But it is also important to realize—or to notice—that Schneemann's work is a kind of archaeology. From the abstraction that she inherited as a painter, she extracts the dynamism of the gesture, the corporeality of the body, the kinetics of making, the temporality of process. She also seeks a rupture from the male gaze that underwrites modernist aesthetics, holding the feminine body—literal or figurative—captive and immobile. If the male painter or beholder (suddenly Fried's term of art takes on a more sinister blush) objectivizes the female model, then, by extension, femaleness itself is objectivized. Syllogistically, one might conclude that since subjects perceive objects—and the male perceives the female—the male is the subject and the female is the object (ipso facto: objects are categorically female). *Meat Joy* and most of Schneeman's work from the 1960s and 1970s reclaim female subjectivity by reclaiming the control of the body (including its liberty to lose control). It also strikes at the framed and framing male gaze by placing the "picture" not in space but in time, by making it mobile, spontaneous, unanswerable to formal queries.

> In 1963 to use my body as an extension of my painting-constructions was to challenge and threaten the psychic territorial power lines by which women were admitted to the Art Stud Club so long as they behaved enough like the men, did work clearly in the traditions & pathways being hacked out by the men. (Schneemann, quoted in Foerschner and Rivenc 169)

Schneemann responds directly to the subject-object problem inherent in male-female relations. Her off-the-canvas work confronts the conflict between the (male) eye and the (female) body. 1963's *Eye Body* stages Schneeman's body as an object for the eye's delectation. But in this series of photographs, Schneemann suggests that her object-body is reclaiming its subjectivity in direct disobeyance of the camera's tacit demands. The images present themselves as discrete slices of a continuous process. Each photograph seems to have been plucked from an ongoing series of movements and actions. The impression is that of documentation of a performance, necessarily incomplete and merely suggestive of the whole. The viewer is fully aware that there is at least as much absent as present in this sequence of images. The work is staged for the camera, but not in service (or subservience) to it. Rather, as with conceptual art or Hoffman's levitation, the camera is invited to catch what it can, while at the same time being forced to admit that it is at the mercy of the performance, of time, of circumstance, and accident. The best the camera can do is to "try to get a light on" Schneemann's metamorphoses, knowing full well that it is bound to fail.

In her notebooks, Schneemann writes,

> *Eye Body* was performed as an Event for Camera: focus in evocation and salvage, concretization of dream images, visions of materials, substances in interchange (paint on flesh, flesh against wood, glass, paint — the ambiguous, shifting dimensionality of the works themselves incorporating the figure) I wanted to experience the expanding action, from that by which I had made the paintings and constructions to turning myself into an aspect of the work. (Schneemann, quoted in Foerschner and Rivenc 169)

Schneemann's work of this era—falling in between the temblor of Checker's "Twist" and the Beatles' seismic touchdown at the recently renamed JFK airport—applies pressure to the frame's joints, testing its solidity, torqueing its plasticity. The frame around the object that is the female body begins to bend, then splinter. The male eye that subjects the female to the frame takes those splinters squarely in the retina, blinding its ability to locate the borders required to contain and constitute its object. In Schneemann's work, the modernist dictum of singularity is replaced by a multiplicity distributed in space, time, and perspectival authority. As Amelia Jones has observed, these performances enact,

> the dispersed, multiplied, specific subjectivities of the late capitalist, postcolonial, post-modern era: subjectivities that are acknowledged to exist always already in relation to the world of other objects and subjects; subjectivities that are always already intersubjective as well as interobjective. . . . it is precisely the relationship of these bodies/subjects to documentation (or, more specifically, to re-presentation) that most profoundly points to the dislocation of the fantasy of the fixed, normative, centered modernist subject and thus most dramatically provides a radical challenge to the masculinism, racism, colonialism, classism, and hetero-sexism built into this fantasy. (Jones 12)

Anna Dezeuze observes that *Meat Joy* (originally presented in 1964) both inherits and responds to the modernism of Schneemann's training, "As performers shift from painting to pouring paint over each other by the bucket, Abstract Expressionism feels very close. The energy of the performers' movements, to which the artist often refers, [echoes] Jackson Pollock's gestural dance on the canvas" (Dezeuze 4). The structure of the *Meat Joy* performance moves from a distanced, pre-theatrical setup—in which performers talk and drink, preparing for the event—to a series of intimate interactions involving art materials and a kind of allegorical staging of art-enshrined subject-object relations, to its final, most (in)famous scene: a writhing mass of nearly naked human bodies entwining with each other, with raw poultry, sausages, and fish. Notably, the work's soundtrack employs numerous pop and rock and roll hits of the day, including, Elvis Presley's "Blue Suede Shoes," Little Richard's "Tutti Frutti," the Supremes' "Baby Love," Lesley Gore's "That's The Way Boys Are," and the Beatles' "From Me To You." Most of the songs in the performance were released in 1963 or 1964. Their use in *Meat Joy* leverages the immediacy of songs that have recently arrived, exploiting their ability to timestamp the moment as "now" while also taking advantage of their inherent ephemerality. The use of rock and roll contributes to an untethered, performative energetics; a transcendence that doesn't believe in, or have use for, a notion of an outside or an elsewhere. Instead, something different, something "other," can be constructed right here, right now, of the same materials from which the old order emerged, but reconceived, rearranged, and reinvigorated. Inspiration can be found within rather than without. Jonathan Edwards's "proof of a God" can be replaced with proof of reality, stripped bare of its blinders, its camouflage, its sanctions and solemn verities.

Amelia Jones recognizes that performance's claim to "radical presence" can sometimes be turned against itself or against the modernism it has inherited. Jones focuses on performance's dependence on documentation to problematize such claims. But she also recognizes that for Schneemann (and others) active engagement in time and space is intentionally complicated in order to reveal the impossibility of anything like unmediated experience. Jones writes that such "desire for immediacy is, precisely, a modernist . . . dream" (Jones 17). The frame of the moment is destabilized in the subversive work of early performance art—paradigmatically Schneemann's.

> In this fin-de-millennium age of multinational capitalism, virtual realities, postcolonialism, and cyborg identity politics, . . . such a dream must be viewed as historically specific rather than epistemologically secure. Body and performance art expose, precisely, the contingency of the body/self not only on the other of the communicative exchange . . . but on the very modes of its own (re)presentation. (Jones 17)

Schneemann's use of rock and roll is not coincidental—or rather, it is precisely coincidental: both in the sense of occurring at the same time, but also faithful to the Latin etymology: her work *falls together with* rock and roll. Both fall into the social, cultural, and aesthetic paradigms of the mid-1960s. Importantly they are not placed, they fall. Lacking the disciplinary structures or languages of trained practitioners, rock and roll allows otherwise uninspired teenagers to scavenge equipment and inspiration and to force into existence an aesthetic response to the clarion call of the times: a jalopy rigged of scrapped parts, frustration, anger, lust, and mimicry. Schneemann's work of the 1960s, emerging in tandem with rock and roll in mass (read: *White*) consciousness, offers the era's most radical rejection of mid-century modern art dogma.

# 4

# The Politics and Ethics of Ecstasy

History's a trickster. Exhibit A: the epicenter of 1967's "Summer of Love" was a street pronounced "hate." Not even a novelist of Joan Didion's talent could make this stuff up. But she could catch wind of it; the stench of something rotting in the flower beds. Didion had visited San Francisco at the behest of the *Saturday Evening Post*, which wanted her to get a light on it, as it were. Middle America knew that something was happening, but it didn't know what it was. The "it" in this case, was the hippie movement. Across the country, kids were opting out of the plans that had been made for them: college, a job, marriage, kids of their own. With no readymade alternative to this readymade future, they decamped to the intersection of Ashbury and Haight Streets in San Francisco, looking for something different. Didion followed them there, hoping to clarify precisely what it was that was happening for the readers of the *Saturday Evening Post*, for the parents of these wayward children.

Didion noticed something that others hadn't. The media had it wrong—these kids were not the cause of the problems affecting the nation's nervous system. The hippies were merely a symptom. The kids, themselves, had it wrong—peace and love were just words, words that are singularly hard to pronounce in a system founded on violence, built by slave labor, supported by might-makes-right relations. So the kids kept mouthing the words, like some desperate incantation. They had little else to do. Without the required knowledge or skills to actually build peace and love, clueless about the world that had to be disassembled first, these kids wandered the streets, hustled for drug money, ran themselves down until the incantation revealed itself to be a whispered lie passed from mouth to mouth like a dissipating joint. Didion understood that the hippies' dreams were bound to evaporate because they had no foundation to rest upon, no atmosphere to breathe, no ground to nourish their roots. Every time such a base threatened to materialize, to offer advantageous conditions for growth, it had been systematically destroyed by the interests of those with money and authority. Didion described the hippies' project as "the desperate attempt of a handful of pathetically unequipped children to create a community in a social vacuum." Once she trained her camera's lens on them, we would be unable to sympathetically picture them as they wanted to be seen, or to see them depicted as the broad strokes of the nightly news broadcasts painted them.

> Once we had seen these children, we could no longer overlook the vacuum, no longer pretend that the society's atomization could be reversed. At some point between 1945 and 1967, we had somehow neglected to tell these children the rules of the game we happened to be playing. Maybe we had stopped believing in the rules ourselves. (Didion 94)

Didion's account is liberally populated by the bands of the San Francisco scene: the Grateful Dead, Quicksilver Messenger Service, Big Brother, and the Holding Company. In the vacuum, the bands supply an otherwise absent center of gravity. They become inadvertent leaders, willfully oblivious to their power, convinced of their own benevolence and of a fictional equality among everyone in the scene: boys and girls, Black and White, old and young, bands and groupies. Unlike so many others on the scene, the bands have a purpose. They are creating, building careers. They are not focused on whatever incipient politics may be brimming in the Haight. But, as Didion informs us, the bands see the politics bubbling to the surface, "because they were often where it was happening."

> "In the Park there are always twenty or thirty people below the stand," one of the Grateful Dead complained to me, "ready to take the crowd on some militant trip." (Didion 93)

Meanwhile, somewhere else, Bob Dylan was playing similar games but with much higher stakes. Rather than play dumb, Dylan played at being smarter and slipperier than all the cameras whose shudders snapped around his chimerical self; a rushing creek slithering through the jaws of a snapping bear trap.

Dylan was a synthesis of multiple strands of American history and culture. He was simultaneously, or alternately, the embodiment of the rural and the cosmopolitan, the naïve and the worldly, the past and the future, folk culture and pop culture. He was uniquely photogenic, but he also assembled snapshots of his surroundings that were unrivalled in their ability to locate the singularity of moments and psychologies. He could outdance the spotlight, rupture each successive frame as it stabilized around him. His songs, recordings, and performances were exercises akin to painting the Golden Gate Bridge: by the time you got to the end, the beginning was already being restarted, generating a loop that confused the sanctity of the task, folding its incipience into its telos; its death situated as a precursor to its birth. Dylan's art, as much as anyone's— Judd's, Godard's, Schneemann's, Warhol's, James Brown's—demanded that we begin again: repaint (if not rebuild) our bridges. If the flower children of the Haight were cut loose in a vacuum devoid of meaning, structure, and value, Dylan was leaning hard on precedents, piecing together a new music and image from spare parts and off-the-shelf familiarities. In 1965, when Dylan "went electric" at the Newport Folk Festival, he was merely adding another joist to his ramshackle Rimbaudian chateau. Unlike folk music, which hearkened to (and retrospectively fabricated) an earlier and simpler time, rock and roll allowed Dylan to answer the whirlwind of his personal and societal present. As early as 1967, Ellen Willis observed that "chaos had become a condition, like the weather, not to analyze or prophesy but to gripe about, cope with, dodge" (Willis 27). (I have my doubts about awarding Dylan the Nobel Prize for literature, but if there were a Nobel for griping, coping, and dodging, he'd be a shoo-in.)

While hippie culture and mass media were embracing Dylan as a kind of elected representative for a new social sensibility, Willis understood that Dylan's true position was not in synch with the Haight demimonde or the beaded boys inserting daisies into the muzzles of M16s. "Dylan was really at cross-purposes with the hippies. They were trying to embody pop sensibility in a folk culture. He was trying to comprehend pop culture with—at bottom—a folk sensibility" (Willis 30–1). Unwittingly, the hippies were making themselves into a type, a form easily emulated by lost souls in search of an identity, but also by Madison Avenue ad men and department store chains. In 1971, Coca-Cola had already produced a TV spot in which dozens of kids: East Asian, Indian, Black, White, boys and girls—in frocks, turtlenecks, and dashikis—adorn a grassy hilltop (apparently in Italy). Their faces glow with the rays of the setting sun. Each of them holds a bottle of Coke. Each bottle displays the international brand's locally customized logo. The kids sing together, in harmony, about harmony. But they also sing about Coke, of course, and about a particularly 1960s vision of peace and love, as filtered through the sensibilities of commerce. The vision is of a folk, living unfettered, at one with their environment. The framing, however, is that of pop: mediated for mass consumption of the ad itself and of the product for which it shills. The ad opens on the face of a girl, blonde and blue-eyed, gazing hopefully into the distance. She begins the song alone: "I'd like to buy the world a home and furnish it with love." It would have been easy, natural even, for the song to speak of "building" or "finding" a home. But buying is what this ad—every ad—is about. So the beautiful, harmonious home will be bought for us by this wholesome young woman. The camera zooms out to reveal the rest of the kids as they join in, singing of "apple trees and honey bees and snow white turtle doves." By the time the ad cuts to an aerial shot of the whole hilltop, dozens of the world's children assembled and singing in harmony, we learn that Coca-Cola is "the real thing, what the world wants today." The ad was such a success that, not one, but two different groups, released expanded versions of the song "I'd Like to Teach the World to Sing (in Perfect Harmony)," removing the references to Coke. Both versions were hits, ascending to number 13 and number 7 on the US charts.

Willis is alert to the tensions between frame and freedom, between official- and counterculture. As with Fried, Mailer, and Hoffman, this tension is not solely produced by opposition but equally by assumptions and desires held in common. The friction is generated by this proximity of ideals; by dialectic inversions of interpretations and responses. "Conservative and utopian ideologues agree that man must understand and control his environment; the questions are how, and for whose benefit" (Willis 32). Willis's analysis balances on the fine fulcrum supporting the antithesis of pop and folk. As she sees it, "pop culture defines man as a receiver of stimuli, his environment as sensory patterns to be enjoyed, not interpreted (literature and philosophy are irrelevant) or acted upon (politics is irrelevant)" (Willis 32). Folk, by contrast, works on its environment. It builds a cabin in the woods. It spins yarn for (and yarns about) itself. Literature is not merely reflective of its environment. Folk tells stories to give meaningful shape to experience. The antagonism is embodied in the structure and subjects of modern society, most starkly perhaps in the figure of the bureaucrat who "defends standardization because it makes a complex society manageable. Yet he thinks of himself as an individualist and finds the idea of mass-produced, mechanized art incomprehensible, threatening—or a put-on" (Willis 32).

In the 1960s, rock and roll was embedded in these contradictions: on the one hand avowedly individualist and on the other confronting traditional media and mediums, forcing them to reconsider their relation to their contemporary cultural conditions. In the rarified climes of the gallery arts, sculpture was losing its footing amidst the increasingly sculptural environment of postwar commodity culture. Technology and the ubiquity of consumer goods situated the perceiving body in a fortress of three-dimensional objects designed to promulgate desire. Many of these objects were mobile, either portable or ambulatory, not sitting still for the contemplation of the perceiving body, but manically traversing its space and attention. Cars, moving pictures, conveyor belts, shelves of jars, radios, electric toys, neon signs, public address systems, elevators, escalators, lights across the night sky: rock and roll was the equal of these twitchy gadgets. Dylan figured this kinetic moment like electricity in a downed wire. He was, himself, both wired and wiry, constantly moving in space and time; constantly forming/deforming/reforming; never the same figure twice. Constantly inconstant. Ultimately, it was not his sound, his syntax, nor his semantics that would influence the trajectory of rock and roll, but his twitchy recalcitrance. The sacred, static, sculptural form is ill-suited to respond to this newly erratic, motile world. Rock and roll, however, makes perfect sense. It is both the reflection of restless technological commodity culture and a tool for subduing its most unnerving features.

Too many commentators want to frame Dylan, to stabilize him as an image, to concretize him and his work as a form. When Christopher Ricks (and others) grab for Dylan with their poet gloves, and the Nobel committee anoints him with their laureate wand, they essentially misapprehend the nature of his art. Unlike the stable page, the song doesn't hold still. It vibrates in time and when you reach the end, the beginning has already restarted, different from last time or next time. You cannot look at it synoptically, holding its top and bottom, its inner core and outer extremities, all equally in focus. Cameras falter in the presence of music, especially Dylan's. Because it is Dylan's voice, not the words it sings, that is his most powerful weapon. When others sing his words they almost always lose their charge. The Byrds; Peter, Paul, and Mary; Sonny and Cher; Joan Baez; The Staple Singers: the list goes on.[1] So many cover versions of Dylan songs stumble awkwardly into the ravine of righteous intentions. When these versions work, it is almost always due to something peculiar to the performance, something that sidesteps the burden of the words and the cultural specificity of Dylan's original.

When Dylan sings his own songs, he approaches the task with the insouciant disregard of a pipefitter working in the basement of a man he dislikes. He distorts the structures of the songs with contortionistic gusto, insuring that the material can indeed travel from point A to point B, but without instrumental concerns for efficiency or strain upon the system. His phrasing tortures individual syllables

---

[1]  For an exhaustive (but still probably incomplete) list of artists who have covered Dylan's songs, see: https://en.wikipedia.org/wiki/List_of_artists_who_have_covered_Bob_Dylan_songs

and sounds. Tellingly, when his voice is absent, he goes for the harmonica like a petty thug in an alley brawl retrieving the dagger from his ankle sheath. Allen Ginsberg once described Dylan as a "column of air." The harmonica is all air, all breath: exhale and inhale. It is the lungs without language. Listen to the live ten-minute and forty-four-second version of "Mr. Tambourine Man" on the *Rites of Spring* bootleg. The harmonica reels out beyond the boundaries of the song, daring something else to land in the space the song has created, to colonize it, to recast it, to reengineer its innards such that its heart is routed directly to its lungs. The harmonica begins manically repeating a simple phrase, falling out of time and phasing against the strumming guitar (beating Steve Reich to the punch by a matter of months), then after a long moaning howl which simultaneously conjures the two great beasts of the Western desolation of Dylan's myth: the coyote and the locomotive, the harmonica escapes the tether of the chords into a territory that Ornette Coleman might have called harmolodic. At the end of the song, the harmonica and the guitar—without Dylan's voice, without his words— tear at and torment the song, pulling its skin away from its bones. It sounds for all the world like a one-man-band version of the Velvet Underground's "Sister Ray." Music trying to destroy the very idea of music.

Not only the commentators, but also the fans, the cameras, the headlines, the glossy magazine covers, wanting to concretize Dylan as an image, also wanted to define him as a figure: social, cultural, political, historical. He was the voice of his generation. Or else he was the conscience of the 1960s. He was a poet, a ragamuffin, Charlie Chaplin, Woody Guthrie redux. When audiences looked at him, they saw an answer. They saw a composite of the society's most alluring dreams: honesty and theatrics, hard work and escapism, ethical intuitions and personal liberation, conviction and comedy. The picture they collaged together, like the cover of the September 1968 *Esquire* magazine—featuring a composite face constructed of one-quarter each of the faces of Malcolm X, John F. Kennedy, Fidel Castro, and Dylan—was not so much an actually existing person in the world, as a dream of something that the audience themselves needed.

Willis, ever on point, notes that the audience's "passion told less about Dylan than about their own peculiar compound of aristocratic and proletarian sensitivities" (Willis 28).

The threat of this dream is that it cannot abide self-doubt. The dream inflates itself with purity and insulates itself in the impenetrability of faith. As James Baldwin warned, "No one is more dangerous than he who imagines himself pure in heart: for his purity, by definition, is unassailable" (Baldwin 277). As kids in the Haight and the mass media alike discovered or invented heroes—like *Esquire's* Franken-zeitgeist—it became almost inevitable that gods would emerge among men. A "San Francisco psychiatrist" offered this observation to Joan Didion:

> Anybody who thinks this is all about drugs has his head in a bag. It's a social movement, quintessentially romantic, the kind that recurs in times of real social crisis. The themes are always the same. A return to innocence. The invocation of an earlier authority and control. The mysteries of the blood. An itch for the transcendental, for purification. Right there you've got the ways that romanticism historically ends up in trouble, lends itself to authoritarianism. (Didion 93)

Dylan was one of the gods *du jour*. He came out of nowhere, seemingly unaware of his gifts and his magnetism. He conjured a past that was as innocent and as true as it was fictional and willfully blind to its own barbarity. Greil Marcus calls it "the old, weird America." Dylan tapped into something uniquely American, something in the soil, something bigger than himself, something that presented itself as lost and recovered; messianic in its gravity. Marcus observes that Dylan, "embodied a yearning for peace and home in the midst of noise and upheaval." Rather than presenting a kind of emotional utopia, neatly boxed for consumption, Dylan's songs,

> located both peace and home in the purity, the essential goodness, of each listener's heart. It was this purity, this glimpse of a democratic oasis unsullied by commerce or greed, that in the late 1950s and early 1960s so many young people began to hear in the blues and ballads first recorded in the 1920s and 1930s, by people mostly from small towns and tiny settlements in the South, a strange and foreign place to most who were now listening—music that seemed the product of no ego but of the inherent genius of a people—the people—people one could embrace and, perhaps, become. It was the sound of another country—a country that, once glimpsed from afar, could be felt within oneself. (Marcus 2011, 21)

When Dylan veered off course, zigzagging aimlessly, the listeners—the people— took it personally, because the path was not his alone. Moses couldn't just go off for a wander, while the Israelites followed their destiny to Jerusalem. Dylan was the one who knew the way and he was expected to lead them. He received the commandments and he was expected to follow them.

Thou shalt not amplify.
Thou shalt not don a herringbone suit.
Thou shalt not accept thirty pieces of silver.

On December 3, 1965, KQED television in San Francisco broadcast a one-hour program simply entitled "Press Conference Bob Dylan," hosted by Ralph Gleason, a music critic for *The San Francisco Chronicle* and, later, a founding editor of *Rolling Stone*. Gleason enters KQED's studio with Dylan and begins speaking to those assembled. His first few sentences are difficult to make out. Almost comically, Gleason, a doyen of the printed page—not the camera and the microphone—seems blissfully oblivious to the fact that they're trying to get a light on him. Only after he points to a microphone positioned on a stand just behind him and asks rhetorically, "oh, I'm supposed to be talking to this microphone?" can we clearly make out his words: "Mr. Dylan is a poet. He will answer questions about everything from atomic science to riddles and rhymes. Go" (Bob Dylan San Francisco Press Conference 1965). What follows is fifty-one minutes of absurdist theater that neither Abbie Hoffman, Antonin Artaud, nor Samuel Beckett could have conjured.

The first question is posed by Eric Weill, an amateur photographer, well known in the Bay Area counterculture.[2] Weill cuts a figure almost satirically of its times: heavy dark-framed glasses, a Garibaldi beard, and a head of curly hair to rival Dylan's own. Weill asks Dylan about the photograph on the cover of the album, *Highway 61 Revisited*, mistakenly referring to it as "the one with 'Subterranean Homesick Blues.'" Weill is over-eager. "I'd like to know the meaning of the photograph of you wearing the Triumph T-shirt. That's an equivalent photograph," Weill says, "it means something. It's got a philosophy in it" (Bob Dylan San Francisco Press Conference 1965). When Dylan, amused by the specificity of Weill's inquiry, replies, "Um, I haven't really looked at it that much," Weill shoots back, "I've thought about it a great deal." The camera cuts from Dylan to Weill whose eyes have turned inquisitorial, accusing. He ominously licks his lips—a cartoon wolf moving in on the chicken. Above him the boom microphone momentarily breaks the frame. They're trying to get a light on him as he's trying to get a light on the photograph the camera took of Dylan in his Triumph motorcycle shirt. "It was just taken one day when I was sitting on the steps, you know," replies Dylan as he reaches into his jacket for a pack of cigarettes, "I don't really remember too much about it."

---

[2] To identify those in attendance at the press conference, I've relied on the painstaking work of someone using the screen name "cripes." The information was first posted in 2007 and most recently updated in 2018. The fascinating documentation is compiled here: https://kripes.proboards.com/thread/1 (last accessed March 1, 2021).

The scene defies easy characterization. It is at once casual—the inhabitants of a particular milieu gathering to chat about their mutual interests—and formal, the press—many of them not of the scene—putting stiffly formulated questions to the 24-year-old singer. Laughter often erupts unexpectedly and exaggeratedly. There is a palpable nervousness, not just on Dylan's part, but throughout the room. The scenario is part celebrity meet-and-greet, part visitation with a holy man, part-slapstick comedy, and part interrogation of a master criminal in which the detectives already know they can't make the charges stick. At 13:30 of the YouTube clip, Claude Mann of KTVU in San Francisco says, "Mr. Dylan, I know you dislike labels and probably rightly so, but for those of us who are well over thirty, could you label yourself and perhaps tell us what your role is?" This question seems self-aware of its own squareness and once Dylan speaks it almost seems like a setup for a punch line. Dylan responds, "I sort of label myself as well under thirty [laughter] and my role is, you know, just to stay here as long as I can [more laughter]."

It is a strange question. Bob Dylan is a songwriter, a singer, and a musician. The labels could not have been more clear. And as offbeat and square as the first part of the question is, it takes another second to register how strange the second part is. In the context of a team or a group effort of some sort, one might reflect on one's role. But in the context of this press conference with a young singer-songwriter, the question hardly makes sense. That is, unless we acknowledge that the culture of the time was beginning to see Dylan as having a role (even if he himself did not). Returning to Ellen Willis's foregoing observation, the questions of those assembled at KQED "told less about Dylan than about their own peculiar compound of aristocratic and proletarian sensitivities" (Willis 28). As a devotee, Eric Weill seeks insights from the eye of the storm. "What's it like in there?" "What can you see or feel or think that we can't?" As a responsible journalist, Claude Mann is compelled to enter the lair of the untamed beast and to return to civilization with pronouncements that the plumbers and parents, the principals and politicians, might understand. From this perspective, the question makes subtextual sense. Mann is simply asking the questions a good journalist would ask of any would-be messiah: "Are you what they say you are?" "How do you plan to exercise your power?" "Will this all end well?"

Once we make sense of the questions themselves, we can zoom out to see just how ludicrous the whole picture is. Jean Gleason, wife and collaborator of Ralph, citing a recent article by Phil Ochs in *Broadside* magazine, asks Dylan—the 24-year-old singer-songwriter—if he fears for his life.

At 15:35, Dylan is asked if he is planning any demonstrations. He hesitantly describes a protest in which 25,000–30,000 cards are printed up with pictures of "jack of diamonds and the ace of spades, pictures of mules, maybe words . . . [people] carry the signs and just picket." Someone at the press conference asks, "what words?" The first thing that pops into Dylan's head is "camera"—understandable given that a pair of them are just then staring him in the face (Figure 4.1). The second word, equally understandable, is "microphone." At 26:50 he is asked how he would define folk music. He answers, "as a constitutional replay of mass production." He is asked if protest songs are folk songs, to which he replies, "I guess, if they're 'a constitutional replay of mass production.'" The only definitions that make sense are tautological. "This is a portrait of Iris Clert if I say so." At 43:07, Rollin Post of KPIX, asks Dylan if he can explain his popularity. Something about Post's tone strikes Dylan's ear, his eyebrows dip as he locates Post in the room. "What do you want me to say?" he bristles. "Tell me, I'll go along with you. If I can't go along with you, I'll find somebody to go along with you." Post wants an explanation, a frame, around this phenomenon; a way to name it and to hold it steady. But Dylan is in synch with the capriciousness of the times. He knows that not everything has a name.

**Figure 4.1**  Bob Dylan press conference, KQED San Francisco, 1965.

That even things that do have names, change their names. "It happened," he says of his popularity, "it happened like anything else happens. It's just a happening. You don't figure out happenings. You dig happenings" (Bob Dylan San Francisco Press Conference 1965). And, finally, almost as if by design, the most revealing and earnest answer of the press conference comes in response to what turned out to be the last question. KGO news anchor, Jerry Jensen asks, "What's more important to you, the way that your music and words sound or the content, the message of the work?" Dylan doesn't snicker while he tries to explain to Jensen and the rest of the room that the old form-content dichotomy just doesn't hold anymore. "The whole thing, while it's happening," says Dylan, his eyebrows arch with the word "happening" and he nods a little to make sure we understand that he believes what he's just said. "The whole, total sound of the words. What's really going down. It either happens or it doesn't happen, you know? Just the thing which is happening there at that time. That's what we do, you know. That is the most important thing. There really isn't anything else." For the first and only time, Dylan confesses, "I don't know if I'm answering your question." He then tries to clarify. This point seems to be the only thing he's cared to communicate directly—rather than through irony and sarcasm—over the entire hour.

> Most of the time it does come across. Most of the time we do feel like we're playing. That's important to me. The aftermath, or whatever happens before and after is not really important to me. Just the time on the stage, and the time that we're singing the songs, and performing them. Or, not really performing them even, just letting them be there. (Bob Dylan San Francisco Press Conference 1965)

This emphasis, this insistence really, on what is happening is the triangulation of form and content, or their explosion in time and as time. Jensen's question is thoughtful enough. It makes perfect sense in the modernist paradigms of 1965. It is a question that—slightly reformulated—Jackson Pollock could have answered, or Ezra Pound or Arnold Schoenberg. Even Greta Garbo, Muddy Waters, Charlie Chaplin, or Gertrude Stein. But Dylan isn't working in that paradigm. Beyond the form and content of his work, there is the liveness. Not the same thing as the presentness beloved of Michael Fried. This *happeningness*, if you'll tolerate the coinage, can't be framed. It can't be put away in storage. Like Robert Morris's mirrored cubes it only happens while it's happening. And this happeningness is what Dylan prizes, what he's at pains to communicate to those gathered for the 1965 press conference. In the mid-1960s, "happening" was a radically everywhere word. Dylan wasn't the only one realizing that a happening or the quality of happeningness was fundamentally different than what modernism had wanted and been satisfied with. By 1965 "happening" was understood as both a verb and a noun, sometimes simultaneously. Recall the chorus of Dylan's "Ballad of a Thin Man," from *Highway 61 Revisited*—a staple of his sets at the time: "You know that something is happening, but you don't know what it is, do you, Mr. Jones?"

In 1965, John Berryman won the Pulitzer Prize for poetry for his book, *77 Dream Songs*, the fourteenth of which begins:

> Life, friends, is boring. We must not say so.
> After all, the sky flashes, the great sea yearns,
> we ourselves flash and yearn,
> and moreover my mother told me as a boy
> (repeatedly) "Ever to confess you're bored . . .
> means you have no
>
> Inner Resources." I conclude now I have no
> inner resources, because I am heavy bored.
> Peoples bore me,
> literature bores me, especially great literature . . . (Berryman)

By the arrival of the 1970s, you could reasonably conclude that the existential threat of the times wasn't nuclear annihilation, racism, colonialism, misogyny, or economic exploitation, but plain old boredom.

> Abbie Hoffman: "One of the worst mistakes any revolution can make is to become boring."
> Michel Fried: "Literalist work is often condemned . . . for being boring. A tougher charge would be that it is merely interesting."
> Norman Mailer: "The decision is to encourage the psychopath in oneself to explore that domain of experience where security is boredom and therefore sickness."

Boredom is assuredly not the first thing that comes to mind when we think of the artist Chris Burden. The man had himself shot with a .22 caliber rifle, had himself crucified on the back of a Volkswagen Beetle, toyed with electrocution and drowning, and crawled naked through broken glass. He was sometimes referred to as "Modernism's Evel Knievel" (*New York Times*, "Chris Burden, a Conceptualist with Scars, Dies at 69"). But it is easy to see Burden's daredevil aesthetics as a response to pervasive boredom. Another current in his work courted boredom more directly.

For his Master's thesis in 1971, Chris Burden interned himself for five days in a school locker measuring two by two by three feet. In the locker above his, a five gallon jug of water was accessible via a hose. A similar arrangement led to an empty jug in the locker below. One would be hard-pressed to imagine a more literal enactment of the feeling of being trapped, contained, restrained, framed, captive to models of experience woefully unsuitable for the rancor and rebellion playing out on the canvas of society.

He followed this with similar works, such as *Bed Piece* (1972), in which Burden occupied a bed for twenty-two straight days at the Market Street Program in Venice Beach, California. In *Documentation of Selected Works, 1971–74*, Burden explains that the piece is included to "offset the more dramatic pieces in this tape."

> To me this piece remains in my mind as one of the strangest and most interesting piece that I've ever done. At first it was very hard. The first two days were very boring, very painful. And I realized I wasn't anywhere near the end. And I didn't see how, how I could go on. But by the end, or the middle of the second week, I had begun to establish a routine. And I began to sort of enjoy it there. My days were very full, very rich. And I had a very peaceful feeling. And as the piece neared ending, neared closing, I started feeling regret about leaving. I started feeling like I wanted to stay. And I actually considered staying but I knew that if I stayed that I would be forced to leave anyway and that people would consider me crazy. I mean, I knew that they were going to end it for me. But the fact that I was tempted and that I was very seduced into it. To me, that is the strangest part about this piece. (Burden *Documentation of Selected Works*)

Three years later, in 1975, Burden lived for twenty-one days on a triangular platform raised some ten feet above one corner of the Ronald Feldman Gallery in New York. This piece is titled *White Light/White Heat* after the 1968 Velvet Underground album. It may be hard initially to connect the dots between Burden's stasis and the Velvet Underground's ecstatic freneticism (more on this in Chapter 7). But again, if we think of either Burden's or the Velvets' work as different formulations of responses to creeping boredom, perhaps Burden's titular homage begins to make some sense.

Burden's work of the 1970s can be seen as a reaction formation to the boredom that threatened to subsume society, politics, art, and music; that suffused the kind of life that the postwar West was constructing to ward off the evils of the bomb, the war, the Nazis, bad conscience, and historical ghosts. The mind-body dialectic of Burden's work plays itself out—not in Burden's flesh, as one might be tempted to conclude—but in the thoroughgoing submission of mind to body and of body to mind. In the end each disappears, only to reappear as a composite entity—thought and material—that we must call a "situation." It is not, in the end, the flesh of Burden's palms or the will of his mind that is tested in *Transfixed* (1974), but the assignments meted out by the specificities of the situation to his assistants, to the Volkswagen Beetle onto which he was nailed— spikes driven through his palms—to the garage and the alley where it all took place. But more directly, more crucially, the situation of *Transfixed*, like all of Burden's indispensable work of the 1970s, assigns to us, the audience, a host of tasks and obligations. We must bear witness, even if we weren't there (and for most of his pieces, most of us weren't). We must testify. We must assume the moral implications of his choices even if he cannot, will not, or denies the actuality of such implications. It is hard to believe that his name was "Burden" because this is what his crucial work was about: the burden of being alive, of being responsible for and to the mind and the body within which we've landed. The abdication of these very responsibilities is what James Baldwin mourned in Norman Mailer's facile "White Negro." We land in our skin, our bodies, our minds, and, as Joan Didion observed in 1970, we must play them as they lay. In 1974, Punk rocker Richard Hell sang, "it's such a gamble when you get a face." That gamble, everything that rides on it and how it plays out, is for each of us, our particular burden. Before there was "the virtual," before avatars and screen names, Burden stood in our stead. He tested the limits of what we—each of us individually, and all of us collectively—are willing to accept: as art, as moral behavior, as agency in the context of situations in which we unwittingly put or find ourselves. While the 1964 murder of Kitty Genovese still haunted our collective consciences, Vietnam disabused us of the inviolability of our moral positions, and Nixon's betrayals lacerated the constitution of the body politic, Chris Burden substituted his conscience, his morality, and his body for ours and allowed us to play out and play through our direst disquiet.

# 5

# Funk Lessons

If the internet were to disappear tomorrow, taking with it all the social media, the e-commerce, Wikipedia, blogs, and websites, surely something would be lost. But so long as one particular YouTube clip was spared, left to stand as the lone survivor of this webpocalypse, then we would be entitled to still consider ourselves fortunate. We could take solace in the understanding that, ultimately, the internet had served the interests of history and humanity. This clip dates from 1969, from *Music Scene*, a television program that briefly aired on ABC, canceled in the midst of its first and only season. It opens with host David Steinberg, sitting down at a drum set to introduce the next performer while attempting an awkward rim shot. He tries to bounce a stick off the snare drum and catch it, but it sails out of reach. He looks on helplessly as the stick clatters to the floor. His introduction is succinct; artist and song title: "James Brown 'Mother Popcorn.'" A quick cross-fade takes us to a low angle, across the laps of Brown's twin drummers, John "Jabo" Starks and Clyde Stubblefield. The song begins and the camera moves to the right around the backs of the drummers, locating James Brown, standing on a small platform—maybe three-by-three feet. The rest of the band is sitting. The stage-set background is burnt orange. Plexiglass dividers with yellow and black angled lines are interspersed in and around the band, like cordons at an accident scene. The band wears loose-fitting, light blue tops—a cross between hospital scrubs, dashikis, and Star Trek uniforms. Brown is set off in a white v-neck with gray trim, belted above the waist to maintain the image of his trim physique for the camera. His outfit too has something vaguely sci-fi about it, and the whole stage arrangement suggests an alternative-reality deck of the Starship Enterprise. This is Afro-futurism with its feet firmly on the ground.

It may seem counterintuitive to ask James Brown's band, the funkiest band going, to sit down while playing; downright dopey to ask James Brown to contain his pinball energy within the confines of a three-by-three platform.

Yet, these production decisions tap into the very qualities that make Brown's music of this period so radical and so effective. Brown recorded a number of songs meant to take advantage of the then-popular dance "the popcorn." But it seems self-evident that Brown also seized on the metaphor of popcorn to guide his and his band's approach to composition and performance. Toward the end of the *Music Scene* clip, Brown—as he often did in the late 1960s and early 1970s—turned his vocals from a carrier of content to a director of form. Rather than singing about something outside of the song, his vocals become instructions to the band and to the listener. His famous exhortation, "take it to the bridge," is a communique both to his band: "transition from the current part of the song to the bridge," and to the audience: "we're going to the bridge now, come with us, you're part of this movement, this transition, this happening."

At 2:21 of the YouTube clip of "Mother Popcorn," Brown is singing, "Sometimes / I'm feeling low / Call another brother / Talking about Maceo / Maceo, come blow your horn" (Brown "Mother Popcorn"). These lyrics are so sly. They start by describing Brown (or the song's narrator) feeling low and requesting the company of a friend. Then they shift to introducing Maceo Parker's saxophone solo. To borrow film language, the lyrics start off as diegetic—occurring within the context of the song's narrative—and then move outside of any portrait the song is painting, referring pedantically to the structural components of the song. At that point, Brown starts to offer instructions to Parker, giving him guidelines about what he wants him to play. "I don't want no trash / I don't want no trash / Don't want that mess / Play me some popcorn." Parker launches into a solo, punctuated by Brown's various species of hoots, squeals, "hey"s, "ha-ha"s, and "come on"s. At 3:29 Brown brings the rest of the horns back, exhorting, "hit it now." Parker's solo is all short, percussive bursts, no long plaintive melodies. Despite the backgrounds of many of Brown's band members, this isn't jazz. It's something new, a brand new bag. Parker's solo is the corn in the pot, dozens of tiny explosions. The pent-up energy hiding in the kernel releases in staccato ricochets.

As Jonathan Lethem wrote in *Rolling Stone*,

> James Brown seemed less a musician with an imperative either to entertain or to express his own emotional reality than one driven to push his musicians and listeners to the verge of a sonic idea, and then past that verge, until the moment when he became, more or less officially, the single-handed inventor of an entire genre of music called funk. (Lethem 280)

Without much harm, Brown's sonic idea could be reduced to the metaphor of popcorn. Sitting his band down in chairs, confining him to that tiny platform, these uncredited decisions on *Music Scene* reinforce this sonic idea. The energy of Brown and his band is not garish or ecstatic. It is never fully released. Something is always held in reserve. The band impales the beat like master swordsmen, but they do so without ever leaving their seats. Brown gyrates a tempest in his teapot. Although, contrary to the colloquial use of that phrase, what he whips into shape is not nothing, but a sublime something, a happening—too vital for the rest of us to process. Lethem quotes the critic, Robert Palmer, as having said that "the rhythmic elements became the song . . . Brown and his musicians began to treat every instrument and voice in the group as if it were a drum" (Palmer, quoted in Lethem 280). Maceo Parker's saxophone solo on "Mother Popcorn" is a drum solo, built not from melodic or harmonic ideas, but rhythms: where and when the hits of the reed fall against the drums' emphases, sliding in and out of synch with "Sweet" Charles Sherrell's serpentine bassline and Jimmy Nolen's percolating rhythm guitars, and—after Brown summons them back into the song—bobbing and weaving with the other horns as they hammer on the upbeat-*and* between the four and the one, rescuing the rhythm's subconscious from an oblivion most bands never plumb.

Lethem is not quite right in this respect: James Brown did not single-handedly invent funk. Starting in 1965 with "Papa's Got a Brand New Bag," Brown's bands were his bricklayers, his welders, and his electricians, constructing the sonic idea from his blueprints. The drummers, Stubblefield and Starks, are the foremen of this project. But in order to provide both the skeleton and the power for the construction of this new architecture, they had to reimagine their role and their playing. If every instrument is a drum, then how much territory and responsibility is left for the actual drums? And what if there are two drum kits? In response, Stubblefield and Starks tap into the most fundamental understanding of rhythm: that it is a binary code: ones and zeroes, on and off, snap and silence. As much as they create music, they create space. Wicked absences at the upstroke. Targets for the other instruments to hit. Bait set in the bear trap. The band builds itself in these spaces, its form defined by what the drummers allow.

What made Maceo Parker and Fred Wesley, Brown's two great band leaders, so intrinsic to James Brown's sound, was their ability to tap into the popcorn, the particular evolutionary turn in Brown's music—the one that is the spawning of funk. Parker and Wesley know what Brown means when he says "don't give me no trash, just give me some popcorn." No excess. Just the moment the kernel pops. Just the singularity of mutation: an impenetrable surface releasing and becoming energy. When brothers Bootsy and Catfish Collins joined the band in the early 1970s, they introduced something else to the mix, a little butter, a little salt. Their playing suggests a libidinal freedom that Brown never allows to surface and that the Collins brothers would pursue more fully in Parliament-Funkadelic. But at the core of all of James Brown's best tracks from the late 60s ("Mother Popcorn," "Say It Loud—I'm Black and I'm Proud," Stubblefield's signature number, "Funky Drummer") is a rhythmic stringency. The drumming is an exercise in repression: a struggle against an energy that wants to detonate. This energy is never allowed to come truly to fruition, because Stubblefield and Starks realize that what counts is tension and anticipation; not more, but the possibility of more. The repression is ultimately more powerful than its lifting could ever be. The power of the internal combustion engine is predicated on pressure and intermittent release. While the conditions for a climactic explosion are all present, the engine is designed to repress it. James Brown and his band understand this and make of their music a motor.

The "genius of James Brown"—to repurpose Lethem's title—is to make the frame visible by pressing up against it, applying pressure without puncturing it. It is possible to read his music as a kind of metaphor for, or performance of, African Americans' experience of the strictures constantly bearing down upon them from above, below, and both sides; from the past, in the present, prohibiting passage to the future. Michael Veal has made a similar argument about Jamaican dub music, writing that "the privileging of rupture in dub music comes to symbolize the disruptions in cultural memory and the historical shattering of existential peace, encoded into the cultural nervous system and sublimated into musical sound" (Veal, 462). I'll confess, even as I propose the equation, that this mapping of experience onto musical form is a pretty speculative gambit. Reading Veal, I find myself sympathetic, but skeptical. Nevertheless, there may be some value in wondering aloud, as it were, if James Brown's popcorn—the musicalized experience of repressed energy—functions as either a representation of, or a response to, the ruthless repressions of Brown's own life experiences and, through a kind of cultural-genetic transmission, the subjugations of African American and African diasporic experience in general. It may have been possible for a White middle-class man—say Norman Mailer or Abbie Hoffman—to destroy, deconstruct, or simply ignore frames. But recall James Baldwin's words,

To become a Negro man, let alone a Negro artist, one had to make oneself up as one went along. This had to be done in the not-at-all-metaphorical teeth of the world's determination to destroy you. The world had prepared no place for you, and if the world had its way, no place would ever exist. Now, this is true for everyone, but, in the case of the Negro, this truth is absolutely naked: if he deludes himself about it, he will die. (Baldwin 279)

James Brown must have understood this as palpably as Baldwin did. Like the sheet on the otherwise invisible ghost or the hands of the mime designating the box by pressing against its invisible walls, Brown's music makes the frame available by reaching but not exceeding it. Listening to the ever-so-tightly ratcheted arrangements of Stubblefield, Starks, Parker, Wesley, and Brown et al. brings the frame into a kind of proximal visibility, more felt than seen, more pressure than form. As with Schneemann and Dylan and Burden, Brown's work is more about process than product, more about something happening in time than about stabilizing the contours of that something in space. It is about, as Dylan put it, "the whole thing, while it's happening."

In 1967, President Lyndon Johnson convened an eleven-member panel chaired by Illinois Governor Otto Kerner. The National Advisory Commission on Civil Disorders was tasked with investigating the 1967 race riots that plagued US cities, including Tampa, Cincinnati, Atlanta, Newark, and, most destructively, Detroit. The Commission's report, which runs to over 400 pages, was published in 1968, becoming a national bestseller. Although the report adopts a patronizing, paternalistic attitude typical of its time, it also tries to frankly describe and diagnose the structural antecedents of racism in America. The report identifies multiple factors contributing to the racial tension erupting in US cities: lack of economic opportunity, failed social service programs, police brutality, and racism. One section of the report is dedicated to "The News Media and the Disorders," concluding that "the media report and write from the standpoint of a white man's world. . . . This may be understandable, but it is not excusable in an institution that has the mission to inform and educate the whole of our society" (Kerner Commission 203). In the section entitled, "Reporting Racial Problems in the United States," the report states pointedly, "the so-called 'white press' is at best misunderstood and at worst held in contempt by many black Americans. Far too often, the press acts and talks about Negroes as if Negroes do not read the newspapers or watch television, give birth, marry, die, and go to PTA meetings" (Kerner

Commission 210). The report notes the scarcity of Black editors in the news media and suggests that,

> Television should develop programming which integrates Negroes into all aspects of televised presentations. Television is such a visible medium that some constructive steps are easy and obvious. . . . For example, Negro reporters and performers should appear more frequently—and at prime time—in news broadcasts, on weather shows, in documentaries, and in advertisements. . . . In addition to news-related programming, we think that Negroes should appear more frequently in dramatic and comedy series. (Kerner Commission 212)

Problematically, the Commission generally equates Black life with the ghetto, poverty, and social problems. It is easy to construe the intentions and tone of the report as an attempt to get a light on the lives and living conditions of the Black "other." Of course, this doesn't do anything to challenge the media's bias toward the "standpoint of the white man's world." It merely reinforces the division between society's constructed identities: "us" and "them." The mass media's—especially television's—rigid framing of content demands that each story takes the form of a capsule: small, tightly packed, brightly colored, clearly identified, and easily swallowed. Never mind that the very phenomena that necessitated the formation of the Kerner Commission were none of these things. Race in America, the strife of 1967, the Civil Rights Movement, halting efforts at desegregation, expanding wealth and generation gaps: none of these things fit neatly or comfortably on a TV screen, in a half-hour time slot, beneath a Walter Cronkite voice-over. Nevertheless, Black deprivation is a story that White networks, producers, presenters, and audiences can get their heads around. Stories of complex Black life, thought, and culture were less easily packaged because White media possessed no readymade frame for this image.

In 1968, the same year that the Kerner Commission Report was published, the program, *Soul!*, premiered on New York's, WNDT (later WNET), Channel 13. *Soul!* ran for five years—thirty-nine one-hour broadcasts—available on Public Broadcasting Service (PBS) stations around the country. Created by, and hosted for most of its run, by Ellis Haizlip, *Soul!* was the only US television program dedicated to Black cultural expression and Black social and political life (Figure 5.1). As Gayle Wald points out in her book on *Soul!*, Haizlip's vision broke from mainstream, White TV, not just in terms of content, but in the conception of what a television show can and should do.

**Figure 5.1** *Soul!* host, Ellis Haizlip, second from right, interviews director Mario Van Peebles, 1971.

> *Soul!* televised a richly heterogeneous cast of artists and public figures, expanding opportunities for black performing artists and intellectuals on television while critiquing the notion that a TV show—let alone a weekly one-hour broadcast produced on a shoestring budget—could adequately or fully represent the black collective. (Wald 4)

As Gil Scott-Heron famously announced in 1971, "the revolution will not be televised" (Scott-Heron 1971). The revolution—political or personal—does not avail itself of the singularity for which a spotlight is designed. The camera's single-point perspective, its boundedness, limited to zooming, dollying, panning make it an inadequate spectator, unable to show or tell, represent or map the revolution. As Scott-Heron later explained in a 1990 interview, "the thing that's going to change people is something that nobody will ever be able to capture on film" (Scott-Heron interview).

The episode of *Soul!* that aired on October 24, 1968 pushes as hard as anything before (and possibly since) against television's framing. As was often the case with *Soul!*, the episode shuffles between multiple performers and discussion segments. The episode's guests include gospel singer, Marion Williams; Barbara Ann Teer, founder of the National Black Theater; and the Last Poets (David

Nelson, Gylan Kain, Abiodun Oyewole, and percussionist Nilija). Haizlip opens the episode—the show's first to be broadcast live—by preparing the audience for the unpredictability of live TV: "We hope you'll kind of bear with us. We can go up or we can go down, but we hope it runs evenly" (*Mr. Soul!*). Almost immediately, we gain inadvertent insight into anxieties circulating through the studio about what is to come. Haizlip turns to the Last Poets' manager, Russell Pitchford, and asks "what are they going to do for us now?" Pitchford responds, "The Poets are going to do, now, a piece they call, 'Die Nigga!!!'" (*Mr. Soul!*). There is laughter in the room, some of it nervous, some of it righteous. Haizlip turns back to the camera, "alright, very good. So, we have the Black . . ." he misspeaks, "the Last Poets, now, doing 'Die Nigga!!!'" There's a brief pause and a look of confusion on Haizlip's face. Off camera, a woman's voice (probably co-host, Loretta Long) says, "They're doing 'Waking Waters.'" Pitchford, realizing his mistake, covers his face with his hand. Haizlip recovers quickly, smiling at the camera and announcing, "first goof on live television."

Later in the episode the moment that had set everyone on edge arrives. This time Haizlip tells us, "The Last Poets are going to do a piece for us now, and I can only beg that everyone can accept it in the spirit that it's delivered, it's called 'Die Nigga!!!'. The Last Poets and 'Die Nigga!!!'" (*Mr. Soul!*). The Last Poets deliver something that television is not built to capture: angry, ecstatic, a journey into the despondency of historical oppression to rescue the materials required for redemption and self-realization. The prohibited word "nigga" is recuperated, redefined, clarified. When it is used by Whites, it absorbs everything that is, and everyone who is, Black. But for the Last Poets, it is a term invented by Whites to define the symptoms of subjugation, the aspects of Black life that are not endemic to it, but imposed upon it by White supremacy. "Die nigga" then is détourned from a damning epithet to a kind of surgery, the removal of an alien aspect in the midst of Black American life. The piece ends in a furious climax. Kain and Oyewole chant "die," Nilija plays an increasingly frenetic roll on the congas, Nelson declaims "Die nigga!," and everything stops, clearing space for the final line and the piece's denouement: "So Black folks can take over." The Last Poets don't simply paint a picture of the revolution, they initiate it. At the risk of hyperbole, I want to emphasize this point. The performance of "Die Nigga!!!" on *Soul!* was not a performance in the everyday use of that term. It was performative in the way that the word has been used in linguistics and later in performance studies. It is an action that makes something so, in the way that saying "I do" at a wedding makes the speaker married. The Last Poets are acting out and acting upon the final line of the poem. They are the Black folks taking over. They are killing the word and the concept "nigger." As Oyewole tells us in the documentary, *Mr Soul!*, "That was important, because we knew that you can't just say 'I'm Black' and go with that. You've got to *do* something, you've got to show how Black you are by your actions" (*Mr. Soul!*). The revolution starts in a dozen different places, or a hundred, or a thousand. But each beginning is a singular event, a burst, an epiphany, a pop. No camera is there, but for the camera that each of us is. And that camera has to shut itself down to allow the revolution to get cracking. As Wald describes it, the Last Poets' performance on *Soul!*

> is poetry as exorcism, a nearly three-minute piece that requires Nelson to say the word "nigga" dozens of times, in rapid-fire variations of the title phrase. . . . As he raps, Nelson doesn't just speak the words to the poem; he spits them, as though to rid himself of the unclean taste of the racial epithet and the unwelcome images of the violated black body (assassinated, lynched, raped, and suicidal) that the poem conjures. (Wald 90–1)

Umar Bin Hassan, who joined the Last Poets in 1970 (after the *Soul!* performance) explains, "We were definitely trying to de-niggerize our people" (*Mr. Soul!*).

Consider what *Soul!* and the Last Poets were up against. Not only was television a medium designed by and for "the standpoint of a white man's world," but the form and content of the Last Poets' performance was something without precedent in the cultural experience of most viewers. To make sense of what you were watching you had to process the Blackness of *Soul!*; the confrontation of the Last Poets' performance; the litany of dead Black men: Medgar Evers, Emmett Till, Bobby Hutton, James Chaney; and the blunt, unforgiving repetition of the taboo epithet. "The N-word." We sidestep the historical violence of the word with this synecdochic replacement.

Three years after *Soul!* broadcast the Last Poets' "Die Nigga!!!," the *New York Times* published a long response to CBS's hit sitcom, *All in the* Family. The piece, penned by Laura Z. Hobson, author of the best-selling novel, *Gentleman's Agreement*, begins by explaining that for twenty-four years—since the publication of her novel about anti-Semitism—she has avoided writing about bigotry. "I've stuck to it," she writes, "No lectures, no articles, no books about discrimination against Jews, against blacks, against whites, against Puerto Ricans" (Hobson). But this changed when *All in the Family* rose to the top spot in the Nielsen ratings. Hobson felt she had a responsibility to see what all the critical and commercial fuss was about. "The Number One Nielsen, I'm told, means an audience of some 40 million families per week. Forty million families means about 100 million people. Old people, young people, black, white, Protestant, Catholic, Jewish, well-educated, ill-educated, secure, insecure—100 million people every week" (Hobson). She surveys the critical responses to the show, noting that one written by Whitney Young, shortly before his tragically untimely death, "came closest to what I felt." Young decried *All in the Family*'s "Gratuitous insults." "It is irresponsible," he writes, "to air a show like this at a time when our nation, is polarized and torn by racism" (Young, quoted in Hobson). Hobson goes on to offer her own critique of the show, "I have a most peculiar complaint about the bigotry in the hit TV comedy, *All in the Family*. There's not enough of it" (Hobson).

Again, this is 1971, three years *after* the Last Poets' appearance on *Soul!* This response in the *New York Times* offers a glimpse of how unequipped American television was to deal with endemic racism and its visual, narrative, and linguistic representations. Hobson condemns *All in the Family*'s soft-peddling of racism, challenging producer, Norman Lear, to accurately represent the bigotry the show purportedly denounced. Hobson details her careful accounting of the language employed by the show, noting that the most offensive epithets are assiduously replaced by less common and (probably because they are less common) less offensive name-calling.

> But do the bigots of this world really talk about spades moving in next door, or not breaking bread with no jungle bunnies, or signing petitions to keep black beauties from ruining real estate values on the street? You know the word they use. The one word, the hideous word. Unthinkable too. Don't even print it. Nigger. [. . .] Were the honest producer and the responsible network trying to make bigotry more acceptable? Were they trying to clean it up, deodorize it, make millions of people more comfy about hearing it, indulging in it? (Hobson)

Maybe it's 1986. Maybe you are Black. Maybe you walk into a gallery in New York or Berlin or some other global art metropolis. Maybe you approach a plinth to inspect the two small displayed objects. They are stacks of printed cards, the size of conventional business cards. They rest in Lucite cradles, the kind you might find on the counter of a local restaurant, beside the toothpick dispenser. One stack is printed on white cardstock, the other on light brown, the color of a paper grocery bag. Each presents only text and no images. Although both are worthy of attention, let's focus on the one on the right. The text begins:

Dear Friend,

I am black.

I am sure you did not realize this when you made/laughed at/agreed with that racist remark. In the past, I have attempted to alert white people to my racial identity in advance. Unfortunately, this invariably causes them to react to me as pushy, manipulative, or socially inappropriate. Therefore, my policy is to assume that white people do not make these remarks, even when they believe there are no black people present, and to distribute this card when they do.

I regret any discomfort my presence is causing you, just as I am sure you regret the discomfort your racism is causing me.

Adrian Piper, *Calling Cards*, 1986

Adrian Piper, the artist responsible for these *Calling Cards*, began working in the late 1960s. She adopted the logical concerns and methods of the first generation of conceptual artists. Sol LeWitt, twenty years her senior, befriended and mentored the young Piper. However, after a few years of working with philosophical issues—contradictions between spatial and linguistic descriptive systems, for example—Piper shook off the framing devices of conceptual art. The late 1960s work of LeWitt and his contemporaries assumed a kind of neutral position relative to the world. Cameras on tripods, merely pointing themselves at systems, processes, permutations, or progressions. To take the world as given, to take one's own position as equally given; to assume a horizontality relative to things and other subjects, unimpeded by hierarchical relations, by power, pecking orders, status, or historically determined positionality, is a privilege that is not distributed equally. As a Black woman, Piper realized that she could not pretend to be entitled to such privilege. LeWitt could concern himself with geometry because, as a White man, his subjectivity integrated seamlessly with history and society as constructed by other White men. LeWitt and his conceptual art brethren were entitled to make art from an unmarked position. Only the unmarked hand can make a mark that is only a mark. Conceptual art can start from the assumption that a form is a form. But to be Black, to be a woman, at the turn of the 1970s, was to live in a palpable relation with forms as reinforcements: reinforcements of power, reestablishments of hierarchies. The borders establishing inclusion and exclusion are traced in the land, in the architecture, in the art of the society. They don't need to be stamped "Whites Only" in order to convey their implicit interdictions. The city bus. The water fountain. The school house. The fire hose. The white collar. The red lines of the residential security maps commissioned by the Federal Home Loan Bank Board in 1935 and used to deny mortgages to Black neighborhoods until the Home Mortgage Disclosure Act of 1975 and the Community Reinvestment Act of 1977. The form taken by the red line is a mere form to the White banker who draws it. To the Black family, it is a sword: slashing violently at their present and hanging with Damoclean menace above their future.

Piper quickly realized that to assume the neutrality of first-generation conceptual art constituted a kind of "passing." She could pretend to sit on the tripod of identity-neutrality, like LeWitt. But doing so would enact a complex betrayal of her identity, her history, and her art. So, in the early 1970s, Piper began to repurpose conceptual techniques to explore her identity and the institutionally embedded attitudes of society.

A few years before the *Calling Cards*, Piper made a series of performances in which she gathered people, typically in an art institution, and taught them the rudiments of dancing to Black music. Piper's *Funk Lessons* seek to address racial social divides through encounters with a cultural form conventionally associated with Black communities. The performances begin with Piper teaching the fundamentals of funk dancing. A handout distributed to participants provides the "Characteristics of Black Dance":

1. Relaxed back.
2. Bent knees.
3. Whole foot on floor.
4. Isolation of body parts: feet, knees, hips, shoulders, head, and so on.
5. Polyrhythmic: different rhythms carried by different body parts.
6. Unification of music with dance: Each kind of music has its own appropriate dance style.
7. Personalistic: variation and play on fixed dance conventions for individual self-expression (Piper 1996, 213).

Piper stands at the front of the room with a sound system and a white board, assuming a role familiar to her mostly-White audience. She is the instructor, the teacher, the expert. The situation, too, is familiar: the lecture, the classroom, the symposium. The sly intervention in 1982 is to conceal a Black cultural form in a White cultural wrapper in order to smuggle the former into the institutions of the latter. *Funk Lessons* pushes against the framing devices of the museum, the gallery. With a conceptual stiffness, an artificial formality, Piper introduces the participants to the apparent spontaneity and naturalness of funk dancing.

> The basic means for moving around is a simple two-step. And that's simply where you, say, shift your weight onto your left foot, and then step on it, shift your weight onto your right foot, step on it, left foot, step, right, step. (Piper *Funk Lessons*)

A clutch of assumptions is called surreptitiously into question. Can White people dance, after all? Is funk verifiably "Black music"? Why is the majority of the gathered audience at this art institution White? Why are Black people implicitly prohibited from this space? Does introducing funk here transform it into "fine art"? Or does it transform the institution into a popular venue? Funk, here, does a lot of work very efficiently. The musical genre functions as a cultural signifier that conveys volumes of information about race, class, gender, cultural hierarchies, and the histories that produce and are produced by them. The *Funk Lessons* harness the pent-up historical energy in James Brown's popcorn and redirect it at cultural and institutional assumptions. Like Brown, Piper makes the frame visible, not by transgressing it, but by pressing up against it; by reaching but not exceeding it. The *Funk Lesson* performances generate tightly ratcheted situations that bring the frame into a kind of proximal visibility, more felt than seen, more pressure than form, more about something happening in time than about stabilizing the contours of that something in space. Of course, this is an even more radical move to make in the visual arts, where stabilized spatial form is the traditional name of the game, than it is in music.

In 1987, at Randolph Street Gallery in Chicago, Piper exhibited video documentation of a *Funk Lessons* performance in Berkeley, California. This screening, which she called *Funk Lessons Meta-Performance,* is then presented, in turn, as video documentation. The setting for the *Meta-Performance* is even more academic than the original *Funk Lessons*. The audience sits in front of a video monitor to watch the documentation and then discusses the piece with Piper and among themselves. They analyze the place of funk in White society. They discuss funk as a marker of class and leisure. The all-White audience responds to the original *Funk Lessons* performance by analyzing the music, at one point concluding collectively that George Clinton's work with Parliament-Funkadelic parodies racial stereotypes as well as the work of other artists who have appropriated his comedic-theatrical take on Afro-futuristic funk. The staid academic setting encourages discussion of the social, political, and economic meanings of both funk and the *Funk Lessons*. One participant, says,

> I don't want to be a bore and say that class is a big issue, but class *is* a big issue. Class is the issue that Americans don't talk about. I remember when my roommates were all Party members [. . .] they went out and took disco lessons because it dawned on them that they'd all been taking such pains at school to master essentially upper-middle class skills but they couldn't dance. And not being able to dance and not being in their bodies at all was a real barrier between them and the people they were trying to reach. (Piper, *Funk Lessons Meta-Performance*)

We witness the White audience embrace the convenient obfuscation of the racial component of class politics. The divide between Black and White, between body and mind, between funk and disco on the one hand and rock and roll and classical on the other is swept under the class rug. In modernity, as Cedric Robinson clarifies in *Black Marxism*, class is constructed, first, from racial distinctions.

> The delusions of medieval citizenship, which had been expanded into shared patrimony and had persisted for five centuries in western Europe as the single great leveling principle, were to be supplanted by race [. . .] Race became largely the rationalization for the domination, exploitation, and/or extermination of non "Europeans" (including Slavs and Jews). (Robinson 26–7)

We don't even need to leave Chicago, site of the *Funk Lessons Meta-Performance*, in order to locate a salient, bracing example of this uniquely American distortion of race and class played out through a musical proxy. The year is 1979, three years prior to Piper's first *Funk Lessons* performances. We cameras are trained on Comiskey Park, where the Chicago White Sox will meet the Detroit Tigers for a doubleheader (two games back-to-back). The White Sox owner, Bill Veeck, a baseball showman in the tradition of P. T. Barnum, was already famous for staging unorthodox promotions. In the 1950s, as owner of the St. Louis Browns, he sent the three-foot, seven-inch Eddie Gaedel to the plate to pinch hit. Gaedel wore the jersey number "1/8" and, due to his smaller-than-average strike zone, walked on four pitches. St. Louis staged a "Grandstand Manager's Day," in which the team made strategic game decisions based on real time fan voting. In Chicago, Veeck introduced the Major Leagues' first "exploding scoreboard" and experimented with alternative uniforms (one had players in shorts—a dubious choice for a game in which base runners slide across the infield dirt to avoid a fielder's tag). On this hot July day, at Comiskey, the fans are promised ninety-eight cent admission if they donate a disco record to be destroyed on the field in between the two games.

Comiskey Park is located in the Bridgeport neighborhood, a White, Irish Catholic enclave on Chicago's otherwise predominantly Black south side. Bridgeport is home to Chicago's most powerful family, the Daleys. The promotion, known as the "Disco Demolition," was conceived and promoted by radio DJ, Steve Dahl, who spun rock and roll records at Chicago's WLUP. The event, in both conception and execution, is concisely the performance of the precise cultural prejudices that Piper's *Funk Lessons* is meant to address. Dahl uses disco music as a code word for an intertwined set of threats to White, heteronormative identity, for which rock and roll is the musical signifier. In a late 1970s television interview, Dahl's choice of adjective is telling. He says of disco, "it's an intimidating lifestyle, it's an intimidating culture" (Red Bull Music Academy, "Disco Demolition"). In the short documentary, "Disco Demolition: Riot to Rebirth," produced by the Red Bull Music Academy, numerous White fans and White Sox officials express their "hatred" for disco, describing it as the "bane" of their existence and "an assault on what we grew up on, which was rock and roll" (Red Bull Music Academy, "Disco Demolition"). Over the subsequent years, Dahl has taken a number of argumentative tacks to defend himself from accusations of racism and homophobia. In an interview from around the time of the Comiskey event, he responds with blithe irony, "I hate disco because I can't find a white three-piece suit that fits me off the rack that hangs well. I can't dance." Frederick Dunson, executive director of the Frankie Knuckles Foundation, offers the necessary retort:

> That's a really stupid attitude to take, "Oh, because they've got on white polyester suits on and I can't dance, I don't like disco." Well, shit, don't go. It's a choice. It's so easy. (Red Bull Music Academy, "Disco Demolition")

The documentary's subtitle suggests that the Disco Demolition backfired; that disco, reborn as "Chicago House" music, was forced out of the prying camera lenses of the mainstream and back into the creative ferment of the relative invisibility of underground clubs from whence it could become the single biggest influence on the development of electronic dance music. "It didn't do what it set out to do," says Dunson, "because out of disco came house music." More concretely, Vince Lawrence, one of the originators of Chicago House, worked as an usher at Comiskey Park and was on duty the day of the demolition. As he describes it, the records that were sacrificed that day were not strictly or even primarily disco records, but simply records in various genres produced by Black artists. The fourteen-year-old Lawrence hung out by the bins used to collect the vinyl and plucked records that interested him, stashing them in his locker until after the game. Ironically, this distorted version of crate digging—White baseball fans handing off their Black records—is a founding moment in the birth of Chicago House.

Between the two games of the doubleheader, Dahl took to the field in military uniform and helmet (the image, I trust, requires no elucidation), led a chant of "disco sucks," and then detonated a large box of records, tearing a hole in the outfield grass. The crowd, whipped into a frenzy of White-hetero-privilege, stormed the field, ripping up bases and handfuls of turf, lighting a bonfire in centerfield and raiding the teams' dugouts to steal bats and gloves. Despite the pleas of the stadium announcer and broadcasting legend Harry Caray, and the efforts of the White Sox staff and Chicago Police, the mayhem carried on for more than twenty minutes. After the mob dispersed, Major League Baseball found the field unsuitable for play and forced the White Sox to forfeit the second game.

For decades after the event, the Disco Demolition was generally seen as a madcap promotion that got charmingly out of hand. True White Sox fans bemoaned the forfeited game, but many more accepted it in the spirit of kids-will-be-kids. It is only in recent years that the Disco Demolition has been recognized for what it really was: a performance of White, heteronormative aggression against Black and gay populations as represented by disco records. Again, I want to keep what happened at Comiskey Park that day in a kind of dialectical equilibrium with Adrian Piper's *Funk Lessons* from three years later. While there is no evidence to suggest that Piper devised *Funk Lessons* as an explicit retort to the Disco Demolition, the two events nevertheless function as mirror images. Ultimately, it is more instructive to understand Piper's piece as a response, not to a single event, but to a set of pervasive attitudes and associations baked into the culture. Lawrence recalls White fans screaming at him on the way back to the safety of his locker area, "'see this?' and showed [him], like, a Cameo record and broke it in half. And what is that? That's not like 'I hate disco'" (Red Bull Music Academy, "Disco Demolition"). In the documentary, various people describe the effects of the Disco Demolition in Chicago. People felt unsafe going to dance clubs, venues shut down; two interviewees mention disco clubs being converted into Country and Western bars. Dahl, for his part, has been unable, or unwilling, to acknowledge the bigotry that motivated the Disco Demolition.

I think it's hard to reframe history from a present day standpoint. People say that it was racist and homophobic. But it wasn't. I had no issue with anybody with respect to that. Now, some people might have that went there and who did things before, during, or after. But my part of it was just making fun of disco. That's it. (Red Bull Music Academy, "Disco Demolition")

In the Red Bull Music Academy documentary Dahl's comments are presented immediately after Frederick Dunson laments the historical racism of Chicago, and Vince Lawrence recounts a story about walking his first girlfriend, "who wasn't Black," home to the border of Bridgeport. After dropping her off, a car approached. The White driver threatened him. When Lawrence ran, the driver and his friends chased Lawrence and beat him.

I never really knew that that hate was real. That that was something that actually happened, you know? It turns out that his father was a Bridgeport cop and they wanted this to go away. And they asked me if I would take money to drop the charges and, honestly, I had synthesizer on the brain, and that was pretty much what happened. I forgave his racism in exchange for a piece of my dream. (Red Bull Music Academy, "Disco Demolition")

The Disco Demolition is not an isolated incident. If we scan the cultural landscape between 1965 and 1985, we can identify numerous instances in which music functions as a kind of litmus test for cultural assumptions and class, race, and gender affiliations. In many cases, music acts as a vehicle for political sentiment. Sometimes music even strikes the match that sets off revolutionary actions or for reactionary crackdowns.

Formed in the wake of the 1968 Prague Spring, the Plastic People of the Universe tested the flexibility of Alexander Dubček's reformist legacy and the resolve of Czechoslovakia's Soviet minders. In 1970 Fela Kuti returned to his native Lagos with his band, Africa 70, and established the Kalakuta Republic, comprised of housing for himself and members of his entourage, a free health clinic, and a recording studio. Kuti later declared the Kalakuta Republic an independent state, free of the rule of the Nigerian military junta. In 1977, after the release of the song "Zombie," a critique of the Nigerian armed forces, the military raided the Kalakuta Republic. Kuti was badly beaten, and the compound was burned to the ground. His mother, Funmilayo Ransome-Kuti—a well-known women's rights activist— was thrown by soldiers from a second-floor window and later died of her injuries.

After sprouting in the State of Bahia, on Brazil's tropical east coast, a musical movement blossomed and withered, all within the course of 1968. Known as either Tropicália or Tropicalismo, the movement ignited fierce debates throughout Brazilian culture, mass media, and politics. Eventually, its two most popular artists, Caetano Veloso and Gilberto Gil, were jailed and then exiled by the military dictatorship. As a movement, Tropicália was fundamentally multimedia, intercultural, and voracious in its appetite for influence from multiple spheres. This is already evident in the movement's name. As Christopher Dunn explains, "After hearing one of Veloso's untitled compositions in late 1967, the cinematographer Luís Carlos Barreto detected affinities with an installation called Tropicália by the visual artist Hélio Oiticica. Despite Veloso's initial reluctance, he agreed to use 'Tropicália' as the title of his song, which subsequently became a key song-manifesto of the movement" (Dunn 8).

Tropicália, as the name suggests, plays with the image of Brazil as a tropical paradise and, simultaneously, as a backwater whose dense rain forests defend their riches from the clutches of globalist extraction. The tropical is an emblem of both desire and discontent. The movement, born under the shadow of autocratic rule, developed sophisticated positions relative to a burgeoning global consciousness of both anti-colonialism and capitalist cultural exchange. Like Bob Dylan in the United States, Veloso, Gil, and their compatriots worked both with and against tradition, unabashedly fusing folk forms with new pop forms. They found encouragement and precedent for this approach in Oswald de Andrade's *Manifesto Antropófago*, published in 1928, which argued that Brazilian culture should consume the cultures of its colonizers and digest them in its own way, thereby making something new of them. Antropófagia (cannibalism) became a motto and method for Tropicália. "The idea of cultural cannibalism fit us, the tropicalists, like a glove. We were 'eating' the Beatles and Jimi Hendrix" (Caetano Veloso, quoted in Dunn 74). Tropicália negotiated a space between the Música Popular Brasileira (MPB), on the one hand and the so-called Jovem Guarda (the young guard), on the other. The MPB championed the legacy of Bossa Nova, a style derived from Samba, that emerged in the 1950s and 1960s and was popularized by João Gilberto. The MPB equated the cultural specificity of Bossa Nova with traditional Brazilian culture and an anti-colonial nationalism. The Jovem Guarda embraced American and British rock and roll and, with it, a mass-mediated global cosmopolitanism. As with the folk versus rock and roll debates surrounding Bob Dylan, the divide between the MPB and the Jovem Guarda pitted a nostalgic, generally leftist, modernism against an aggressively postmodern embrace of the possibilities of media and the commodity form.

Dunn notes,

> the tropicalists contributed decisively to the erosion of barriers between *música erudita,* for a restricted audience of elite patrons, and *música popular,* for the general public. Tropicália was an exemplary instance of cultural hybridity that dismantled binaries that maintained neat distinctions between high and low, traditional and modern, national and international cultural production.
>
> [. . .]
>
> On a discursive level, the tropicalists proposed a far-reaching critique of Brazilian modernity that challenged dominant constructions of national culture. Instead of exalting the *pouo* (masses) as agents for revolutionary transformation, their songs tended to focus on the quotidian desires and frustrations of "everyday people" living in the cities. Ultimately, the tropicalists would give impetus to emerging countercultural attitudes, styles, and discourses concerning race, gender, sexuality, and personal freedom. These issues were becoming increasingly salient in countercultural movements in the United States and Europe but were manifested in distinct ways in Brazil during the period of military rule. (Dunn 3–4)

For the tropicalists, the camera was a periscope, granting access above and beyond the horizon of the equator and onto New York, London, Paris, and the increasing internationality of styles, sounds, and images. But the camera was also a vehicle that could transport their styles, sounds, and images across, and eventually beyond, Brazil. The jostling and jockeying of the MPB and the Joven Guarda played out on Brazilian television. Numerous programs hit the Brazilian airwaves in the late 1960s to capitalize on the new energy and attention being devoted to Brazilian music. These shows tended to align themselves with one or another camp and to not-so-subtly goad the opposing camp. Keeping the fires stoked was good for ratings.

The televised music festivals were enormously popular. An estimated 47.3 percent of the viewers in São Paulo tuned in for the finals of the 1967 TV Record festival on October 21. "Success in the festivals translated into record sales as well. The three-volume set of festival songs, released by Philips during the final round, briefly supplanted the Beatles' *Sgt. Pepper's Lonely Hearts Club Band* as the best-selling LP in early November" (Dunn 64). When Caetano Veloso and Gilbert Gil appeared on the 1967 TV Record festival, they had not yet coined the term Tropicália. At the time, they were merely two rising stars among many in Brazilian music. Gil's "Domingo no Parque" won second prize at the festival and Veloso's "Alegria, Alegria," placed fourth. But Veloso's path was not as smooth as this might suggest. In the qualifying rounds that were held for three weeks leading up to the selection of twelve songs for the broadcast, Veloso performed with the Argentine rock band, the Beat Boys. Bucking bluntly against the accepted sounds and modes of performance and fashion, Veloso piqued the ire of audiences who routinely jeered him. As Dunn points out, "artists and critics of the nationalist left regarded the experiments of Gil and Veloso with suspicion, if not hostility. Their use of electric instruments, their open celebration of the mass media, and their highly subjective and fragmentary songs departed from the norms of MPB" (Dunn 68).

By the time of the 1968 Festival Internacional de Canção (FIC), sponsored by TV Globo, Tropicália had arrived. The collective album, *Tropicália: Panis et Circensis,* has been released in July to much fanfare. Veloso, Gil, Gal Costa, Tom Zé, and the trio Os Mutantes were the figureheads, not only of the movement but of much bigger transformations in Brazilian society. During the qualifying rounds for the FIC, Gilberto Gil performed "Questão de Ordem" ("Question of Order"), a garage rock rave-up featuring distorted trebly lead guitar lines reminiscent of bands like the Seeds or the Sonics. Wearing a Senegalese-style kaftan, Gil yowls and grunts in the sections preceding the verses, which espouse a mix of political and personal liberation. The judges decided that the performance veered too far from Brazilian norms and disqualified Gil from the competition. In an interview conducted shortly after his disqualification, Gil explains,

> These clothes are my nudity. Since I can't walk around naked, just as any person would like, I disguise nudity. I am certain that if I seek beauty in my negritude, clothes cease to be an abstraction. . . . On the stage, my outfit is part of the spectacle. This is important: spectacle. It's a contradiction: in this festival, many accepted my music but jeered at my outfit. Why? I don't want to be judged according to my lyrics, my music, much less my clothes. The arrangement is like the outfit, the presentation is an integral part of the spectacle, the spectacle is the spectacle. (Gil, quoted in Dunn 131)

Also in the qualifying rounds, Veloso, backed by Os Mutantes performed his song, "É proibido proibir" ("It is Prohibited to Prohibit"), at the Catholic University in São Paulo. Earlier in the evening a tropicalist had incited the crowd—largely composed of students sympathetic to the traditional styles and leftist politics of the MPB—with a placard reading, "Folklore is reaction!" The students recognize Veloso's performance as an opportunity for retribution. They turn their backs on the performers, hissing and booing at the tops of their lungs. Recordings reveal the event to be genuinely menacing. Although the FIC is supposed to be a "song" contest, Os Mutantes opened the performance with a minute or so of discordant noise, making the prospect of a song seem unlikely. By the time they segue into "É proibido proibir," the crowd is already frenzied. Veloso gamely tries to shepherd the song through the maelstrom, but when he reaches the chorus, intoning "it is prohibited to prohibit," he loses his shit. For more than two minutes, he berates the audience. They shriek back at him. And Os Mutantes soundtrack the mayhem with a kind of dissonant, swinging noise. The Stooges, at their most feral, have nothing on this pandemonium. Veloso's lecture-rant is a marvel of fierce emotion and intellect loosed in a moment of half-madness:

So, this is youth who says it wants to take power? Do you have the courage to applaud a song this year, the same kind of song that you didn't have the courage to applaud the year before? You are the same youth that will always, always kill tomorrow the old enemy who died yesterday. You don't understand anything, anything, anything—nothing at all! Today there is no Fernando Pessoa. Today, I came to tell you that the one who had the courage to take on the structure of the festival, not with the fear that Mr. Chico de Assis recommended, but with courage . . . the one who had the courage to take on that structure and make it explode was Gilberto Gil! And it was me! Nobody else, it was Gilberto Gil and me! You're out of it. You don't understand anything. But what kind of youth is this? What kind of youth is this? (screams) You will never stop anyone. Do you know who you are like? Do you know who you are like? Is there sound in this microphone? Do you know who you are like? You are like those who went to "Roda Viva" and beat up the actors. You are no different—no different in any way from them. You are no different. And speaking of that, long live Cacilda Becker! Long live Cacilda Becker! I'm committed to declaring this homage here. It has nothing to do with you. The problem is this: you want to police Brazilian music. Maranhão presented, this year, a song with a Charleston arrangement. You know what it was? It was "Gabriela" from the year before, which he didn't have the courage to present last year because it was American. But Gil has already been on this road. What do you want? I came here to put an end to this. I want to say to the jury: disqualify me! I have nothing to do with this! Nothing to do with this! Gilberto Gil. Gilberto Gil is here with me, so that we can put an end to this festival, to all of the idiocy that reigns in Brazil. To end it once and for all. We only participated in the festival for that, right, Gil? We don't pretend. . . . We don't pretend here that we are unaware of what the festival is, no. No one ever

heard me talk this way. Understand? I only wanted to say that, baby. You know
how it is? We, he and I, had the courage to go inside all the structures and leave
them all. And you? You, if you are . . . if you are the same in politics as you are
in aesthetics, we're done for! Disqualify me along with Gil! Along with Gil, do
you understand? And as for you . . . In this . . . the Jury is very nice, but it is
incompetent. God is free! (sings): "Give me a kiss, my love, they are waiting for
us, the automobiles burn in flames, knock down the shelves, the bookshelves, the
statues, the glass cases, the dishes, books, yes, and I say yes, and I say no to no, and
I say, it is forbidden to forbid." Off key, without melody. What do you think, jury?
You didn't get it? Did Gilberto Gil's melody qualify? You're out of it. Gil melted
your brains, huh? And that's the way I want to see it. Enough! (Veloso 1967)[1]

The role of television in the rise (and, some might say, the fall) of Tropicália
hearkens back to James Brown on *Music Scene*, to Ellis Haizlip's *Soul!*, to Adrian
Piper's video documentation of *Funk Lessons* and the video of her "meta-
performance," to the broadcast of the Disco Demolition on WSNS TV-44 in
Chicago. All of us cameras. It takes us back to Bob Dylan's KQED press conference
and to Iggy Pop on WLWT. We are reminded of Abbie Hoffman staging events to
be teleported by the camera from the streets of America to its La-Z-Boy recliners.
Television nominates itself as the paradigmatic medium of modernism that,
here, we are putting into productive opposition with rock and roll. Television
divides the rush of time into thirty minute cubes. It weaves its commodity form
immediately into its content: programs sponsored by commercial firms (*Texaco
Star Theater, Colgate Comedy Hour, Mutual of Omaha's Wild Kingdom*) and the
insertion of discrete advertisements into the broadcasts themselves. It appears
to us on framed screens, making clear distinctions between what is in and what
is out. TV programming extracts itself from the rest of life and isolates itself in
what was once called the "idiot box" and now, I suppose, should be dubbed the
"fatuous screen." You know the litany as well as I do: phones, tablets, laptops,
blah-blah-blah. But what also proliferates is the screens' framing perspective;
how they clearly establish an "it," distinct from "not it."

Our mediated modernism is far from dead. Rock and roll didn't kill it.
Nor did minimalism or happenings or Abbie Hoffman or even a dawning
recognition of our saturation in, and existence as, data. Still, we can zoom in on

---

[1]   This transcription can only do so much to convey the sound and fury of this moment. To understand
    the sonic chaos and the anger of Veloso's upbraiding of the audience, nothing can take the place of
    the audio recording of the event, available here:
       http://tropicalia.uol.com.br/wordpress/wp-content/uploads/2010/10/e_proibido_proibir.mp3.

the moments we've been highlighting here. We can connect the dots like latter-day Greeks detecting constellations in the singular flickerings of sui generis disavowals. Caetano Veloso's appearance on the 1968 TV Globo broadcast of the Festival Internacional de Canção offers compelling evidence of the double-bind of rock and roll. Never distinct as an art form from its status as commodity; never simply music, but always image too; always a product of cultural, racial, and national, miscegenation and just as often of cultural, racial, and national misrecognition: of mistaking the meaning of a gesture as it travels the byways of international media circuits, subject to the framing of producers, presenters, and of the exigencies of the medium itself. The "versus" that stands between rock and roll and modern life is not a drawbridge that can be closed to repel the invading horde, it is rather more like a cat door that allows passage between one side and the other. Of course, sometimes, it's not our cat who emerges from beneath the flap, but the neighbor's cat, or a racoon, or even Teddy Adorno, on hands and knees, determined to raid the root cellar for pickled beets.

Ever since 1790, when Immanuel Kant laid down the laws of Western aesthetics in his *Critique of Judgment*, we have been taken with objects. The art object. The sonic object. So many objects of our affection; and disaffection, and defection. We've even seen objects of our defecation (see: Piero Manzoni). Music, quite obviously, isn't an object like a painting or a sculpture. But that hasn't stopped all manner of composers, performers, critics, and musicologists, from seeking to objectify music. The publishers and record companies, of course, have been the drivers and most successful objectivizers of all: music objectized in the form of the score, the piano roll, the wax cylinder, record, tape, CD, MP3. But it would be too easy to attribute this entirely to the demands of commodity. There is a more general, more benign, urge to understand things as things. We quite understandably want to know what we're talking about when we talk about "Beethoven's Fifth," *What's Going On*, or "Stairway to Heaven." So we unfairly and inaccurately lop off the spider's legs to fit it in our box.

Kant asked us, when looking at the painting, to ignore the frame. But Jacques Derrida demonstrated how this was literally impossible. In order to know where the painting stops—where our consideration of it should stop—we need the frame as a marker of that divide between inside and outside, between the "it" and the "not it." The frame, then, is neither properly in nor out of the painting, neither it nor not it. Metaphorically, this is true, as well, for a whole host of other frames. The title, for instance, tells us what we are looking at and how to look. If we allow our camericity to fall away, if we open our apertures wide enough to take in the frame, and then the frame of the frame, and so on, we expand much more than the breadth of our screen. We expand our understanding of what we might be inclined to call an object. We take in all its non-objectival framing; that which accompanies the object: aspects embedded in history, culture, biography, provenance, and genre. "Mother Popcorn" is not just what happens between 0:01 and 6:16. It is a vehicle and an environment. It is a happening. All of what we watch when we watch James Brown on *Music Scene* doesn't fit on the screen. Adrian Piper showed us that. Funk ain't just funk. Disco Demolition proved that disco's not simply disco. "É proibido proibir" cannot be reduced to "É proibido proibir." Kant can't frame out the frame. He can't direct the spotlight solely on the painting or the song or the poem, such that the rationality of enlightenment illuminates the surface evenly and perfectly, stopping precisely at the boundary of the object proper. There's always a little overflow; a little seepage, spillage, sloshing-out. The object doesn't obey its boundaries. It bleeds.

# 6

# Gnostics of the North, *or* Music to Recolonize Your Anxious Capitalist Dreams by

In 1975, the Venezuelan terrorist known as Carlos (born Ilich Ramírez Sánchez) and six accomplices, calling themselves the Arm of the Arab Revolution, raided the annual meeting of the Organization of Petroleum Exporting Countries in Vienna. Demanding the liberation of Palestine, they took more than sixty hostages, including the Oil and Energy ministers of most of the OPEC member states. The OPEC kidnapping is the most notorious entry in Carlos's resume of political violence. The geopolitical complexities of the event, its motivations, and its ramifications tell us much about global interconnectedness, mass media, economics, and leverageable power in the 1970s.

Starting in the late 1950s, a wave of decolonization swept across Africa, the Middle East, the Caribbean, and Asia: Cambodia in 1953; Malaysia and Ghana in 1957; Cameroon, Togo, Mali, Nigeria, Congo, and others in 1960; Kuwait in 1961; Jamaica, Trinidad and Tobago, Rwanda, and Uganda in 1962; Singapore in 1963; Barbados in 1966; Qatar, the United Arab Emirates, and Bahrain in 1971; the Bahamas in 1973. Rather than beat a hasty retreat, the former colonial powers reconceived the ex-colonies as emerging markets and as locations of natural resource extraction. Individual territories were no longer the property of one or another imperial nation, rather they were sites of contestation, of market competition. Initially, this put the newly independent nations of the Global South at a disadvantage. Without robust national economies, durable infrastructures, and stable governments, these countries were at the scant mercy of the industrial economies of the North. Between 1971 and 1973, when US president Richard Nixon finally instituted a floating exchange rate, international exchange rates began to fluctuate wildly. Recently, decolonized nations, without the tools to hedge against such fluctuations, found themselves at a significant, new disadvantage. But this emerging economic order was not played out strictly between nation states. Multinational corporations took advantage of these changing dynamics, stepping into gaps vacated by colonial powers. As Giovanni Arrighi argues, the expansion and consolidation of corporate activities "created an additional powerful vested interest—the interest of the corporations themselves—in preserving maximum present and future flexibility in the use of Third World resources for the benefit of First World states" (Arrighi 332).

At the same time, as the newly sovereign states began to claim autonomy and agency with regard to their natural resources, "the pressure on supplies generated by the expansion of the US regime of accumulation would inevitably implode in the form of 'excessive' competition within and among First World states" (Arrighi 332). In other words, once decolonized states began to control the extraction, output, and prices of their valued resources, the price mechanism of capitalist markets would drive down real returns on capital investment to levels deemed unacceptable by Northern corporate interests. Crucially, it is in this context that oil becomes a critical global commodity. As the North and West become increasingly dependent on oil for the manufacture and distribution of goods, oil-producing nations find themselves newly empowered. In 1973, for the first time, OPEC utilizes the tool of embargo, forcing the price of oil to quadruple in a matter of months. As Arrighi points out,

> The price of crude oil had already begun to rise prior to the "shock" of 1973. But it was the virtual acknowledgment of defeat by the US government in Vietnam, followed immediately by the shattering of the myth of Israeli invincibility during the Yom Kippur War that energized OPEC into effectively protecting its members from the depreciation of the dollar and in imposing on the First World a substantial oil rent. (Arrighi 333)

According to Quinn Slobodian, "The oil shock of 1973–1974 placed postcolonial actors at center stage. Robust demands for economic redistribution and stabilization were enshrined in the Declaration of a New International Economic Order championed by the world's poorer nations and passed by the UN General Assembly in 1974" (Slobodian 18). Needless to say, the powers of the Global North did not lay down and die. Instead, they imagined into being a new model of capitalism, based on the rhetoric of anti-totalitarianism and freedom: of individuals and markets; and on the material reality of policies and practices constructed to insure that markets would be insulated from the untoward influence of the "unwanted" actors of the newly unshackled Global South. Slobodian refers to this effort as the "encasement" of markets. Rather than freeing markets from all the tethers of regulation, oversight, and state interference—

as the story has been told through successive mouthpieces: Von Mises, Hayek, Reagan, Thatcher, Friedman, Greenspan, Sarkozy, Merkel, Blankfein, Dimon, Geithner, and Summers—Slobodian suggests that what neoliberals have actually done is to build a political economy whose primary responsibility is to encase the market in a shell, protecting it from outside influences such as governments, electorates; indeed from the corruptions of democracy. The result is not a market that freely responds to evolving realities of lived experience, but a market that obeys only its own, hermetic self-perpetuating logic, continuing to serve the same actors it has always served.

Olivier Assayas's 2010 film, *Carlos*, is an epic examination of the events of which Carlos was both a cause and effect. The film—which was released simultaneously in its five-and-a-half-hour theatrical form and as a three-part miniseries on French television—traces the woven structure of Carlos's activities and of international affairs, the ebbs and flows of global power distribution. Key scenes are soundtracked by music that had not yet been produced during the times represented in the film. Instead, at significant junctures, Assayas uses Post-Punk music, recorded five to fifteen years after the facts depicted(Assayas). About this music, critic Greil Marcus has written,

> the songs raise the question of whether the best and most adventurous music of the late 1970s and early 1980s was itself as animated by international terrorism, by the specter of a world where, at times, it could seem that only a few armed gnostics were in control, as by anything else. (Marcus)

We are justified to ask: What kind of claim is this: aesthetic, legal, ethical, historical? What does it mean to say that music is animated by terrorism? How might such a claim affect our understanding of the music in question, of international terrorism, of the task of the critic? A first step might be to decode the terms invoked: "the best and most adventurous music of the late 70s and early 80s"; "international terrorism"—specifically the terrorism of that era, the terrorism that historically speaking could have served as the music's animating force; we need to decode the notion that "only a few armed gnostics were in control"; and last, we need to understand how and why this music is used in Assayas's film.

The music in *Carlos* that Greil Marcus characterizes as "best" and "most adventurous" is part of a big, amorphous moment in popular music known as Post-Punk. The soundtrack includes songs by the Feelies, New Order, the Dead Boys, and a number of songs by the band, Wire. Of these, the Feelies and Wire bear the most immediate similarities to each other: arty, nerdy, fast, and nervous. New Order is less of each of these things, but via their emergence from the ashes of the band Joy Division, who all but invented arty, nerdy, fast, and nervous, they bear genetic similarities to the Feelies and Wire. Cleveland, Ohio's Dead Boys would seem to be the true outlier here. Their contribution, the song "Sonic Reducer," predates the other Post-Punk songs, and the designation of the movement itself, by a few years. The song was released in 1977 but had been written and performed some years earlier, originally by Rocket from the Tombs the protopunk group that spawned not only Dead Boys but also the Brechtian art-Punk ensemble, Pere Ubu. Dead Boys qualify as fast and nervous, but rejected arty and nerdy in favor of more classic rock and roll adjectives like *Young, Loud, and Snotty* (which happens to be the title of their debut album).

Surely, what Marcus has in mind when he claims that "only a few armed gnostics were in control" is the fast-paced, virile, cinematic vision of sunglassed, bereted, militants on tarmacs beside the airliners of jet travel's golden age; lone wolves and romantic fighter figures piercing the stability of the world order like scimitars through snake-filled baskets. But the facts of the global geopolitics of the 1970s immediately and irredeemably complicate this myth. First, for Marcus, international terrorism and armed gnostics in control are meant to live on the same side of history's ledger. The gnostics *are* the terrorists. But as we've just rehearsed, there is another group of gnostics, with far greater access to the levers of power, knowledge, and value production: oil ministers, CEOs of petrochemical firms, central bankers, the International Monetary Fund. History's ledger might then put these gnostics in one column and the terrorists in another: debits opposed to credits. Or, thinking historically, chronologically, syllogistically: the gnostics of colonialism, the King Leopolds and their progeny, might be conceived as the cause of the effect that was international terrorism. If we register the gnosticism of the prime ministers and presidents of the era of decolonialization and their cousins—the CEOs of British Petroleum, Exxon, Tate & Lyle, General Motors, Halliburton, Unilever, Nestle . . . along with their caretakers, the WTO, the World Bank, the IMF—we are forced to concede that it was not the terrorists who possessed the esoteric knowledge employed to lubricate and motivate the works of history's machine.

Max Weber famously defined the State as that entity which maintains a monopoly on the legitimate use of violence. But under neoliberalism, with so many traditional State functions offloaded to the private sector, this monopoly on violence is extended to the board room. As Judith Butler notes, "the physical blow cannot be the only model for thinking about what violence is. Anything that jeopardizes the lives of others through explicit policy or through negligence—and that would include all kinds of public policies or state policies—are practices of institutional or systemic violence" (Butler). The colonial powers ceded authority to multinational corporations. As a result, violence no longer takes the form of the whip hand, but of economic oppression, restricted access to health care and education, and barriers to democratic participation, all implicitly sanctioned by the State in its abdication of the mechanisms of security, provision, and control. Under neoliberalism, the loci of legitimate violence include the board room of the multinational corporation, but exclude the jungle encampment, the barrio, or the equally multinational "terrorist" organizations with divisions focused on markets—black and otherwise—in arms, banking, and drugs. Perversely, this untenable distinction is precisely the one that tautologically defines the "international terrorists" as those without a claim to legitimate violence, thereby designating their actions as "terrorism."

Gnostics, it seems, are everywhere, bearing different arms, but armed nonetheless. And when we track the details of the OPEC kidnapping, which ended with none of its intended executions, with no political concessions, and with supposedly friendly Arab states denying the Arm of the Arab Revolution permission even to land their hijacked DC10, we start to see that the gnostics in control were not and had never been synonymous with the terrorists. So Marcus isn't simply wrong when he says that it seemed "that only a few armed gnostics were in control." He is complicatedly wrong. There is some truth in his assertion, but it is a different truth than the one he has in mind. Via a similarly tautological loop, equating the "best" and "most adventurous" music with a glamorous-televisual-hipster imaginary of the global terrorist, conjures a vision borrowed from the mythology of rock and roll itself, hearkening back to the very image and ethos that Punk and then Post-Punk allegedly disavowed. Carlos is a rock star in all the banal senses of the term.

A more nuanced understanding of the dynamics of 1970s terrorism and of post-punk's various splinter groups shifts the meaning of Marcus's claim. But one has to do quite a bit of cultural math in order to work out this formula for the music used in *Carlos*. If the Feelies and Wire were "arty," "nerdy," "fast," and "nervous," Carlos, as depicted in the film, is none of these things. Rather he is professional, cool, deliberate, and steady. What we hear is interestingly at odds with what we see. If the music is animated by anything germane to the film, it is not Carlos as "armed gnostic," but the anxiety of the age; an anxiety felt most acutely by the "gnostics" of the North. This is the anxiety we hear in the skittery, caffeinated rhythms of the Feelies—the guitars strummed as if by pistons, but self-consciously human. There is no pretense to virtuosity or godlikeness. Instead, the Feelies present as the attentive kid in chemistry class. Their music suggests machinicity, but it's faulty, pre-industrial: more art than science, a product, not of the Taylorist assembly line, but of the suburban garage and all its quotidian insufficiencies. The anxiety that pulses through the Feelies reflects not the itchy Marxist trigger finger, so much as the clattering stock ticker and the flailing efforts of economists to diagnose and tame unforeseen beasts (think: "stagflation") as we wait in line at the gas pumps in the "way back" of the family station wagon. What animates this music is instability and perturbation. It is not renegade or revolutionary, or even so much as directly critical. Rather, it reflects a disturbance that juddered through the commonplaces of 1970s European and North American culture: the recognition of shifting centers of power, a new awareness that comforting Keynesian certainties were unexpectedly tenuous, Nixon's televised demonstrations of the paranoiac desperation for power. In short, this music announces, in a neo-Attalian manner, the advent of the precarity endemic to what we now recognize as the era of neoliberalism.[1]

The music chosen by Assayas is taken from the artier, art-schoolier, end of the Post-Punk spectrum, what Simon Reynolds describes as "the playful process-oriented art school sensibility that informed Wire and Talking Heads, . . . post-Eno art punk as 'formalism,' decadent and disengaged, arty for artinesses' sake" (Reynolds 181). This brand of Post-Punk is animated by aesthetic modernism, experimentation, Poundian exhortations to "make it new," and Adornian convictions that formal invention embodies a politics even when the specific nature of that politics remains unspoken. The agitations and antagonisms of the political economy of the 1970s are more directly evident in the music of other bands of the era.

Gang of Four was an agitprop advertising agency for a kind of funky Marxism that could flourish on the dance floor, even if it was floundering on Britain's picket lines and at the ballot box. Their airtight angularity and penchant for sloganesque choruses are the inevitable products of a generation that Jean-Luc Godard dubbed "the children of Marx and Coca Cola." Gang of Four performed the contradiction of commodified dissent. Whether such a contradiction cancels out political efficacy or forces a reckoning with its own constitutive

---

[1]  See, Jacques Attali, *Noise: The Political Economy of Music*, University of Minnesota Press, 1977, in which Attali argues that impending societal changes are first perceptible in shifting musical forms.

estrangement is, of course, in the ear (or false consciousness) of the beholder. Crass were a gutterpunk commune; representatives of a romantic, rejectionist anarchism. Their insistent anti-commercialism kept them determinedly out of the mainstream. Unlike, Gang of Four, they received little attention from outlets like the NME, Melody Maker, and the BBC. This has always been the dilemma of leftist aesthetics: participate in the corrupting mechanisms of capitalism in order to communicate to a broad audience, or resist commodification and limit the reach of the work to those already in the artistic- and political-know. Nowhere is this tension played out more dramatically than in the career of Scritti Politti, a squat-dwelling collective who named themselves in tribute to Antonio Gramsci's politics and Little Richard's glossolalian glee. They made skittery, skeletal, deconstructed music with occasional wisps of sweet melody sung by primary songwriter, Green Gartside, who as a teenager had founded a branch of the Young Communists in his hometown of Cwmbran, Wales. They wrote songs called "Hegemony," "Skank Bloc Bologna" (referencing multi-racial ska music, Gramscian theory, and the seat of the Italian Communists), "Jacques Derrida," and indeed "Opec—Immac" (in which Gartside sings, "14 nations and they're all producing oil"). Scritti Politti traveled a Tiresian path, their early years spent in the underground of British Post-Punk, critically lauded but decidedly uncommercial, and then, after a conscious decision to reach the masses, a rise to the top of the British and American charts accompanied by a visual makeover and an embrace of electronic instruments and Black American dance music. We will return to Scritti Politti in more detail in Chapter 9.

There are many other overtly political Punk and Post-Punk bands to choose from, which is what draws curious attention to both Assayas's soundtrack and to Macus's critical claim. The Clash's Joe Strummer, for instance, made a habit of wearing a Red Army Faction star, leading West German Punk bands to adopt the symbol of radical leftist militancy as a standard element of their aesthetic iconography (Shahan 372). Film critic Manohla Dargis suggests that rather than an analogy of terrorist violence or as a representation of the tenor of the times, the songs constitute an imaginary, self-curated soundtrack compiled, not by Assayas, but by the self-absorbed Carlos,

> as the guitars [of New Order's "Dreams Never End"] carry over into the next scene—a seemingly unremarkable yet crucial pause in the action in which Carlos listens to a report about the bombing and then clutches his genitals while gazing in a mirror—the music feels a lot less like an empty device, one used

simply to pump the story, and more like the soundtrack you might expect to be playing inside the head of a world-class self-mythologizer like this one. (Dargis)

If, as Dargis suggests, Assayas chose the music he did, not to soundtrack the desperate rationale and violent results of the film's terrorist acts, but to establish Carlos's rock star pretensions, then this would still seem the wrong batch of songs. The Feelies, New Order, and Wire were self-consciously countercultural. Their music and self-presentation were constructed as overt rejoinders to rock star mythologization. If Carlos had, in fact, played a self-serving soundtrack in his head in the mid-1970s, in all likelihood it would have relied on the tough, hedonistic, libertine, imaginary of classic rock and heavy metal: AC/DC, Led Zeppelin, the Rolling Stones.

Assayas's use of Post-Punk makes more sense if we think of these songs as animating, not the activities or self-regard of the gnostic terrorists bursting into meeting rooms with machine guns and berets, but on the effects disseminated by those seated at the meeting room table just before the doors fly open: the gnostic capitalists of the Global North and those recently liberated from the North's oppression by dint of their sudden access to global markets. The post-punk on the *Carlos* soundtrack is understood most productively as animated by the disease and the dis-ease of late capitalism as it suffers the contortions of its metamorphosis from the stabilized system of the postwar welfare state to the jittery, destabilized realities of 1970s malaise at the moment of friction between Thatcher and Reagan's ascendance and the declaration of a New International Economic Order.

To align Punk and Post-Punk with the moment of international terrorism is to position this music as expressive of the neuroses of life under global capitalism, colonialism, patriarchy, and the authoritarian tendencies of Western liberal democracies as they transitioned from World War to Cold War to the US War on Terror (waged to quell the accumulating power—and oil—of the so-called Third World). But such an alignment overlooks the salient fact that Punk and Post-Punk also positioned themselves very consciously against the previous generation's modes and methods of resistance to the same social, economic, and political forces. Punk was just as much anti-hippie as it was antiauthoritarian. Looking back at what animated the music of the late-1960s offers meaningful counterpoints from which to assess Marcus's claims about Post-Punk and the terrorism of the 1970s.

These counterpoints come immediately to the surface in Jean-Luc Godard's 1968 film *One Plus One*. The film is a bricolage of footage, characters, settings, and signifiers. It juxtaposes footage of the Rolling Stones recording the follow-up to *Their Satanic Majesties Request*, their dalliance with psychedelia. Due perhaps to tepid critical response to that album, the Stones subsequent albums herald a return to their roots in Black American music. Nevertheless, the Stones appear in the film in *haute* hippie splendor: flouncy shirts, pink flares, and red leather boots. Footage of the Stones working on preliminary arrangements of the song, "Sympathy for the Devil," alternates with staged *tableaux vivants* related to the socio-political events of the late 1960s. A group of Black men loiter in an automobile junkyard in London's Battersea neighborhood, reciting revolutionary texts by African American activists including LeRoi Jones (Amiri Baraka) and Eldridge Cleaver, distributing rifles, assaulting and murdering a trio of White flower-child women dressed in flowing white gowns. In a paperback bookstore, the proprietor reads aloud from *Mein Kampf*, while patrons pay for their purchases with Nazi salutes and by slapping the faces of two teenage hippie-boy hostages who spout Maoist and Marxist slogans. A three-man film crew—with camera and microphone—traipse through the forest at the heels of an interviewer lobbing political and philosophical questions at a young woman named Eve Democracy (played by Godard's then-wife Anne Wiazemsky).

The film abruptly confronts its own representations. The Stones' pastiche bluesiness crashes into Jones's *Blues People*, and, shortly thereafter, his essay "The Changing Same" in which Jones/Baraka declares that "not only the Beatles, but any group of Myddle-class white boys who need a haircut and male hormones can be a pop group." He accuses such Myddle-class white boys of "stealing Music . . . stealing energy (lives): with their own concerns and lives finally, making it White Music" (Jones 1967, 205). The viewer is enticed with the sumptuousness of a rock group in an expensive London studio—multi-colored baffles, Vox amplifiers, Gibson guitars—recording what we now know to be a classic rock anthem, while a 35-mm film crew trains its cinematographic eye on the creative labor that attests to the band's genius. But the basis of that enticement is cut off at the knees by Jones's indictment. What are we to make of the Stones' bourgeois luxury, evidenced by the ample studio time, which allows them to figure out their new song and experiment with different instrumentation and arrangements while the record label foots the bill for the studio's ticking clock? We are aware, of course, that this luxury is bought with the spoils of the very theft of which Jones/Baraka has accused them. The Stones, named after a Muddy Waters song, learned their craft and made their name in obsequious devotion to African American bluesmen like Waters, Robert Johnson, and Howlin' Wolf and to the nascent rock and roll birthed at Chicago's Chess Records by Bo Diddley and Chuck Berry. And what of the song they are constructing before our eyes and ears? These Myddle-class white boys play at being the devil himself, pulling the strings of a cast of historical puppets ranging from Pontius Pilate to the Bolsheviks storming the Winter Palace to a Nazi General and the Kennedys' assassins, Lee Harvey Oswald and Sirhan Sirhan. The song doesn't so much tap into the late 1960s zeitgeist as proto-tweet about it. The Stones don the revolutionary garb of the times. But as Godard seems intent on demonstrating, their investment is wholly in the vestments.

Yet, it would be a mistake to see *One Plus One* as a simple bad-versus-good-portrait of the Stones and the Black militants. The later scenes inevitably complicate such a view by placing side by side (one plus one) Maoist hippie boys and a neo-Nazi book seller (played by the film's producer, Iain Quarrier) and then the idyllic Eve Democracy (portrayed as a pre-Raphaelite-hippie version of a Socialist Realist peasant) in contrast to the crass film crew with their media apparatus and their banal yes/no questions that deny access to the thoughts of Democracy herself. When we add up all these one plus ones, we don't arrive at clean twos. Rather, we must filter each element through the mesh of the other. In every case, the mesh is media—books and broadsides, cameras and tape recorders, the baring of Godard's own filmic apparatus—all assuming the role of the facilitators of messages, of action, of the construction of subjects. The Black militants are produced by the Jones and Cleaver texts that they recite and record with handheld tape machines. The Rolling Stones are produced (in the vernacular of their field) by the rolling of tape, by the producers and money men roaming watchfully about the periphery of the studio. Eve Democracy is produced by the film crew (filmed, of course, by Godard's film crew)—screens within screens, cameras within cameras. As Patrick Burke notes,

> In *One Plus One* Godard takes a wary view of rock's revolutionary and racial rhetoric. Rather than assume a direct, uncomplicated correspondence between the energy and style of rock and political and cultural revolution, Godard's film pushes viewers to acknowledge the then unfashionable possibility that both rock music and revolutionary politics are social and textual constructions created through the circulation of borrowed texts rather than rooted in any essential reality. (Burke 277)

Godard asks us to see all the revolutionary posturing of *One Plus One* as commensurate. The Stones are no less—but no more—radical than the junkyard militants, the bookstore Maoists, or verdant Democracy strolling through the forest. Nor are the Black radicals the real deal and the Stones the posers. Mediated by technology, by character typology, by language, by a locus of tropes, every identity and identity position is constructed: reclaimed readymades with readymade intentions and destinations. This can't be seen as a condemnation or a dismissal of any of the film's characters. None is more-or-less real than any other. None is more authentic or more artificial. None is true or false. Rather, in the final analysis, each must be judged by how it passes through the mesh of its context, by what it allows to pass through its own mesh, and, thus, by its effects in the world. Eldridge Cleaver, minister of information for the Black Panther Party, and Mick Jagger, singer in a British rock and roll band: each knows how to play his part, each knows how to literally walk the walk and talk the talk. And each passes through the other.

Just a month before the start of filming of *One Plus One* in London, Conservative British MP, Enoch Powell, delivered what has come to be known as the "Rivers of Blood" speech in Birmingham. Powell's belligerent paranoia about immigration to Britain, especially from the recently independent colonies of the Commonwealth made headlines across the country. Quoting Virgil, he speculated about a future in which "Like the Roman, I seem to see 'the River Tiber foaming with much blood.'" And citing a conversation with a constituent, he predicted that "in this country in 15 or 20 years' time the black man will have the whip hand over the white man" (Powell, quoted in Yeginsu). It is unclear if Godard was aware of Powell's speech. But the film's scenes of Black men molesting and killing White women while reciting incendiary texts in a junkyard that resembles a cinematic dystopia play like a Swiftian satire of Powell's racist delusions. While Burke interprets the Black revolutionaries in the junkyard as "obviously archetypes" (Burke 290), it is also important to recognize them as grotesqueries born of White Britain's declining-Empire paranoia.

The deliberate staging of the scene constructs a kind of reciprocal relationship between media and message. "They speak not in their own words, but only through quotations from such writers as Baraka and Cleaver, often read directly from their sources. These quotations are filtered through layers of alienating technology, dictated into microphones and tape recorders that create an artificial distance between the speakers and their speech" (Burke 290). Information is formed by the allowances and limitations of given media and the ways in which these media-formations effect the messages they convey. The mass market paperback commodifies Cleaver's dissent, transforming the rhetoric of revolution into the kind of dime store pulp we encounter later in the bookshop scene. Burke draws our attention to Raymond Durgnat's review of *One Plus One*, in which he argues that "all the impedimenta of communication (from books through tape recorders to a-camera-before-the-cameras) signaled that 'an iron (or safety) curtain' of theory has dropped across the world's stage. Life is reduced to footnotes about the theory of life's possibility" (Durgnat, cited in Burke 290). Burke goes on to compare Godard's use of recording technology to Antonioni's *Blow-Up* (1966) and Coppola's *The Conversation* (1974), "in which photography or audio recording lead their users into paranoia and confusion rather than an enhanced understanding of the world around them" (Burke 291).

Godard's emphasis on recording and inscription devices (audio, film, text) saturates *One Plus One*. Cameras and microphones frame Eve Democracy during her sylvan interview. And in the film's final scene, introduced by a title card bearing a punily modified Situationist slogan, "Under the Stones the Beach," Eve Democracy reappears, rifle in hand, scampering frantically across a beach. She is shot by a White man in a leather jacket, who is shot in return by a Black man in a dashiki. The Black man helps Democracy to her feet. They run across a set of camera dolly tracks. Democracy falls again and is assisted again by the Black man. Godard himself enters the scene, urging the two actors forward. She falls a third time, at the wheels of a camera crane. Godard takes a jar of red paint from an assistant and pours it across Democracy's prone body.

**Figure 6.1** *One Plus One*, Jean-Luc Godard, director (1968).

The Black man helps her onto the camera-end of the crane's arm where two flags, one black (anarchist) and one red (communist), flap noisily in the seaside wind. Democracy is hoisted up on the crane's arm and the film ends with us gazing up at her lifeless body splayed at the feet of the camera and the billowing flags, all set against the blue sky (Figure 6.1).

Of course, such baring of the device is typical of Godard. It is, in many ways, his signature gesture. But here the emphasis on technological inscription and recording are just as much content as form. The Stones and recorded popular music more generally are the most technologically embedded of cultural constructs. Pop music is a form that lives only in and for recording with no life outside of that context. A recorded pop song has no existence prior to its recording. There may be live performances. But the song as an artifact only comes into being with and by the recording process. Think of the myriad hits of the 1960s, written by staff songwriters, recorded by session musicians, and attributed to fabricated band names. (The Velvet Underground emerged from just such a concoction, attributed to "The Primitives.") Cinema, on the other hand (or at least cinema prior to computer-generated imagery), always starts from preexistent reality. Even if Godard can correct a misguided viewer, saying, "your difficulties stem from the false idea you have that people on the screen are made of flesh and blood. Whereas what you see are shadows and you reproach these shadows for not being alive" (quoted in Elshaw), it is still true that cinema builds on a foundation of real people and objects in real space. As Samuel Thomas adds it up, "faces and names deliver momentary associations and impressions; associations and impressions become networks and structures; networks and structures become nation states; nation states become entities in a much larger game of geo-political chess and so on" (Thomas 472). Pop music, conversely, builds from no preceding reality and is inextricably bound to its status as recording. While the Black radicals in the junkyard may be *partially* constructed by the texts they recite and the machines they use to record themselves, and while Eve Democracy's life and death may be *partially* products of cameras and microphones (she was, as we've noted, played by Anne Wiazemsky, who was married to Godard and presumably accompanied him home when shooting wrapped), a song like "Sympathy for the Devil" is *entirely* made by the form of the information as recorded. This is, perhaps, the most striking aspect of Godard's studio scenes. We witness all the false starts and what-ifs of the song's unborn twins. And this is why Godard punched out producer Quarrier at the film's London debut. Against Godard's wishes, Quarrier recut the film to include the Stones' finished version of "Sympathy for the Devil." For Godard, leaving the song unfinished, contingent, one of many possible outcomes, is fundamental to the film's meaning. The realization of any potential version is *totally* beholden to its capture and storage on magnetic tape. There is no song independent of its recording. In both cases—cinema and pop music—the medium is inexorably engaged in a feedback loop with the world, with history, politics, economics, and so on. But the role played by media and mediation and the specific influence it exerts is qualitatively different. Godard orbits his film around the Stones in the studio because they represent the strongest form of recorded media's sway over the meaning and manifestation of information.

If we ask what animates "Sympathy for the Devil" or the Rolling Stones' music more generally, *One Plus One* replies with a more complicated diagnosis than the one that Marcus offers about Post-Punk. Global interconnectedness cuts in more than one direction. Or, more accurately, like a Molotov cocktail, shards discharge in unpredictable trajectories and velocities, igniting intended and unintended targets. At the same time that Eldridge Cleaver is recognizing that the conditions driving the struggles of African Americans are part of a planetary movement of colonized peoples against their capitalist, imperialist oppressors, the Rolling Stones are transporting the sounds and styles of African Americans to the capital of the British Empire, converting both the labor and the culture of slavery's descendants into unimaginable wealth. Russian tanks trundle into Prague. Bullets end the lives of Martin Luther King and Robert Kennedy. Harrowing battles immolate the streets of Chicago. The filming of *One Plus One* is interrupted as Godard returns to Paris to participate in the events of May, France erupting in a fury of unprecedented scale and speed. It is at once too easy and woefully inadequate to claim that such complicated currents have either a single origin or a unified destination. Liberation and domination often progress in tandem along parallel tracks. King's assassination prompts Lyndon Johnson to sign the 1968 Civil Rights Act. But a few months later Richard Nixon is elected president on a platform of institutional racism that he calls, using a code still transparent to all, "law and order."

As much as Punk and Post-Punk rejected the naïveté of the Summer of Love, they had no choice but to accept the inheritances of 1968. It was Nixon, after all, who removed the US dollar from the gold standard, allowing alternate markets to compete for economic dominance via monetary policy. When Marcus says that Post-Punk is "as animated by international terrorism, . . . . as by anything else," he is, perhaps unknowingly, connecting the music of the

*Carlos* soundtrack to the complicated contexts of *One Plus One*; to the Black Power movement, to the Rolling Stones, to the Blues, to the unprocessed fumes of fascism in Europe, and to a radical Leftism to which Godard was becoming increasingly dedicated. It is not difficult to connect the dots of global anti-colonialism (including anti-Vietnam War protests and the Civil Rights Movement) to the Cold War's new varieties of imperialism, to the burgeoning generation gap, to growing awareness of institutionalized wealth inequality, and, finally, to the emergence of violence as a political tool in the Middle East (the PLO), Italy (the Red Brigades), Japan (the Red Army), the United States (the Black Panthers and the Weather Underground), and elsewhere. Many of Carlos's comrades in the 1970s emerged from the same radical German Left that spawned the Baader Meinhof Gang (also known as the Red Army Faction). Their cause was both internationalist and, given Germany's recent past, anti-nationalist.

> German terrorism of the 1970s shared many of the revolutionary fantasies of German students that linked their struggles against capitalist oppression of "third world" countries and against former National Socialists in positions of political or economic power (such as Chancellor Kurt-Georg Kiesinger and industrialist Hanns-Martin Schleyer), for example, with those of the Vietcong against American capitalist imperialism. (Shahan 369–70)

It is only amidst the tumult of such concatenations that a figure like Carlos could emerge. Named Ilich Ramírez Sánchez by his Marxist father, the Venezuelan studied at Patrice Lumumba University in Moscow and graduated to the Popular Front for the Liberation of Palestine, training in Jordan and Syria. He adopted the nom de guerre, Carlos, in tribute to President Carlos Andrés Pérez Rodríguez, who nationalized the Venezuelan oil industry. So in 1975, when he carried out his most famous mission, storming the OPEC meeting in Vienna, and kidnapping some sixty hostages including ministers of more than ten Arab nations, we have a Venezuelan, named after Lenin, renamed after a Venezuelan progressive, schooled in Moscow at a University named after the first prime minister of the independent Democratic Republic of the Congo, kidnapping Arab leaders—newly powerful due to their oil reserves—on behalf of the Palestinian cause. As Samuel Thomas notes, Carlos is a "name that is deeply connected to both the traversal and reassertion of the boundaries between fact and fiction, the interchange between overground and underground, and indeed the boundaries of the law, the nation state and so on" (Thomas 460–1).

Assayas's use of Post-Punk in *Carlos* similarly traverses and reasserts. On the one hand, the music allows the film to traverse time and history, to fast forward, as it were, from the mid-1970s of oil embargoes, terrorism, and the destabilization of First World dominance to the early 1980s of Reagan and Thatcher's ensconcing of neoliberal priorities and policies, the encasement of First World market dominance over the mechanics of global geopolitics. On the other hand, the music reasserts a use of rock and roll that owes allegiance to 1970s filmmakers like Scorsese and Coppola. By the same token, this reassertion recasts the traversal of time as yet another reassertion of the claim staked by neoliberalism over everything within its market purview. This neoliberal "everything" is often imagined, by champions and detractors alike, as totalizing; literally everything. Nothing is left behind. "There is no alternative," as Thatcher infamously put it. But Post-Punk was meant to separate itself from that music and the self-assured bravura that led the directors to use it. Post-Punk claimed to represent an alternative. Bands like the Feelies and Wire were supposed to be different from the Doors and the Stones, rejecting self-mythologizing and push-button musical affect in favor of less off-the-shelf sounds and senses. Post-Punk, so the story went, was not so easily susceptible to recuperation by the machinery of mass media commodity.

This is what I meant when I wrote previously that Greil Marcus gets it complicatedly wrong when he asserts "the best and most adventurous music of the late 1970s and early 1980s was itself as animated by international terrorism, by the specter of a world where, at times, it could seem that only a few armed gnostics were in control, as by anything else." The use of the music in *Carlos* does damage to Post-Punk's adventurousness. And Marcus's claim, based as it is on the way the music is used, does further damage, tying the music to the use of the Stones in a film like Scorsese's *Goodfellas* (but *not* to their use in Godard's *One Plus One*). The resulting contradiction may be the most productive aspect of the film's soundtrack. It is the same contradiction that confronts political violence: whatever radical effect such violence might have at first, it is quickly subsumed into political praxis. To smash the State's monopoly on violence requires a usurpation of a violence that starts as renegade and unjustifiable, but, if successful, becomes sanctioned and official. The thing itself remains the same, but its meaning shifts as it moves to the center. Via the coup, the terrorists become the State. Of course, this problem, in both its aesthetic and its political formulations, is the problem that has obsessed Godard for all of his six decades of filmmaking.

In his insightful reading of media representations of Carlos, "Yours in Revolution: Retrofitting Carlos the Jackal," Samuel Thomas has this to say about Assayas's use of Wire's song "Drill,"

> the yelped, incantatory lyrics function as a sort of choric device [. . .] the effect is not intrusively "experimental" and this unlikely "chorus" does not disturb the film's ground-level sense of space and time. Rather, we must recognise such questions as embedded in the raw materials of the film's composition and in the theoretical/experiential processes of the editing suite. (Thomas 474)

This observation passes with the alacrity of a jump cut. But it's worth slowing it down and comparing it with Marcus's claim. Thomas notices that the experimentalism that is usually explicit in Wire's music is neutralized by the way it is integrated into the scene. Even the cut-and-spliced lyrics, desperate and accusatory, settle down at ground level. What animates the music here is not international terrorism, or at least not only or simply that. It is animated at least as much by the allowances and limitations of the editing suite; of sitting in a darkened room for days on end, beholden to the exigencies of the medium of film and of the noun "film," the particular object being constructed with images and sound. The music in the film is animated by a certain conception of what cinema is, what a film is, what a soundtrack is: by the demands of the market, by producers' investments, by a directorial career in progress. In other words, it is animated by the vast complex of capital as it feeds and is fed by the conversion of use into exchange, of labor into commodity, of life into lifestyle.

So perhaps, in the end, Marcus is not so much complicatedly wrong as complicatedly and inadvertently right. There are indeed gnostics in control. But they are not the armed gnostics that Marcus has in mind: Carlos and his band. They are the gnostics of the board room, the stockholders' meeting, the television executives, the movie theater chains, and the financers who green-light Assayas's five-and-a-half-hour film. Punk and Post-Punk may begin as renegade and unjustifiable, but before long they are sanctioned and official. The thing itself remains the same, but its meaning shifts as it moves to the center. Arty, nerdy, fast, and nervous, vacate the periphery as they turn up in car ads, as radio bumper music, over supermarket sound systems, on television and film soundtracks. Via the coup, the terrorists become the State.

# 7

# All the Needles Are on Red

I am a microphone. You are a microphone. All of us, microphones. Sorry, I've switched horses midstream, mixing my metaphors, and transgressing time-honored boundaries between organs of perception. But, if this is a book about what things sound like when we look at them and what music looks like when we listen to it, then I think the crossed wires are not only excusable, but inevitable. From the late 1960s through the early 1980s—more or less the span of time with which we are presently concerned—the verb *taping* and the noun *tapes* took on specific meanings. Newly portable and affordable tape recorders meant that nearly anyone, from the president of the United States to a suburban kid attending rock and roll shows, could afford to tape myriad goings-on; to capture, to archive, and to revisit the ephemerality of sound. The Swiss company Nagra introduced the first portable audio tape recorders in the 1950s. But they were prohibitively expensive and heavy. Nagra III, introduced in 1959 and capable of cinema synch sound, weighed 10 kilograms (22 pounds). In the early 1960s, with the development of transistors, portable tape recorders became smaller and lighter, but not significantly less expensive. The Dutch company Philips developed the compact cassette tape in the early 1960s and made the patent freely available (imagine that!) to other manufacturers in 1965 (Kimizuka, 217).

It is commonplace among the literature on sound and vision that "hearing is spherical, vision is directional; hearing immerses its subject, vision offers a perspective." It is so commonplace, in fact, that Jonathan Sterne has dubbed these, and a set of related presumptions, the "audio visual litany" (Sterne 15). It might be true, when standing in a forest, that the calls of birds, the rustle of wind-rippled leaves, or the buzzing of insects is experienced as spherical and immersive and that the visual identification of any specific source of such sounds would emanate from a directional perspective. But if we think about our rapidly expanding experience of recorded sound from the 1940s to the present, we must reckon with the fact that such sounds are both captured and recapitulated in very directional ways. Microphones are sonic cameras, pointed at sound sources, with framing patterns characterized as "cardioid," "figure-of-eight," and "omni-directional."

On the one hand, we can think of the speaker—as Pierre Schaeffer, the inventor of *musique concrete*, urged us to—as a curtain that separates us from the source of sound. But it makes precisely equal sense to think of the speaker as a sound screen, onto which sound—and some image of its source (a bird or Bird's saxophone or Charlie Parker himself)—is projected. Think of our home sound systems, how we point our speakers at ourselves, and ourselves at our speakers.

Lighter, cheaper tape recorders allowed us to point microphones at more things, more often. Take, for example, Andy Warhol, the quintessential artist of the 1960s. Between 1964 and 1985—again, conveniently, the time period covered by this book—Warhol was rarely without his beloved cassette recorder. The Warhol archive is home to nearly 3,500 tapes, 70 percent of which are cassettes. As Judith Paraino notes, "In addition to capturing conversations and the occasional cabarets and rock shows he attended, these tapes provide a sonic trace of Warhol's own body moving through different spaces. [. . .] The tapes archive Warhol's being in the world by way of sound" (Paraino 403). Warhol's first tape recorder was a Norelco Carry-Corder 150, which hit the market in late 1964. For Warhol, the acquisition was momentous. He referred to the machine as "my wife," writing in *THE Philosophy of Andy Warhol (From A to B and Back Again)*, "I didn't get married until 1964 when I got my first tape recorder" (Warhol 26).

A photo in the January 1966 issue of the magazine *Tape Recording* features Warhol in his de rigueur sunglasses, wearing headphones, and a superhero costume—briefs-over-tights and cape. A picture of Warhol, himself, is emblazoned on the costume's chest. Warhol, hands on hips, is looking down at the photo of himself on his chest. While the smaller, photo-within-the-photo-Warhol is holding a microphone and looking up at his larger version as if speaking to him through the closed circuit of the self (Figure 7.1). It's all here, everything this book's about, save the rock and roll. But, of course, that's easily fixed. At the moment this photo was taken, Warhol was on the verge of bringing the Velvet Underground into his fold.

An argument can be made that Warhol's association with still images, the soup cans, Brillo boxes, electric chairs, and Marilyns, is the lesser part of his oeuvre. Or, more precisely, that they mattered less to him and were less representative

**Figure 7.1** Andy Warhol, *Tape Recording* magazine, January 1966.

of a properly Warholian aesthetic radicality than the kinetic, dynamic aspects of his practice. This is not to say that Warhol would not have been pleased that the soup can is the image that launched a thousand museum shop tote bags, but that the image is not the source of Warhol's intervention. Rather, it is the bag, doled out to countless visitors, each going their separate ways—to boardrooms and two martini lunches, to downtown parties and impromptu sleepovers, to the shopping mall and the beach. It is the bag itself, as a passenger in the lives of strangers, crossing the thresholds of one milieu, entering another. The bag as unobtrusive company in the world is Warhol's vehicle. The image is just the permit, so to speak, that authorizes its operation. You can't put the Exploding Plastic Inevitable on a bag. But the bag becomes a kind of small-scale, portable version of the EPI, subject to lights, sounds, bodies, and motion.

Warhol was fascinated with images in transit. His tape recordings, his movies, his prints of newspaper photos, his importation of the Velvet Underground into the filmic-performance-party of the EPI are all displacements of images—visual images, sonic images, informational images. Warhol was fascinated with mass media's transportation and equalization of images. Any image could go anywhere and be swapped with any other: the Queen of England for the local pharmacist, Marilyn Monroe for the FBI's most wanted, Elvis Presley for a pair of ruby slippers.

> He was fascinated by the ways sounds grew big by traveling through everyday publicity channels like vinyl records, radio, and the gossip and chatter of celebrity culture. More literally, he embraced the agglutination of individual particles of human sound—especially words and voices—into an aural mass. (Stadler 429)

What Gustavus Stadler refers to as Warhol's "queer ways of listening" signifies a relation to sound, especially recorded sound, that defies the normative frames that regulate, define, and separate talk from music, gossip from discourse, pop from "serious" music. Commenting on a passage from Warhol's book, *POPism*, in which Warhol describes his own experience among the competing sounds of his studio, the Factory, Stadler writes,

> Warhol can't prioritize or hierarchize the sounds; he can't formulate an aural version of perspective, relegating some sounds to the background while keeping others in the foreground. These sonic effects precipitate a sense-traversing breakdown in the ability not only to separate humans from machines but also to separate real people from represented ones. (Stadler 430)

Warhol listens like a microphone, stripped of subjectivity and the accompanying ability to frame experience. While the microphone is used by the filmmaker, the journalist, the disc jockey, as a kind of camera, Warhol uses it differently. He's not trying to get a light on it. His audio recordings restore the horizontality of real time and real space. Iggy slips back into the crowd, where his microphone is equally available to the star's grunts and the fan's entreaties. The microphone doesn't give a shit about this distinction or other mythical binaries. Rather, for Warhol, the wonder of recording is the breaching of frames; the merging of miscellaneous perceptions. Of the Factory, Warhol writes, "I'd sit there and listen to every sound,"

> the freight elevator moving in the shaft, the sound of the grate opening and closing when people got in and went out, the steady traffic all the way downstairs on 47th Street, the projector running, a camera shutter clicking, a magazine page turning, somebody lighting a match, the colored sheets of gelatin and sheets of silver paper moving when the fan hit them, the high school typists hitting a key every couple of seconds, the scissors shearing as Paul [Morrissey] cut out E.P.I.

[Exploding Plastic Inevitable] clippings and pasted them into scrapbooks, the water running over prints in Billy's [Linich, aka Name] darkroom, the timer going off, the dryer operating, someone trying to make the toilet work, men having sex in the back room, girls closing compacts and makeup cases. (Warhol, quoted in Stadler 430)

Taken in this context, Warhol's collaboration with the Velvet Underground becomes more legible. As the story goes, Warhol discovered the Velvets on the night they were fired from the Café Bizarre in New York for playing "The Black Angel's Death Song" after being explicitly told by the club's manager to never play it again (Fricke 17). Surely, it's easy to believe that Warhol was impressed by this act of impudence. But consider the song itself. John Cale's sawing viola revolves like the gear at the heart of a faltering motor. Lou Reed's and Sterling Morrison's guitars lurch against the gear in 6/8, a time signature like a handmade wheel. The effect is akin to walking on broken heels through cobwebs. And then walking through them again. Sprung against this viscid incessance, Reed rattles off an amphetamine screed of cut-and-spliced phrases. Two distinct signals, seemingly from independent sources, collide in the space of the song. For Warhol, this would have been a familiar experience, reminiscent of the sonic montage of the Factory, where the aural inventory above was mixed with radio and multiple record players, all sounding simultaneously. As Warhol describes it, "the radio and the record player would both be blasting 'Don't Let the Sun Catch You Crying' mixed with *Turandot*, 'Where Did Our Love Go?' with Donizetti or Bellini, or the Stones doing 'Not Fade Away' while Maria Callas did *Norma*" (Warhol 93).

Stadler's characterization of "queer listening" hinges on this kind of overload. Warhol's mode of listening gravitates toward saturation, the loss of discrete signals among a tumult of inputs. For Stadler, Warhol's predilections are "evident in the most celebratory, extended description of a song in [*POPism*], his account of the Rolling Stones' single '(I Can't Get No) Satisfaction'" (Stadler 436). The warm months of 1965 were, according to Warhol, "the summer of 'Satisfaction'"—the song "coming out of every doorway, window, closet, and car" (Warhol, quoted in Stadler 436). The song becomes part of the urban landscape, merging with the city itself to create a kind of gimcrack-gesamtkunstwerk. But Stadler also notes that "Satisfaction" announces itself instantly with its now-iconic overdriven guitar riff. Stadler suggests that overdrive is another form of saturation,

created by flooding an amplifier's circuits with too much signal from the guitar. In other words, the song's sound registers the presence of more information than the apparatus can recognize or process in the moment. The guitar's aesthetic of informational overload is the sound of mediation itself—that is, the eminently Warholian sound of an uneven, not fully containable encounter between two modes of mediating sound, in this case the guitar and the amplifier. (Stadler 436)

"Information" became an early 1970s buzzword, indicative of a new mode of interfacing with the world. Rather than positing a phenomenological relation to our environment, "information" suggests that we interact, first and foremost, with data, with categories, with signs. Information meets apparatus. Light hits lens. Sound vibrates the microphonic membrane. In the 1960s and early 1970s, these were locales of fascination. For artists, they were fecund sites of exploration. In 1970, the Museum of Modern Art presented an exhibition—curated by Kynaston McShine—with the matter-of-fact title *Information*. In fact, the show took information as a matter of fact. One hundred international artists contributed projects that engaged not primarily with visual, sonic, or haptic stimuli, but with text and numbers, grids, and systems. As Eve Meltzer points out, the exhibition's thesis is evident in the images which adorn the cover of the catalogue.

A grid of abstracted lithographic images of contemporary technologies of communication—an instamatic camera, an IBM Selectric, cruise ship, Volkswagen Bug, a portable television—together proposed that all forms of discourse had similarly achieved and suffered from a flattening and totalising informational consistency. Considered together, the aesthetic of "information" and "information" in the technological sense of word gave rise to the following notion: the world itself had become an information system. (Meltzer, 126)

At every turn, the inevitable conclusion is announced: we are no longer eyes, seeing the world. We are cameras, documenting it. Contemporary experience (*c.* 1970) disconnected the senses from the phenomena of the environment. For better or for worse, the world presented as a data set seen through the viewfinder of the instamatic or on the screen of the portable television. Meltzer fails to note that the cover of the *Information* catalogue also includes an image of a reel-to-reel tape recorder. Our sonic world too had been transformed from an object of perception to a collection of information to be documented, recorded, and played back.

Needless to say, *Information* did not initiate this transformation, but recognized and codified a tendency already afoot in the art world. Prior to 1970, artists were already rejecting the centuries of art history that they'd inherited; a history smug in its acceptance of the world as an offering for our eyes, a visual entity apprehended most appropriately in visual media. The second half of the 1960s witnessed the birth of conceptual art, which among other innovations, rejected the visual basis of visual art. Instead, conceptualists of various stripes engaged with systems that structure the world's phenomena and our understandings of them. Such structures could be mathematical, philosophical, economic, medial, or—most likely—a combination of any or all of these.

Let's start with Christine Kozlov's *Information Drift* (1968), a single reel of audio tape, framed and wall mounted, accompanied by a brief text which reads,

COMBINED RECORDINGS OF NEWS BULLETINS OF THE SHOOTINGS OF ANDY WARHOL AND ROBERT KENNEDY.

*Information Drift* captures two events that might be said to be of both historical importance and of acute personal and social experience. However, rather than depict these events in any conventional sense—a tableau painting, a poem, a song, a documentary film—Kozlov engages the contemporary capture of the information that, for most of us, would constitute the actuality of the events. Kozlov draws attention to the systems that structure the event, rather than to the event itself. *Information Drift* is a presentation of the media of technological reproduction rendered as an object, inaccessible as a conventional conduit of information. These two murder attempts—one successful, one not—took place just two days apart in June of 1968. The public's experience of them is wholly a product of their capture and distribution in the informational packaging of recording and mass media. Yet *Information Drift* does not pass that package along intact. Instead it withholds the content in favor of the material-technological form, leaving us to ponder the status of information in lieu of the information itself. Proof of the existence of information relating to these events, or lack thereof, is circumstantial, based only on what we've been told by the artist. Still, the probability that the tape is what it claims to be is based on other things. It is based on the readiness and receptivity of the media. In some fundamental way, unexposed film and unrecorded audio tape are not yet themselves. They are, to a greater extent, even, than unpainted canvases or blank paper, mere possibilities. Only when they receive the information for which they are intended are they realized as the kinds of things they are. Tape might be thought of as a kind of Derridean arche-writing; a format that behaves in ways that are similar to Jonathan Sterne's description of the header syntax of an MP3, but also like Douglas Kahn's third internal sound: a discursivity that precedes Cage's hearing of low and high pitches in the anechoic chamber.[1] Every medium is a prepared ground for a contextually constrained (if not quite pre-determined) set of marks to be made.

The probability of the existence of information is based on the artist's word. When Kozlov tells us what is on the reel of tape, we are obliged to accept this information, not as certain but as probable. After all, what would be gained by deception? Or, more to the point, what would be lost if *Information Drift* did not, in fact, contain recordings of news bulletins of the Warhol and Kennedy shootings? Critics often misunderstand such works as "solipsistic" and "tautological." Pavel Pyś, in the catalogue for an exhibition of Kozlov's work at the Henry Moore Institute, proposes that Kozlov's "sculptures are governed by a hermetic logic" (17), and Jo Melvin, in the same catalogue, says that "Kozlov set out to represent 'nothing,' to reject concepts, and to consider the parameters of silence" (5). But these critics get it wrong. They're looking for information in all the wrong places. *Information Drift* isn't a media work about silence. It's a silent work about media; about mass media and about recording media. It's a work about information and apparatus. The basis of probability is itself based on the fact that these seemingly blank media are not, in fact, blank. They do carry content, even if not in the conventional manner. *Information Drift* may be blank tape for all we know. Yet, even if it is, it is still about the shootings of Warhol and Kennedy. And it is about news bulletins. And about audio tape. And it is about technological reproduction and blankness and about the art world of the late 1960s and its fixations on technological reproduction and blankness and conceptualism. It is about all these things that I am talking about right now. And I am talking about Kozlov's *Information Drift*.

Critics had a hard time pivoting to this new relation to information. In a review in the *New York Times*, the famously conservative reviewer, Hilton Kramer called the show "unmitigated nonsense." He dismissed the informational turn, sarcastically suggesting that "the relevant and meaningful thing to do in the face of this grave political crisis is, apparently, to go to town with the Xerox machine" (quoted in Meltzer 132). Kramer already had a chip on his shoulder about photocopying. Earlier in 1970 he had published a review of a show at the New York Cultural Center with the headline "Xeroxophilia Rages Out of Control" in which he dismissed some of the young artists as "Xeroxomaniacs" (Kramer).

---

[1]  See Jonathan Sterne, *MP3: The Meaning of a Format*, Duke University Press, 2012, pp. 196–7; and Douglas Kahn, *Noise Water Meat: A History of Sound in the Arts*, MIT Press, 2001, p. 190.

As it turns out, both photocopying and audio recording were waiting in the wings, ready for their cue. Within a few short years they would both play an unexpectedly significant role in the political history of the 1970s. Daniel Ellsberg would spend countless late nights at the copier in the office of a colleague's girlfriend. His children—aged 13 and 10—collated, as he copied 7,000 pages of classified documents that would come to be known as the "Pentagon Papers." Meanwhile, the end of Richard Nixon's unraveling presidency was hastened by the revelation of a network of hidden tape recorders in his offices at the White House and the nearby Executive Office Building. When an eighteen-and-a-half-minute gap was discovered on one of the tapes, inevitable conclusions were drawn by prosecutors and the public alike.

Warhol straddles the perception-information divide. His affection for the cacophonous collisions of multiple sound sources certainly derives from the distortions of information as it grates against the limits of the apparatus. But it also takes pleasure in the resulting perceptual experience. Unexpected sonorities and timbres, unpredictable Frankensteinian forms, emerge as artifacts of chance. Information denies the injunctions of the apparatus and the teleology of intention disintegrates. Not only does the sensibility—both the ability to make sense and the simple perceptibility—of the experience lose its apparent cohesion, but cohesion in general, notions of rationale and propriety, starts to lose their determinative power. Not the museum shop tote bag, but the bag loosed into a thousand contexts, each unpredictable, acquiring its own intention-defying form.

As different as the work of Kozlov and Warhol may be, they share a conviction that information lives at multiple levels. The old form-content divide cannot successfully relegate information strictly to the content side. Rather, information emerges from form as well, whether from conventional notions of composition or as a product of apparatus: media, contexts, containers, interpretation. Both Kozlov's work and Warhol's capitalize most fruitfully on the friction created by conventional content, or information, and conventional form, or apparatus. It's no accident that both were drawn to the tape recorder as an embodiment of the synthesis of information and apparatus. Each uses the tape recorder in distinct, idiosyncratic ways. Yet both understand the tape recorder as a kind of anti-spotlight. While the TV crew of WLWT was compelled to obey the modern mandate of "getting a light on" Iggy Pop as he disappeared into the variegated mass of the Cincinnati Pop Festival audience, Kozlov and Warhol embrace the lack of focus, favoring disorder as a reflection of contemporary experience and a source of "happy accidents," which defy the imperatives of intention, planning, teleology, and self-contained, self-justifying form.

When Warhol witnessed the Velvet Underground grinding their way through "The Black Angel's Death Song," and then starting it over again, he heard another version of this friction. Language against noise. Order against chaos. Stasis against progress. The clock against eternity. The Velvet Underground were capable of conjuring a kind of anti-teleological magic. Their miracles had no source, no master plan or master planner. They delivered no tidy moral-of-the-story. In place of the modernist compulsion to get a light on it, the Velvet Underground flooded the visual field with white light, casting everything in equally blinding relief. This is not merely an inversion of the worldview that modernism inherited from Judeo-Christianity, in which every effect has a cause and every cause is a lesson and every lesson is god. This is not democracy's teleological recourse to freedom. It is not the law's recourse to justice. It is not capitalism's recourse to profit. The Velvet Underground abandon the miracle. They pursue, instead, the epiphany of the epiphenomenon. "Some people work very hard," Lou Reed sings, "but still they never get it right" (The Velvet Underground, "Beginning to See the Light"). You can't plan to have your mind blown.

The Velvet Underground recorded their second album, *White Light/White Heat*, at the in-house recording studio of Scepter Records, home to a diverse array of artists including Dionne Warwick, the Kingsmen, Tami Terrell, the Isley Brothers, and the Guess Who. The studio's location at 254 West 54th Street in New York would later become home to the legendary, Studio 54, famously frequented by Andy Warhol. Despite the fact that the band had severed their ties with Warhol, *White Light/White Heat* stands as the most radical test yet conducted of information and apparatus. As guitarist Sterling Morrison explained to Mary Harron,

> We didn't want to lay down separate tracks, we wanted to do it studio live with a simultaneous voice, but the problem was that the current state of studio art wouldn't let us do it. There was fantastic leakage because everyone was playing so loud and we had so much electronic junk with us in the studio—all these fuzzers and compressors. Gary Kellgran the engineer, who is ultra-competent, told us repeatedly: "You can't do it—all the needles are on red." And we reacted as we always reacted: "Look, we don't know what goes on in there and we don't want to hear about it. Just do the best you can." And so the album is all fuzzy, there's all that white noise. (Harron)

Nowhere is this more salient than on "Sister Ray," *White Light/White Heat's* seventeen-and-a-half-minute opus. The largely improvised maelstrom was a fixture of the Velvet Underground's live sets, often stretching to half an hour or longer. The song provided a forum for pushing and shoving, for trials and errors, for tantrums and doldrums. No two performances are alike. The song resembles a blank canvas more than it does a finished composition. In the studio, the band faced the same quandary faced by improvising jazz musicians: Does fixing it in the amber of a studio recording decimate the spirit of the song as a living organism, an open question? The band rejected the possibility of doing multiple takes and then choosing among them. Instead, as Morrison recounts,

> we stared at each other and said, "This is going to be one take. So whatever you want to do, you better do it now." And that explains what is going on in the mix. There is a musical struggle—everyone's trying to do what he wants to do every second, and nobody's backing off. I think it's great the way the organ comes in. Cale starts to try and play a solo. He's totally buried and there's a sort of surge and then he's pulling out all the stops until he just rises out of the pack. He was able to get louder than Lou and I were. The drums are almost totally drowned out. (Harron)

The result is unmatched in the annals of rock and roll. For the better part of an album side, the band is locked in mortal combat—with each other, yes—but more crucially and more vigorously, with the moment. They know that this is it: the one chance they'll get to commit this song, this *thing*, this something happening, to tape; to lock it down for the eternity of a vinyl groove and to do right by it. We can also hear each of them wanting to do right by themselves. There is Cale's organ, as Morrison describes it. But there is also Mo Tucker, ratcheting the tempo, like the captain/the engineer/the pilot/the driver in the climactic scene, pushing the boat/the train/the plane/the car to the brink in order to escape or save the day or both or something else. The laws of narrative demand that the machinery fails. The engine blows in a billowy flash and the gears claw each other's insides and the whole careening carcass comes to rest in a heap of failed intentions. Yet, as every script confirms, all is not lost. The denouement must still arrive, if by other means. Somehow, the effort continues by alternate energies, by reinvigorated will.

"Sister Ray" follows the script. But what's truly revelatory about the song as it appears on *White Light/White Heat* is that, despite ourselves—enlightened modern listeners though surely we are—we don't realize that we are watching *that* script. We don't know, or else we've forgotten, that the laws of narrative apply to this particular experience. The Velvet Underground disabuse us of our expectations. They suspend the suspension of disbelief. Here, in this specific universe—the one in which the Velvet Underground are building their ship inside the bottle inside the crate inside the hold of the ship submerged in the ocean in a diorama built inside a bottle in the hold of a ship—here in this specific universe that is "Sister Ray," we have no right to expect release, but only tension and tension and tension in this ever-expanding universe without end.

So, when, at three or four different moments, the band sounds as if that's it, that's all they've got, only to churn back up, to rise like a fallen monster/boxer/ drunkard back to their feet, we are truly surprised. Surprised that there is more noise, more friction, to be extracted from the information as it scrapes against the boundaries of the apparatus. "All the needles are on red." It's the opposite of "We're trying to get a light on him." There's no "him." There's only that which is happening. And the light is not external to it, but activated by it. Likewise, there's no "we." There's only that which is happening and of which we are a part. And "it" is never complete, never finished. As information and apparatus merge, as content and form conflate, subject and object fold together into an indiscernible entity, less spatial than temporal; an *it-that-is-happening*.

None other than Jean-François Lyotard, preeminent theorist of the postmodern, identifies this question of happeningness as a critical exception to modernist, formalist understandings of the aesthetic. For Lyotard, Kant's aesthetic category of "the beautiful" describes the effect sought by the modern arts. The alternate category of "the sublime" describes the experience of postmodern art. And the sublime is predicated not on form, but on dynamism and transformation. Lyotard argues that the sublime is the more potent and necessary of aesthetic categories. The sublime occurs when pain is transformed into pleasure, when cessation and death are forestalled, allowing life and time to revivify in the very time and place where death has announced its dominion. The beautiful takes the form of a statement: *it happened*, whereas the sublime can only be a question: *Is it happening?* (Lyotard, passim). The question mark defies resolution. So long as the question is open, the case cannot be closed.

It's no coincidence that so many theorists of the 1960s and 1970s offered formulations of this inconclusiveness. Roland Barthes writes variously of "the punctum," "the neutral," and "that which outplays the paradigm." Gilles Deleuze's entire project focuses on modes of experience that escape the constraints of conceptual and institutional systemization. Julia Kristeva defines the abject as the result of a breakdown of the stability of foundational categories such as subject and object. And Jacques Derrida insists on the apparent essentiality of the apparently inessential; on differences, on the trace, the supplement, or the parergon. He employs the word "hinge" ("brisure") to suggest a component that is neither door nor frame; a part that is incidental to the whole, and yet a piece without which the whole cannot function, indeed cannot remain whole. Derrida confirms the ongoingness, the happeningness, of the question mark. The hinge retains the indeterminacy of any whole, any apparatus, any thing (anything). It can't all be there because it is always revising itself in the inconclusiveness of the question, in the dynamic, temporal interactions of door and frame, subject and object, signifier and signified.

> The hinge marks the impossibility that a sign, the unity of a signifier and a signified, be produced within the plenitude of a present and an absolute presence. (Derrida, *Of Grammatology*, 69)

Of course, there are less highfalutin ways of saying all this. Graffiti in Paris implores, "Soyez réalistes, demandez l'impossible." ("Be realistic, demand the impossible.") From a stage in São Paulo, Caetano Veloso declares, "É Proibido Proibir." ("It is forbidden to forbid.") In New York, the Velvet Underground sing "I'm beginning to see the light." (Not the other way around.) "Sister Ray" is the Velvet Underground's greatest enunciation of the sublime. In fact, one is hard-pressed, upon scouring the recorded history of rock and roll since Muddy Waters's first electric recordings in 1948, to find a better example of rock and roll's happeningness, of its fugitivity. The song, as it appears on *White Light/White Heat*, all the needles on red, is the equal of Iggy Pop submerged and subsumed by the audience in Cincinnati. There's no getting a light on it. The seventeen-plus-minute duration makes it impossible to concisely define it. No tidy schematic of the song's form is available. No exhaustive discursive formulation is forthcoming. (The description you are reading presently can do no more than to conjure the beat-around-the-bush, but hardly the bush itself.)

No god's eye perspective is possible because "Sister Ray" rejects the possibility of being heard or seen or experienced from outside. Derrida again: "Il n'y a pas de hors-texte." ("There is no outside-the-text.") (158–9). The only perspectives available are already embroiled with and interpolated into the song itself, with its happeningness. If we want to know "Sister Ray" differently (we can't say more completely), we can't step outside of it. The only direction is in. We must intervene, zoom in, and perform invasive procedures. As luck would have it, such a procedure has already been performed on our behalf. On March 15, 1969, at a venue called the Boston Tea Party located at 53 Berkeley Street, the Velvet Underground's Boston-based home-away-from-home, an unknown punter concealed a microphone in the back of Lou Reed's amplifier. Perhaps this anonymous surgeon of the sublime was merely trying to hide the apparatus from detection. Or perhaps this was a knowing acknowledgment that we are all microphones and that the only possibility of gaining greater purchase on the Velvet Underground's deluge was to dive into it as into a pool, as Iggy into a crowd. In the dark, secreted away from the mandates of illumination, embedded in the what goes on, one can ask the only question that matters; the one that gets at the heart of the matter: *Is it happening?*

The recording made that night in Boston circulated for years as "The Legendary Guitar Amp Tape." We are inside Reed's amp, closer to its din than we are to the rest of the band, who have been relegated by the microphone's placement to a perennial elsewhere. At the start of the song "Heroin" John Cale's organ drones in stasis, denying all notions of before or after. But Mo Tucker's drums force their way in, the rhythm of time pulsing its way forward. Shadows of words are cast on our cave wall. The listener's ear is a fly on the song's closed eyelid. Most of the space is filled with Reed's mildly out-of-tune guitar as it arpeggiates across the verses of "Heroin" and chugs into its choruses. Eight minutes in, Reed shunts a new chord onto the track. "Sister Ray" spills across the cosmos, consuming time and space. The maelstrom of Reed's amplifier is now unrecognizable as either arpeggios or chords, it is distortion: the apparatus of vacuum tube and speaker cone aggrieved by the information of vibrating strings. The apparatus has been organized to disparage the information. What goes out bears no resemblance to what came in. What's more, in the context of "The Legendary Guitar Amp Tape," the listener is keenly aware that the distension of Reed's amp is but one apparatus-information source, artificially isolated from other apparatus and other information and from the feedback of all these sources as they call and respond to one another. A penumbra of tonality can be made out in the distance, like the light necessary to allow the emergence of the relief of a silhouette. But the relation of Reed's sounds to this ambient hum is no more definitive than the relation of a Zippo (or a hippo) to the cosmic background radiation. One follows from the other, but the precise nature of the complex chain of cause and effect evades facile grasping.

To borrow an observation that Lester Bangs made of the Stooges, the Velvet Underground "work deftly with musical ideas that may not be highly sophisticated

(God forbid) but are certainly advanced" (Bangs, 1987, 39). Approximately twelve minutes into the "Sister Ray" portion of this hard-cut medley, Reed's amplifier assumes the identity of a natural disaster. An erupting volcano, a mudslide, a tsunami—something going where it isn't supposed to go. It is hot and heavy and hungry. Things in its path are devoured. Thingness itself is swallowed whole by what is happening. What is happening? "The question can be modulated in any tone" (Lyotard 198). Whatever it is, it cannot be represented by a dot on or between one of five lines. Rather, it quivers in the oscillations of the hand, the string, the current, the speaker, the room, the bodies, the land, the minutes, the edges of each frame that might be used to quantify what it is that is happening; the thin-lipped membrane commanding compliance to one or another preexisting order.

"The Legendary Guitar Amp Tape" is but one legendary tape of the late 1960s and 1970s. The tape landscape includes the "Nixon Tapes," a trove of recordings made in Richard Nixon's offices, documenting the Watergate scandal and its cover-up. But also the "Basement Tapes," a set of 138 songs recorded by Bob Dylan and the Band in West Saugerties, New York, in 1967. These recordings were long considered the holy grail of Dylan's oeuvre, a set of unguarded performances, not intended for release. The "Basement Tapes" are generally understood as a document of Dylan and his fellow travelers (Rick Danko, Levon Helm, Garth Hudson, Richard Manuel, and Robbie Robertson) questing for the lost essence of American folk music. The recordings trickled out across the subsequent decades until their official, complete release in 2014. There is also the video tape, ripped from a television camera in Irvine, California, and doused with acetone by Chris Burden. Like the Nixon Tapes and "the Basement Tapes," this tape housed evidence. During the preceding hour of February 9, 1972, as a guest on the cable program "All About Art," Burden had put a knife to the throat of host Phyllis Lutjeans and demanded that the taping of the show be broadcast live. The station complied as Burden and Lutjeans resumed their conversation. At the hour's end, Burden again threatened Lutjeans, insisting that the station hand over the tape of the show for subsequent destruction. Burden had arrived with his own cameraman in tow. He had documented the hijacking and the destruction of the station's documentation of the event. In "TV Hijack" as the encounter is now known, the vectors of tape documentation and terrorist hijackings meet in the most mundane of modern settings: the cable TV station (Figure 7.2).

What the Nixon Tapes, "the Basement Tapes," and Burden's personal tape of "TV Hijack" have in common is a shared status as magnetic keepers of secrets.

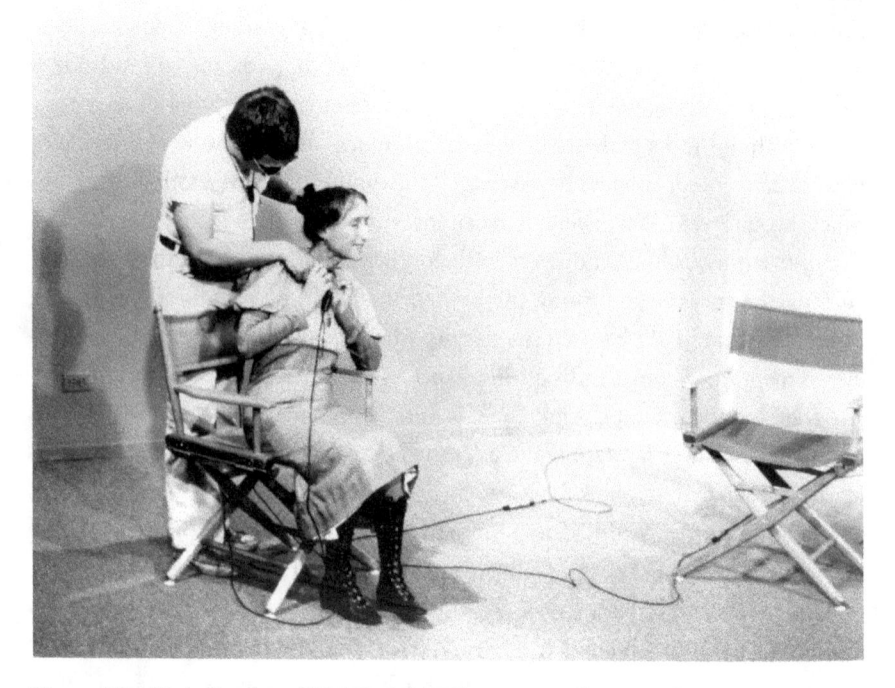

**Figure 7.2** Chris Burden, *TV Hijack* (1972). © 2022 Chris Burden/Licensed by the Chris Burden Estate and Artists Rights Society (ARS), New York.

They are archives not intended for public consumption, each providing evidence of a kind of American unconscious. Surely one can see these tapes as examples of getting a light on previously unilluminated aspects of culture and history. But what they actually reveal is a lack of coherence and clarity. They throw the listener into the unmitigated complexity of psychology, power, and history; the concatenation and confusion that is culture. "TV Hijack" reorganizes the relation of the camera and the microphone to the events they document. The recorder too and the recording are implicated in the violence of the day. Were it not for the presence of the camera and the microphone, the hijack would have never happened. In the absence of the media, terror would be meaningless. "The Basement Tapes" wade into the contradictions of American folklore, mysticism, murder ballads; a pre-modern arcanum of phantasmagoria and ever-lurking death. History floats up through these recordings like a body from the bed of the lake; the story starting at the end. At the core of the Nixon Tapes is the dark heart of paranoiac politics. That heart beats most famously and consequentially during a portion of the tapes dubbed the "buzz section" by The Advisory Panel on the

White House Tapes, which conducted forensic investigations of the tapes. These eighteen and a half minutes were apparently erased to conceal incriminating material. But their erasure proves to be more incriminating than anything that might have been erased. As with Kozlov's "Information Drift," the absences of the buzz section speak. The friction of information against apparatus: magnetic particles arranged to reproduce the conversation had by Nixon and his chief of staff, H. R. Haldeman. Then more friction: the erase-head scrambling the arrangement of those same particles, divorcing apparatus from information. The Advisory Panel determined that the buzz section was the product of a series of between five and nine actions that required manual operation of the tape recorder (Advisory Panel, 4). With a phrase that swings both in and out, functioning as a well-oiled hinge between techne and power, the panel concludes that the buzz is the result of a "dirty power source" in the office of Nixon's secretary, Rose Mary Woods. The evident stasis and the apparent silence of the buzz section pose the inevitable question: Is it happening? History won't take no for an answer.

# 8

# The Wee Hours of Etc.

New Year's Day, 1974. *The New York Times* publishes a harbinger, a prayer, a plea, for the year by the father of so-called "gonzo" journalism, Hunter S. Thompson. The article delights in the crisis of Richard Nixon's presidency like an afficionado savoring a Pinot Noir: aerating it in the mouth, coaxing the tannins, the undertones of brambles and soil, the aftertaste of wet fur—all to be taken account of, to be recorded for posterity; for safekeeping. The illustration accompanying Thompson's essay depicts an outstretched arm, handcuffed at the wrist. The hand forms a tight fist clutching strands of magnetic tape. The tape and the handcuff chain dangle precipitously, both anchored to the plastic reel suspended by the twinned trappings of America, 1974 (Figure 8.1).

The whole world was watching: on television screens, on movie screens, across white picket fences into bedrooms illuminated by the glare of unforgivable trespasses. "The whole world is watching"—the chant reverberated as the noise-cancelling inverse of the coordinated clomp of jackboots on the streets of downtown Chicago, August 1968. Thompson lamented,

> Richard Nixon is living in the White House today because of what happened that night in Chicago. Hubert Humphrey lost that election by a handful of votes—mine among them—and if I had to do it again I would still vote for Dick Gregory. (Thompson 1978, 19)

The vacuum that Joan Didion had diagnosed—the chasm at the heart of the American experiment—could never be filled. It was absence itself that defined the project. The emptiness of the North American continent, an absence that could only be imagined in tandem with the eradication of the people who occupied the land. The vacancy of the African body, generously counted as three-fifths of a European body, leaving two-fifths of it uninhabited in the European imagination and in the Law. The lack anchoring the founding mythology of freedom—never

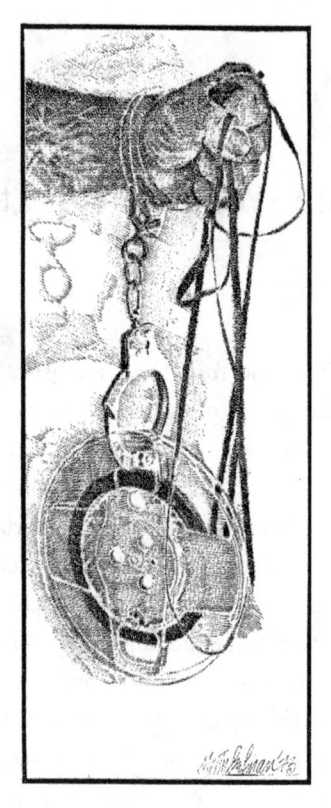

**Figure 8.1** Illustration accompanying Hunter S. Thompson's "Fear and Loathing in the Bunker," *The New York Times*, January 1, 1974.

the presence of something, always the evasion of that something: the rule, the shackle, the command.

Into this vacuum strode Richard Milhous Nixon, nobody's first choice. In 1945, he was approached by the California Republican Party to run for the twelfth congressional district only after their search had failed to attract higher profile candidates. In 1956, when Dwight Eisenhower ran for reelection, he tried to replace Nixon, the incumbent vice president, as his running mate. In 1960, Nixon lost the presidential election to John F. Kennedy. He entered the 1962 race for governor of California and lost, announcing, "You won't have Nixon to kick around anymore" (Aitken 304–5). And yet . . . The chaos of 1968 had struck deep in the American psyche. For many, the knot that held everything together had come untied. With it the sanctity of their warrantied White security frayed to the point of snapping. For others, the chord rang out in a major key, dancing through the wah-wah undulations of a new dawn. The tide was turning because righteousness had finally caught up with history, overtaking the cadaverous impulses of man against man, stone against bone, skin against skin.

Thompson had covered the 1972 presidential campaign for *Rolling Stone.* His admonitions had been taken as journalistic mountains made of political molehills. But as 1973 collided with 1974, the nation had begun to realize, "the truth was turning out to be even worse than my most 'paranoid ravings' during that painful 1972 election" (Thompson 1978, 19). Thompson realized that Nixon wasn't just a bad apple. He was the Johnny Appleseed of bad apples, sowing the seeds of discontent from California to the Gulf Stream waters. Driven by an unholy mixture of lustful ambition, insecurity, bigotry, ignoble ideology, and, yes, deep, disturbing paranoia, Nixon had painted a picture of America that blotted out the bands of the fluorescent rainbow in favor of a darkness that sank into the skin, penetrated the lungs and heart. His politics and his political prospects depended on that darkness. So long as fear stoked the citizenry, his dour disposition had legs. As Thompson understood him, Nixon represented, "that dark, venal, and incurably violent side of the American character" (Thompson, quoted in BBC).

With the arrival of 1974, Thompson—along with the rest of the country—was beginning to see that something like justice might stubbornly prevail. The power had gone to Nixon's head. He had started to believe that he could bend events and ideas to his will. But, like the sweat that beaded on his forehead during his televised debate with Kennedy in 1960, Nixon's administration began to deliquesce and ooze. Thompson grasped that Nixon had brought the whole damn mess upon himself.

> Nixon . . . was blessed with a mixture of arrogance and stupidity that caused him to blow the boilers almost immediately after taking command. By bringing in hundreds of thugs, fixers and fascists to run the Government, he was able to crank almost every problem he touched into a mindbending crisis. (Thompson 1978, 19)

Beyond being the printed press's #1 Nixon-basher, Thompson is widely considered to be the father of so-called "gonzo" journalism. Born, by most accounts, with the essay "The Kentucky Derby Is Decadent and Depraved," published in 1970, gonzo journalism eschews the objectivity and decorum of traditional journalistic codes, in favor of immersing oneself in the action and relating subjective impressions in the native argot of the given milieu. Thompson's Derby piece details a weekend of alcoholic havoc visited by and upon Thompson and his illustrator-sidekick, Ralph Steadman, at the annual run for the roses in Louisville, Kentucky. The goings-on are recounted in the first person, complete with scams perpetrated on unsuspecting punters and a frantic series of escapades to secure press credentials that would grant access, not to the rarified air of the press box or the track, but to the sanctified setting of the open bar. Thompson's purple (black and blue) prose is peppered with memorable characters and characterizations including "the whiskey gentry," "Chemical Billy," "mayblossom senility," and the name of that year's Derby champion, the impossibly apt, "Dust Commander" (Thompson 1970).

"The Kentucky Derby Is Decadent and Depraved" appeared in one of only eight issues of *Scanlan's Monthly*, published between March 1970 and January 1971. *Scanlan's* had been founded by Warren Hinckle, who had previously written for the left-wing magazine, *Ramparts*, and Sidney E. Zion, a lawyer and writer who is perhaps best remembered for outing Daniel Ellsberg as the leaker of the Pentagon Papers. In an editorial in the first issue of *Scanlan's*, Hinckle and Zion outline the motives of the new publication:

> [The] vision of a free, crusading, investigative, hell-raising, totally candid press has been largely consigned to the apologias of the smug publishers who own the working journalists and to the barroom daydreams of newsmen.
>
> The trusts, the banks, and the government teamed up to kill off the muckrakers. Since those murders, we have witnessed the greedy, shortsighted and eventually cancerous reliance of publishers on the financial backing of Madison Avenue. (Hinkle and Zion)

There appears, in the fourth issue of *Scanlan's*, a photo of Nixon lunching with construction union leaders. A large-font, all-caps caption reads, "NIXON AND THE BUMS." An accompanying editorial identifies the figures in the photo and provides each of their criminal records. Unsurprisingly, *Scanlan's Monthly* attracted the attention of the Nixon White House and, equally unsurprisingly, was the subject of an FBI investigation.

*Scanlan's Monthly*—published under the credo "Trust Your Mother, But Cut the Cards"—chronicled the evacuation of American optimism. Nixon was but the straw that broke the camel's back as he forced it through the eye of the needle. The famous 1960s aphorism, "Don't trust anyone over thirty" wasn't really about being over or under thirty. It was about a grappling, desperate quest for someone or something worthy of trust. The phrase could have just as easily been "Don't trust the police" or "Don't trust men" or "Don't trust Republicans" or "Don't trust Democrats" or "Don't trust White people" or "Don't trust the nightly news." The phrase has been almost universally received as a marker of the burgeoning, rapidly widening generation gap. But it is better understood as a statement about loss of trust—in institutions, in traditions, in conventional wisdom, and power, and plain old decency-for-decency's-sake.

Hunter S. Thompson's writing bears witness to this despair. Not only does it offer an account of the crisis of faith, it performs it. Thompson's writing itself conveys a distrust of old ways and old values. Objectivity is a ruse meant to camouflage the White, male, Protestant, moneyed biases of anything presented as "neutral." Justice and honesty are decoys; a magician's misdirection: one hand waving in the air, the other picking every pocket in the room, setting the clocks back, closing the blinds, forging the signature on the deed to the ranch. "Sell the house. Sell the car. Sell the kids," writes Kurtz to his wife in *Apocalypse Now*, a film not so much about the Vietnam War as about the torment of American entitlement during it.[1]

Against this backdrop, it is only a little less surprising that a cadre of cognoscenti Americans of the counterculture would turn for insight to an eighteenth-century Puritan theologian. Jonathan Edwards was born near Windsor, Connecticut, in 1703. At the age of eleven, he published a book on spiders. Just shy of his thirteenth birthday, he enrolled at Yale University. A residential college at Yale bears his name to this day, despite the fact that Edwards was a slave-owner and published a tract that "defended the traditional definition of slaves as those who were debtors, children of slaves, and war captives; for him, the trade in slaves born in North America remained legitimate," even as he maintained that the African slave trade was "a far more cruel slavery" (Minkema 36).

As we learned in the early pages of the present volume, Michael Fried extracted from Edwards's private writings an epigraph for his totemic 1968 essay "Art and Objecthood." Via Edwards, Fried established the stakes of modern art as it fended off the encroachments of the postmodernism ushered in by minimalism. Against the tawdry compromises of everyday objects, Fried invoked Keatsian pieties of truth as beauty and beauty as truth. In the brushstrokes or splatters of a great modernist, one could infer—nay, one could actually *see*—creation itself. One could be present at the moment of creation. As Fried extolled, "Presentness is grace." To be present at a—or, indeed, *the*—moment of creation was to see truth,

---

[1]   See: Linh Dinh, "Apocalypse Lies," *The Guardian*, November 1, 2001. https://www.theguardian.com /film/2001/nov/02/artsfeatures.londonfilmfestival2001

indisputable in its all-at-onceness. Such truth, for a true believer like Edwards, was beauty itself. Such beauty, for a true aesthete like Fried, was the only thing worthy of the name "truth." We must recognize that Fried too was desperate for bulwarks against the vacuum sucking at the soul of postwar culture. But rather than turning toward the happeningness exemplified, if not quite monopolized, by rock and roll, Fried found beauty and truth in the formalist fixity of the modernist canvas.

For Greil Marcus, the "old, weird America" is born with the visions—both transcendent and earthbound—of Jonathan Edwards. Marcus comes to understand the American psyche as a battlefield upon which the release of holy rapture locks in vengeful combat with the basest material wants. Neither side can wholly claim the high ground. The oil man or the automobile magnate is just as beatified as the preacher or the mystic. And each walks the earth possessed of and by a good bit of the other. As far back as 1974, in the "Author's Note" to his first book, *Mystery Train: Images of America in Rock n Roll Music*, Marcus wrote,

> I am no more capable of mulling over Elvis without thinking about Herman Melville than I am of reading Jonathan Edwards . . . without putting on Robert Johnson's records as background music. (Marcus 2011, xiii)

This incapacity was still with Marcus when he wrote *The Old, Weird America*. The book insists that the compact contradiction of heaven on earth, of the divine in the degraded, was the will-o'-the-wisp that Bob Dylan and The Band stalked and hunted at the house known as Big Pink. Far from being matter-of-fact odes to the palpable and the practical, Marcus argues that sense breaks mysteriously down in so many of the old songs: the spark of the divine in "Froggy Went A-Courtin." And in this breakdown, the mystical emerges. Only something like faith or magic allows these songs to cohere and, in fact, to endure across generations, performers, interpretations, and contexts. The folk revival through which Dylan passed as his own kind of phantom was haunted by this magic. And when Dylan crossed over into rock and roll, he smuggled a stash of it through customs.

In his introduction to the 2012 reissue of Gilbert Seldes's 1928 *The Stammering Century*, Marcus describes Jonathan Edwards "as a 'merciless logician,' as subtle a prose stylist as America has ever produced, and a mystic capable of combining both logic and style into an apprehension of nature indistinguishable from sensual ecstasy" (Marcus 2012). Seldes makes a case for the sublime nature of the American imagination, if not always of the actual American experience:

it must be said, he [Edwards] knew the essence of rapture. It is rapture without hysteria, without sham, and it never left him. When he saw Nature he recovered the emotion, because he knew that the world was the world of God. . . . The golden edges of an evening cloud, the sun in his strength, the apparition of comets, the ragged rock, all exalted him.

He lowered himself infinitely, and the infinity of his lowness met, in the infinite, the Infinity of God; met, and became one with it. The two poles of man's life, as Edwards knew them, were to be lower than the dust before God, and to know God: the ecstasy of abasement and the ecstasy of union. (Seldes, quoted in Marcus 2012)

The ecstasy of dust and divinity; the high in the low, the exalted in the exhumed: for listeners like Marcus, this idea lands with the heaviest conviction in their experience of rock and roll.

Before the conceptual artist Dan Graham was a conceptual artist, he was a rock critic. When he moved to New York in 1964, he had already published pieces about British invasion bands like the Beatles and the Kinks (especially the Kinks—Graham really liked the Kinks.) Without prospects or much knowledge of contemporary art, Graham founded the John Daniels Gallery and soon found himself showing the work of nascent conceptualists and minimalists like Sol LeWitt, Dan Flavin, and Robert Smithson. As his own art career ascended, he remained invested in rock and roll, avidly attaching himself to the Post-Punk and No Wave scenes in New York, continuing to publish criticism and making two videos about rock and roll: *Minor Threat* (1983), a rough concert film of the pioneering D.C. straightedge band, and the more difficult to categorize, *Rock My Religion* (1983–4), equal parts conspiracy theory, history lesson, and gonzo visual essay. *Rock My Religion* is a bit like watching a projection of Greil Marcus's dreams as edited by William S. Burroughs (Graham 1983–1984). In a 2004 interview, Graham discusses his initial attraction not just to art and music, but equally to criticism.

My first interest was literary criticism, which was superseded by rock critics like Lester Bangs, Greil Marcus, Sandy Perlman, and Patty [*sic*] Smith. I was very interested in the tradition of rock criticism, and also I was influenced in my art by structures I found in rock music. (Graham 2004, 113)

*Rock My Religion* is an attempt to meet rock and roll on its own terms. Pretense of academic objectivity dissolves before it begins. All anthropology is faux. The first thing we hear is nothing, just the whiteish noise of the audio head insisting on doing its job in the absence of intentional signal. Meanwhile, a grimacing

Henry Rollins shirtlessly bobs and davens like a rabbinical toddler mustering up a tantrum. Twelve seconds in, the audio arrives: a distortion pedal—more than a guitar—decaying, oscillating, and segueing into feedback. The screen goes black replacing soundless image with imageless sound. A terminal chord crashes onto the rocks. And the next two minutes, as described by Kodwo Eshun, establish the mad slice 'n dice methodology that governs *Rock My Religion* for the entirety of its fifty-five minutes and twenty-seven seconds:

> A work song ousts Greg Ginn's distorted guitar and, after a few more seconds, a white text, scrolling upwards, fills the black with the doctrines of Puritanism. A voice-over introduces Ann Lee, the founder of the Shakers, while a second sound channel is abruptly added; it is Sonic Youth's song "Shakin' Hell" (1983), which plays on while archival images interconnect the Shakers with illustrations of the making of the English working class. These shots are in turn interrupted by additional footage of the Black Flag gig and a brief sequence of Joe Strummer performing on stage taken from Rude Boy (1980), a part-fiction, part-documentary film following a Clash fan who becomes a roadie for the band. *Rock My Religion*'s title appears three times in this opening sequence, in yellow capitalised font, firstly for ten seconds at 0:58; then again after an image of an etching of Shakers performing the Ring Dance; and finally for less than a second, just before Black Flag reappears, saturated by a crimson light. The author's name, Dan Graham, can also be seen then in red capitalised font, for one second at 2:11, looking as if it were due to a minor malfunction or seizure of the equipment. (Eshun 1)

Graham's aim is not "to get a light on it," but to rollick in the tumult of the moshpit, the revival tent, the tides of change. Image and sound are often out of synch or mismatched altogether—audio from one source pasted onto video from another. Text imposes itself on everything while voiceovers confuse and cancel the text, the image, and the more-or-less diegetic sound. You can't get a light on rapture, because rapture *is* light. It is heat. It is contact with time, with space. The quarry that Graham pursues cannot be caged. It is less a discrete creature, more a swarm, sublime in its resistance to capture. Thus, alongside Rimbaud and the Sioux ghost dance, we again encounter Jonathan Edwards. At 11:28, against a black screen, we read: "THE PURITANS" in all caps, white, sans-serif font. Seventeen seconds later, the song "A Figure Walks," from *Dragnet* (1979), the second album by Manchester's The Fall stumbles to life. As Mark E. Smith sings "A figure walks behind you / A shadow walks behind you," the screen goes orange and the same all-caps font delivers a passage from Edwards's sermon, "Sinners in the Hands of an Angry God," delivered July 8, 1741 at Enfield, Connecticut.

> Men are held . . . over the pit of hell; they have deserved the fiery pit and are already sentenced to it . . . held captive by Satan . . . [They are] under the power . . . of their lusts, and though they have many struggles of conscience about their sins, yet never wholly escape them.

As its title suggests, *Rock My Religion* positions rock and roll as the latter-day inheritor of ecstatic practices, both indigenous and imported to the American continent. One might describe these practices as religious, but as understood by Dan Graham (and by Greil Marcus and Michael Fried before him) they are equally cultural: expressions of a do-or-die yearning that drives subsequent phases of the American experiment to its lowest lows and its highest highs.

Not only does Graham situate *Rock My Religion* in the flux of the cultural phenomena that function as de facto content in his work, he also allows it to buffet, and be buffeted by, the debates of the early 1980s. As the dust settled on the cultural foment of the late 1960s and 1970s, Ronald Reagan was elected president and the so-called "Culture Wars" heated up. James Dobson founded Focus on the Family in 1977 and Jerry Falwell the Moral Majority in 1979, each preaching a gospel of family values. The first news stories on AIDS appeared in 1981, with the disease acquiring its name in 1982. The Parents Music Resource Center (PMRC) was founded by Tipper Gore, wife of Senator Al Gore, and Susan Baker, wife of treasury secretary, James Baker, in 1985. In 1987, the University of Chicago's Allan Bloom published *The Closing of the American Mind,* perhaps the signal announcement of the rift. The book expands on ideas that Bloom had first road-tested in 1982 in an essay, "Our Listless Universities," in the *National Review,*

> I begin with my conclusion: students in our best universities do not believe in anything, and those universities are doing nothing about it, nor can they. An easygoing American kind of nihilism has descended upon us, a nihilism without terror of the abyss. (Bloom)

Ostensibly, Bloom blames higher education for the woes. But reading the essay, you would be forgiven for concluding that Bloom is actually pointing his finger at students. He accuses the young of "contentless certainty," despite being plagued by "gnawing doubt." Ultimately, he concludes, America's youth have bottomed out in a "true philistinism, a withering of taste and a conformity to what is prevalent in the present. It means the young have no heroes, no objects of aspiration" (Bloom).

*Rock My Religion* opposes this dismal Bloomian view. Graham sees doubt as the fertile ground of questioning and imagination. The Shakers, the Puritans, and Elvis Presley could all be understood shallowly as creatures of contentless certainty. More accurately, they were beings of doubt who acted on and against that doubt, inventing rhythms and reasons to hang their bonnets on. Bloom calls the students of the 1980s "the audio generation," asserting that

> Rock music caused a great evolution in the relations between parents and children. Its success was the result of an amazing cooperation among lust, art, and commercial shrewdness. (Bloom)

It's possible to imagine either Bloom or Graham penning those sentences. But what follows is all Bloom:

> The children have as their heroes banal, drug- and sex-ridden guttersnipes who foment rebellion not only against parents but against all noble sentiments. This is the emotional nourishment they ingest in these precious years. It is the real junk food. (Bloom)

Graham's reception of rock is considerably more sanguine:

> While individual rock heroes (singers) are unrepentant sinners, the rock group is more like a self-sufficient commune. (Graham 1994, 101)

And a little later, Graham expands upon his allegorical thesis:

> The rock club and rock concert performances are like a church, a sanctuary against the adult world. Mechanized, electric instruments unleash anarchic energies for the mass. The rock star stands in a sacrificial position against the regime of work; his sacrifice is his body and life. By living life and performing at the edge, he transcends the values of everyday work. But this transcendence is achieved by sacrificing his ability to become an adult. (Graham 1994, 106)

Fried appeals to Jonathan Edwards to establish what is at stake as the new art of the 1960s threatens to overrun the formal convictions of his beloved modern art. In the "single infinitely brief instant," awestruck before the canvas, the beholder is visited by something that we cannot call an experience. It is more accurately— in Fried's view—a state of consciousness, or indeed of being. It is to such presentness, such grace, that he appeals. And it is Edwards to whom he turns for parallels in the eighteenth-century euphoria of a Christian mindset to which we might reapply Bloom's epithet, "contentless certainty." Marcus and Graham also seek—and find—an ecstatic disposition, but not in the revelatory stasis of Fried's presentness. Their ecstasy might be compared to Kant's conception of the sublime: a feeling of being overwhelmed by the magnitude of a thing or an experience.[2] Marcus and Graham also turn to Edwards for a precedent and for cover. But in place of presentness, their vehicle of transcendence is happeningness, of something going down, of being in the midst of it like a surfer upended and enveloped by the wave. As Graham sees it, art has surrendered its ability—even its desire—to hurl itself upon the surf. In the process, it has given up on whole modes of experience and emotion. Pop art initiated new ways of responding to the commodified world, but rock and roll—as embodied, in Graham's telling, by Patti Smith—reclaims the sacred, ecstatic ground of artistic experience. Toward the end of *Rock My Religion*, the same all-caps font, this time in yellow on black:

IN THE 70S THE RELIGION OF THE 50S TEENAGER AND THE 60S "COUNTERCULTURE" IS ADOPTED BY POP ARTISTS WHO PROPOSE THE END OF THE RELIGION OF "ART FOR ART'S SAKE." PATTI SMITH TOOK THIS ONE STEP FURTHER: SHE SAW ROCK AS AN ART FORM WHICH WOULD COME TO REPLACE POETRY, PAINTING, AND SCULPTURE. IF ART IS ONLY A BUSINESS, AS WARHOL SUGGESTS, THEN MUSIC EXPRESSES A MORE COMMUNAL, TRANSCENDENTAL EMOTION WHICH ART NOW DENIES. (*Rock My Religion*, 52:11)

Dan Graham doesn't set out to make a video *about* rock and roll, but a video that *is* rock and roll. It ain't worth a damn if it doesn't *épater la bourgeoisie*. As every good provocateur knows, a shock to the system is the only thing the system understands. This creates a certain cognitive dissonance for those trained by art history to map new work onto the models of the past. Hal Foster has nagging questions:

Graham cites the Russian formalist Viktor Shklovsky on estrangement. But, for Shklovsky, to estrange convention was to push art ahead—it proceeds "by knight's moves," in his famous phrase. . . . For all his opening to demotic subjects and public settings, then, a question of legibility arises with Graham. How objective is his matrix of allusions? Does its logic exist only in his own head? He

[2] See Kant (2000): "Just because there is in our imagination a striving to advance to the infinite, while in our reason there lies a claim to absolute totality, as to a real idea, the very inadequacy of our faculty for estimating the magnitude of the things in the sensible world awakens the feeling of a supersensible faculty in us" (§25, 250).

refers to his art as "a passionate hobby," and clearly his work is made out of such enthusiasms too. But does the DIY history of one artist extend to others, or are his "hybrids," however, productive for Graham, sterile for others? (Foster 226)

Benjamin Buchloh, too, is troubled:

What the work gains in universality and potential audience access by inserting itself into the mass-cultural totality of floating representations, it loses in material specificity and contextual concreteness, the sources from which avant-garde high culture in modernism had traditionally drawn its capacity of resistance. (Buchloh 220)

Unfortunately for Foster, Buchloh, and their discipline, *Rock My Religion* won't tuck neatly inside the art historical box. There's just too much stuff to close the lid tightly. Graham isn't riffing on Monet or Motherwell or even Robert Morris. He is windmilling his own axe. "I was influenced in my art by structures I found in rock music" (Graham 2004, 113). *Rock My Religion* represents a node in a vast and chaotic network of histories, psychologies, cultural forms, religious fervor, gender politics, lunacies both local and global. What carries *Rock My Religion* is not exposition, but enthusiasm. To engage it as an academic exercise is to misunderstand the work it is doing. Graham's not interested in a calculated exegesis. He wants to fuck shit up.

I've written about Dan Graham's *Rock My Religion* before. Actually, first I extolled about it, offering my "Rock and Roll Lecture Number One" as the opening act at a rock club in Philadelphia. Then I wrote it down and put it in a book.[3] Here's what I wrote:

What did Dan Graham have in mind when he made *Rock My Religion*? He says rock is the great inheritance of American youth. The Shakers thrashed wildly in the throes of religious euphoria. They shook like epileptics. And why not? They weren't built to last, so why save it? The Shakers believed in equality of the sexes. They were founded by a woman, Ann Lee, and they could see Patti Smith coming. Men and women, they thought, should be equal but separate. Utterly separate. No sex. That's what you call an exit plan. One generation, maybe two, if you count the kids the converts brought along for the lonely ride. And then: peace out. Dan Graham says that kind of ecstasy, that kind of expenditure, is what rock and roll is all about. It's not a new impulse. It's been an American urge since the beginning. But with the 1950s and along with the invention of the teenager, America invents teenage angst, followed by teenage kicks. James Dean plays chicken at the cliff's edge and the other kid plays the Shaker. Peace out. Dan Graham trains his camera on the other kid, Patti Smith, the Ann Lee of rock.

Smith's first album, *Horses*, came out in 1975 and it changed Lester Bangs's life. He said so, "*Horses* changed my life, but I've recognized that there was something almost supernatural about the powers it tapped, that no artist or audience can expect that kind of baptism in the firmamental flames every time" (Bangs 1978). So, it wasn't just Graham who warmed his soul by the consecrated heat of Patti Smith. Both he and Bangs found in her sound, in her words, in her person, and her performance, an Edwardsian vibration; a testament to something happening. Whatever it is—this something—it outplays the paradigms of art history. It outwits, at every turn, Fried and Foster and Buchloh: leaves them panting for breath, denied of purchase, stunned, and stunted in the roil of zeal and circumstance.

Smith is no ingénue. She knows what she's after, and on *Horses*, she knows how to get it. Later recordings lose the scent (that's what Bangs is referring to when he says we can't expect the flames every time). In performance, Smith and her group sought to escape the bonds of the simple two- and three-cord structures of their songs. Leaning hard on the rudiments of musical architecture—beats one, two, three, and four—the Patti Smith Group pounded ore into metal and metal into ploughshares. The goal, always, in their early years, was to disrupt the ticking of time, to release energy from inert musical matter. As Smith told Caroline Coon, "Art can exist only in the moment, the anarchical moment. The moment is like an atom which we split. Sometimes" (Coon). Sometimes.

Consider the Patti Smith Group's appearance on *Saturday Night Live* on April 17, 1976. I want to call the performance riveting, not in the keeps-your-attention sense of the word—although it certainly does that too—but meaning that the band drives anchors through the plates of the song, affixing them to the sluice of time as it passes through the broadcast. The seconds slow and soon come to a stop, quivering against their commitments. To witness the five-plus minutes unfold is to have the extremities of your experience thrust through by rivets, affixed to the struggle of time against itself. Smith raves across the phrase "make her mine, make her mine, make her mine, make her mine, make her mine, make her mine"—six times in all—followed by spelling out the name of the song and the object of its affections, "G-L-O-R-I-A" (Smith, Patti 1976).

She gets an all too brief respite while guitarists Lenny Kaye and Ivan Král bellow the chorus, the letters put back together: "Gloria." Smith inhales deeply, her first full breath in four minutes. Her shoulders rise. She exhales. Remember: we are cameras. We focus and zoom in on this moment. The image landing on our lenses insists that the manic rush of syllables, the all-too-much-too-fast, is not about those syllables and the words that they cobble together. The point is not to convey the desperation of making her mine, not about the six discrete letters of her name, but about the expenditure that they require and, even more, about the breath, the recuperation, to follow. The whole galloping din, it turns out, is not an end but a means. The end, we are obliged to conclude, is that moment of response: the raised shoulders and the essential exhale. The song is a vehicle of release, outrunning time, and the body itself, which grasps at the air to supplement its inadequate materiality. The performance—the process— outplays the paradigm of disciplines and dogma in a mad dash for deliverance. Deliverance means simply asking, breathlessly, "is it happening?"

Jonathan Edwards comes up again and again—in Fried, in Marcus, in Graham—because what all of them are after, what the moment was after, is a kind of enlightenment that is not the enlightenment of the spotlight, the microscope, the television camera. The capital-E Enlightenment had it wrong. In essence, this is what is dawning on this age of Aquarius: that precision and form can only get you so far. In France, structuralism, which had ruled the academic roost for decades, was subjected to new critiques levied by a generation of young scholars. In the 1940s and 1950s, structuralism had proven enormously productive as a method for studying complex phenomena (language, societies, the human psyche, the economy) by breaking them down into their elementary particles and then reconstructing them with a new schematic understanding of their mechanics. But in the late 1960s and into the 1970s, a set of "poststructuralist" approaches dug into the aspects of culture that could not be isolated in elementary particles: nebulous qualities like meaning, feeling, sensation, and effect. Jean-François Lyotard's question, "is it happening?" is one such approach, emblematic of not just poststructuralism but of an unease felt throughout the Global North. Answering such a question can easily—probably too easily—slide into the realm of theology. What the poststructuralists are after is an enlightenment not beholden to mysticism, nor to an accountant's tally of modern life, but an enlightenment available exclusively in experience as a time-based, un-atomizable, phenomenon. Such experience does not emerge ex nihilo—literally, "out of nothing." It does not exist in the vacuum of subjectivity nor of the zeitgeist. Such experience is not a discrete unit of anything. Rather it is a node in a complex network of stimuli: history, social relations, class positions, gender, race, contextual meaning, and so on. The answer to "is it happening?" is neither objective nor subjective, but cultural and contextual.

What marks the period of 1965–1985—most notably, although not exclusively in America—is a search for meaning that is unaccountable to religion, hard science, or taxonomic accounting. When Dylan sings, "your sons and your daughters are beyond your command," the word "command" doesn't mean parental authority. It means the command of modern life: of capitalist propriety, of cultural conformity, of patriotic acquiescence. "Command" is command and control: the rationale that informs and enforces the model of the traditional family; of unquestioned loyalty to country and kin; of obedience to arbitrary social conventions; of the limitations of a narrow number of narrow paths through choices of everything from job, home, and partner, to toothpaste, pants, and weekend recreation. The organization of modern life neglects crucial things like the implicit agreement that we'll look out for one another, access to personal and political agency, the time and space to pursue curiosities, frivolities, and enthusiasms—y'know: life, liberty, and the pursuit of happiness. So sons and daughters struck out to find the lost beauty and truth of being alive.

It was no picnic. The Summer of Love was also the summer of Detroit's Great Rebellion. Woodstock was followed by Altamont. Flower power was countered by the National Guard. Efforts to right the wrongs of America's racist past ran headlong into its racist present, embodied by retrograde cretins like Orval Faubus in Arkansas, George Wallace in Alabama, and the 101 of 128 Southern congressmen who signed "The Southern Manifesto," denouncing *Brown v. Board of Education*. As Hunter S. Thompson suggested, the riots of the "Long Hot Summer" of 1967 and the violence at the '68 Democratic National Convention in Chicago played no small part in delivering Richard Nixon to the White House. Thompson's "gonzo" journalism was yet another effort to snare amorphous honesty from the clutches of manipulation and control. "Absolute truth is a very rare and dangerous commodity in the context of professional journalism," he wrote (Thompson 1973, 71). Thompson himself had first used the word "gonzo" in 1971 in *Fear and Loathing in Las Vegas*. How the word gonzo came to describe his subjective, digressive, first-person style is the subject of some dispute. One of the legends traces the term to the song "Gonzo," by New Orleans pianist, James Booker. The organ- and flute-led instrumental was an unlikely hit in 1960. About the song, Booker said,

> It was called that after Edward Frank and myself had seen a movie together called *"The Pusher."* The drug pusher in the film's name was "Gonzo." (Broven 172)

Thompson's influence was taken up by countless imitators. Most of whom lacked Thompson's verve and crackle. But Lester Bangs managed to import a Thompsonesque roguery into the nascent practice of rock criticism. Like Thompson, Bangs was a hunter on the trail of truth. Unlike Thompson, though, Bangs believed himself to have identified truth's natural habitat—a tiny corner of the known universe where the disciplinary hands of capitalism and middle-class politesse and Richard M. Nixon had not yet reached: rock and roll. Thus, unlike Thompson, Bangs's writing stalked liberation and talked of revelation. In rock and roll, Bangs found euphoric moments of happeningness, subject neither to the external validation of authority nor to the verification of double-entry bookkeeping. Bangs felt life in the 1970s as a morality play, a battle between good and evil, between venal lies and ecstatic truth. As Maria Bustillos wrote in *The New Yorker*, Bangs's unhappy childhood merged with the unhappy adult world. He rejected both the cynicism of the establishment and the blandishments of mainstream culture.

> The false Donna Reed visions of a happy, healthy, snow-white America of the postwar years, the disillusionment of the Vietnam war, and Nixon's downfall; everywhere, the rebellion that had begun to precipitate in the Summer of Love now saturated the air and fermented. Bangs developed a pure hatred of the lies and whitewashings of religion and government, his mutiny balanced against a bone-deep love of the truth—no matter how messy or unpretty it might turn out to be—which he equated with the refuge he'd found in literature and music. In fact, the messier, the more "real" art could be, the better. (Bustillos)

The calculations required to assess beauty and truth are not the calculations of the record company accounting department. They are beatific, revelatory, Edwardsian. In a much-cited review, Bangs suggests that Van Morrison's *Astral Weeks* is engaged in "the great search, fueled by the belief that through these musical and mental processes illumination is attainable. Or may at least be glimpsed" (Bangs, "*Astral Weeks*"). Yet, the illumination is not wholly astral. It lives in the folds of human contact; in the power it wields above and beyond the clumsy clenches of institutions, a power that cuts deeper than flesh to something we intimate when we utter the words "heart" and "soul." You don't have to be a Romantic or a zealot to get it.

Here's the rub that rubs both ways: whatever you dub it—truth, beauty, the real, presentness, happeningness, rapture, ecstasy—it starts out with its cutting edge directed at Nixonian paranoia and sclerotic bureaucracy. But before long, the capital-R Romance of the quest starts to chase its own tail and to weave its own tale. The calculations of math are replaced by the fabulations of myth. Rock and roll becomes a surrogate for whatever god used to be a surrogate for. At the bottom, it's freedom: freedom from care, from burdens, from authority, from the clay of mortality, illness, bills, and obligations. When Dan Graham spins the yarns of rock and religion, of an ecstatic, old, weird America, he is tethering the history of the United States to this same freedom. And this is where the blade turns back on itself, cutting against the liberatory pronouncements of rock and roll. If only one were infinitely more acute, a single infinitely brief instant would be long enough to see that this freedom—promised by Michael Fried, awestruck before the AbEx canvas, by Greil Marcus, Dan Graham, and Lester Bangs immersed in the deluge of sound—is a freedom not available to all. It's the same old mistake; Western culture's greatest hit. Each of these White, American, men, blithely accepts his own freedom as universal.

Kodwo Eshun is quick (on page 5 of his book-length study of *Rock My Religion*) to suggest that it is "possible to understand" Graham's piece, "as a video-essay that works with historical images and archival sounds in ways that are not historical, but rather ahistorical and transhistorical; not academic or theoretical so much as associative and speculative" (Eshun 5). Graham's hodgepodge of images and sounds, all overlapping and obscuring each other, bears this out. Likewise, the thesis of the video is conveyed with a self-certainty that is more evangelical than scholarly. This is a work of art, after all, not a peer-reviewed journal article. But in matching rock and roll and Christian fundamentalism, blow for ecstatic blow, Graham's work slips into something more dangerous than speculation. It mistakes subjective responses for universals. It feels its responses as inviolate, absolute, pure. This is where the danger comes in. "No one is more dangerous than he who imagines himself pure in heart: for his purity, by definition, is unassailable," instructs James Baldwin. We would do well to take this admonition very much to heart.

*Rock My Religion* frames the history of rock and roll according to Graham's own experience as a White, American man. It is less concerned with rock and roll's historical origins than with how it fits into a narrative of the push and pull of American culture and counterculture. Early American Shakers, Pentecostals, and Puritans pursued spiritual release through physical exultation and speaking in tongues. Late twentieth-century rock and roll sets aside the theological origin but retains the bodily liberation and glossolalic rapture. Yet, somehow, in all this socio-cultural calculus, Graham loses sight of the specific historical conditions and the individuals that combined to forge rock and roll as a contingent form. The fact that rock and roll emerged in African American communities and cultural practices is all but erased. Eshun writes, "*Rock My Religion* often feels like a white dream of America divested of African presence." He itemizes the slender inventory of Black recognition:

> an appearance by Jimi Hendrix, a single reference to Chuck Berry's "Johnny B. Goode" (1958), a reference to Jerry Lee Lewis's "Great Balls of Fire" (1957) that omits its songwriter Otis Blackwell, Little Eva singing "The Loco-Motion" (1962) and the presence of one unidentified slave spiritual about the day of Jubilee. (Eshun 7)

Benjamin Buchloh finds it

> astonishing that Graham should omit from his construction of the panorama of religious and musical consumption any reference whatsoever to the fact that this history cannot possibly be written without considering the contribution of the black working class and its musicians or reflecting on its cultural contribution in the context of its role as the traditionally exploited and oppressed proletarian class of American society. (Buchloh 220)

In spite of his own reference to "the black working class" as an "it" rather than a "they," Buchloh bemoans "the ensuing instrumentalization of individuals according to the needs of industrial capital" (220). In addition to the exclusion of Black life and Black culture from this story, Buchloh also takes issue with *Rock My Religion*'s failure to recognize that both religion and rock and roll slot comfortably into late capitalist cycles of production and consumption. By offering momentary respites from the capitalist grind, the Saturday night honky tonk and the Sunday morning sermon each provide fantasies of freedom that allow the worker to return to work on Monday feeling a little less indentured.

> [I]t is precisely the mythical quality of that supposed subversion and liberation that qualifies Rock music as a perpetual repetition of the same ritual . . . and as such as an inexhaustible source for industrial production and consumption. (Buchloh 220)

It's one thing for Kris Kristofferson to write, "freedom's just another word for nothing left to lose," and for Roger Miller, Kenny Rogers, and Janis Joplin to sing it (Kristofferson "Me and Bobby McGee"). If you're White, there is always something else to lose—your status as White in American society. So this freedom is at least one enormous step removed from truly having nothing left to lose. As Bob Dylan sang satirically, "A South politician preaches to the poor white man / 'You got more than the blacks, don't complain / You're better than them, you been born with white skin,' they explain" (Dylan "Only a Pawn in Their Game"). But it means something quite different in both scale and kind when Aretha Franklin sings the word "freedom" twelve times in a row. The song "Think" is one of the very few that Franklin had a hand in writing, and it speaks from and to Du Boisian double consciousness, offering two distinct ways to understand what is happening in the song. On the one hand, it can be understood as the plaint of a jilted lover. On the other, it is a demand, directed at the White individual or the White establishment, by those systematically disenfranchised and degraded. The lyrics echo Du Bois when he insisted that anti-Black racism provided a "public and psychological wage" for poor Whites who were "compensated" for their own disenfranchisement by being able to think themselves superior to Blacks (Du Bois 700). Franklin sings, "Let's go back, Let's go back / Let's go way on way back when." This is a developmental diagnosis. The seeds of this condition have been nurtured by the song's addressee. And while Franklin confesses, "I ain't no psychiatrist / I ain't no doctor with degrees." She also declares, "But it don't take too much high IQ / To see what you're doing to me." The song then pleads with its addressee (and its listener) to reject the restraints of the past, of history, of nation, and race, and privilege:

> You better think (think)
> Think about what you're trying to do to me
> Yeah, think (think, think)
> Let your mind go, let yourself be free (Franklin, "Think")

"Think" hammers home its key ideas, repeating the words "think" and "freedom" until they can't be ignored. The freedom the song demands isn't just Franklin's own. She implores the listener to think. Because freedom can't be granted it must be achieved. Blacks' lack of freedom isn't a Black problem. As James Baldwin told an interviewer in 1963,

> We have invented the nigger. I didn't invent him. White people invented him. [. . .] If I am not the nigger, and if it's true that your invention reveals you, then who is the nigger? [. . .] Well, he's unnecessary to me, so he must be necessary

to you. I'm going to give you your problem back: You're the nigger, baby, it isn't me. (Baldwin 41:50)

Franklin's demands don't reside principally in the words. They emerge from the way she pours her astonishment and her outrage into the elasticized contours of the syllables and articulations. How can White America think that this situation could possibly be right? How can they think that this situation can be sustainable? How can they not understand that sooner or later the whole fetid excrescence is going to explode in their throats?

As the phrase, "I can't breathe," has come to represent the literal and figurative strangulation of Black Americans, Aretha Franklin's voice, gloriously full of air, free in a way that so few voices are, takes on added significance. Of course, it's true that when Franklin sings, it is just air—air forced across the fallows and folds of the anatomy. But that simple fact does not diminish the marvel of her voice. On the contrary, to think that each of us also forces air from our lungs and forms it into pitched syllables. And yet none of us—no other singer who has ever sidled up to a microphone—could make air do quite what Franklin made it do. In the depths of her lungs, common air is transformed into a kind of electricity. It is fast. It rises out of nothing. And before you can hear it as voice or as sound or as music, it is already doing its work. Of course, such energy is never sudden, but always the result of pent-up power deprived an outlet. The energy of Franklin's voice is the correlate of the rising anger and righteousness of Black Americans' demands for justice. Her voice, in the space of a vowel or a soft consonant, goes from lying down to standing up. It fills the space of its container. Moments later, in mid-verse crescendo, it devastates that container, like an Ali punch from the inside.

It's often said that Soul music is secular Gospel, a music which replaces religious faith with romantic love. And much of Franklin's music could be described this way. But, such an understanding begs tweaking when we recall that in 1970 Franklin offered to pay Angela Davis's bond while Davis awaited trial on a fabricated murder charge. In 1970, *Jet* magazine reported Franklin, saying,

Angela Davis must go free. Black people will be free. I've been locked up (for disturbing the peace in Detroit) and I know you got to disturb the peace when you can't get no peace. Jail is hell to be in. I'm going to see her free if there is any justice in our courts, not because I believe in communism, but because she's a Black woman and she wants freedom for Black people. I have the money; I got it from Black people—they've made me financially able to have it—and I want to use it in ways that will help our people. (Franklin, *Jet* 54)

Rather than swapping romance for faith, Franklin's songs can be heard as earthly enactments of the great moral demands of religion—the exalted promises of the celestial realm translated to the terrestrial realities of the public bus and the factory floor. When Otis Redding sings "Respect," it is about a working man coming home at the end of the day and expecting love, dinner, sex, and a specifically submissive expression of respect from his woman. When Franklin sings it, it's about something else, something bigger. It is not a demand from the man (much less The Man) for his power to be recognized, but a plea from the disempowered—woman, African American, colonized, enslaved—to be recognized at all.

Lester Bangs thought that not only could rock and roll deliver this message but could engineer its realization. Throughout his brief career, he repeatedly returned to the notion that rock could model a new society by breaking down divisions between Black and White, young and old, rich and poor, male and female, high and low. Recall, that in his review of the 1981 reissue of *Philosophy of the World* by The Shaggs, three sisters from rural New Hampshire, Bangs sang the praises of the Wiggin sisters, calling them

> true one world humanists with an eye to our social future whose only hope is a redefined communism based on the open-hearted sharing of whatever you got with all sentient beings. Their and my religion is compassion, true Christianity with no guilt factors and no vested interest, perhaps a barter economy, but certainly the elimination of capitalism, rape, and special-interest group hatred. (Bangs 1981)

Christianity centers itself on a single point: almighty god as both origin and destination. American capitalism centers itself on the almighty dollar. But rock and roll rejects the single point of god or capital, of the camera or the microphone. Rock and roll does not emanate from the single-point perspective of the Renaissance image of the artist, solitary and endowed with a singular gift. Rock and roll is the result of a thousand inchoate forces converging in the hands and feet and still-developing brains of four or five not-quite-adults. When rock and roll is great, it is not the product of an individual composer, author, or director. It springs not from the mind of the genius but from the clumsy interactions of individuals who each alone could hardly dream of the results. It is a territory being wrestled over as we watch and listen. Not only don't we know how it will end, but neither do the wrestlers.

Rock and roll can't abide by the modernist conviction of *thingness*—that we can point a finger into the universe, say "that," and expect that anyone should know what we're talking about. Rock and roll is not a painting. It won't hold still for contemplation. It can't be framed. It doesn't avail itself of formal Kantian or Greenbergian judgments. (Truth be told, a painting is not a painting in this sense either.) After 1968 and "Art and Objecthood," even Michael Fried realized he had lost the war. Art had become kinetic and conceptual and experiential. And there was no getting that genie back into the bottle. For Lester Bangs, it was the happeningness of rock and roll that promised the only salvation available: the salvation of something going down in real time and space; something involving bodies.

After Bangs died at the age of thirty-three in 1982, Patrick Goldstein wrote in the *Los Angeles Times* that Bangs "was not above picking fights with rock stars in pursuit of a good interview." Richard Meltzer, Bangs's friend, a co-leading light of the early days of gonzo-tinged rock criticism, couldn't let the sleight go uncorrected.

> If Lester (the writer) more than once battled Lou Reed into (and beyond) the wee hours of etc., it was not to *get* a story, it was to *live* a story: to encounter all the rock-related *being* his writerly credentials (as a wedge) were able to afford him (as a person). (Meltzer)

What Meltzer insists we understand is that Bangs's approach to his craft and his life is not incidental to his belief in rock and roll. What Meltzer, in his inimitable—sometimes barely readable—cut-and-splice shuck-and-jive, needs us to know is that he and Bangs and their cohort of first-generation rock journalists could not bring themselves to look passively and objectively upon their object. Only by embedding themselves in the music and the performance, in the incipient demimonde of the club and the late-night, drug-glazed listening session, could a critic claim to have any insight into this new cultural experience. Unlike the jazz critic, it wasn't a matter of providing the time signatures of the album tracks. Unlike the sportscaster, it wasn't a matter of play-by-play. One had to push and pull it, be pushed, be pulled by it, and somehow convey what it feels like to be in its throes. The writing cannot merely reflect; it must reproduce the experience. Bangs engages in what Meltzer refers to as "pugnacity with form."

> [W]hat may most enduringly *matter* about Lester's approach to his chosen profession, way ahead of dandy journalistic touchstones—"courage," "integrity," "pride in craft"— that he ate for breakfast like so much broken glass (but

which, really, you can still get from Nat Hentoff and Howard Cosell), is the "anti-professional," forcibly non-dehumanized *square-one struggle* he by design submitted to—and could not, with any kernel of his humanity, avoid—in order to pump out critical prose of any scale of note. (Meltzer)

In the same review of *Astral Weeks* cited earlier, Bangs comes very near to constructing a comprehensive thesis on rock and roll. In the space of one paragraph, he shuffles across concentric circles of the mortal coil: from facts to truth, life to skin, time to self; from beauty to horror, creation to destruction, the miracle of life, consisting as it necessarily does in hurting others and being hurt. Rock and roll both feels like and, in some crucial sense, *is* a form of comprehension that can only emerge from incomprehension.

What *Astral Weeks* deals in are not facts but truths. *Astral Weeks*, insofar as it can be pinned down, is a record about people stunned by life, completely overwhelmed, stalled in their skins, their ages and selves, paralyzed by the enormity of what in one moment of vision they can comprehend. It is a precious and terrible gift, born of a terrible truth, because what they see is both infinitely beautiful and terminally horrifying: the unlimited human ability to create or destroy, according to whim. It's no Eastern mystic or psychedelic vision of the emerald beyond, nor is it some Baudelairean perception of the beauty of sleaze and grotesquerie. Maybe what it boiled down to is one moment's knowledge of the miracle of life, with its inevitable concomitant, a vertiginous glimpse of the capacity to be hurt, and the capacity to inflict that hurt. (Bangs 1979)

# 9

# The Feeling You've Been Cheated

From 1968 to 1976, a lot of things happened. Not all of them should have. Assassinations. Violence on the streets of Paris, Prague, Detroit, Chicago, and Mexico City. Watergate. The imposition of what is sometimes called "The Washington Consensus," forcing adherence to monetarism, supply-side economics, and minimizing state involvement in both welfare provisions and wealth distribution. Just over the horizon, Margaret Thatcher and Ronald Reagan in wait.

In August 1971, Lewis Powell—at the request of Eugene Sydnor Jr., chairman of the Education Committee of the US Chamber of Commerce—submitted a diagnosis of issues facing the American economy. The "Powell Memorandum," as it is now known, begins by stating flatly that "the American economic system is under broad attack, . . . the assault on the enterprise system is broadly based and consistently pursued." This assault, according to Powell, then a corporate lawyer, was being launched "from the college campus, the pulpit, the media, the intellectual and literary journals, the arts and sciences, and from politicians" (Powell). Powell offers a multipronged solution to the problem: champions of the free market must exert greater influence on college campuses, retraining America's youth in the ideology of laissez-faire capitalism. The mass media—from newspapers and magazines to advertising, television, books, and scholarly journals—should be "kept under constant surveillance." Complaints should be made to the Federal Communications Commission demanding equal time for conservative viewpoints. Powell also suggests action in the courts and in "the neglected political arena" (Powell). He concludes by advising American businesses to take "a more aggressive attitude." The timing of the memo is striking, coming a mere two months prior to Nixon's nomination of Powell for the Supreme Court and eight years before the election of Thatcher, nine before Reagan. Powell is explicit, naming names:

There should be no hesitation to attack the Naders, the Marcuses and others who openly seek destruction of the system. There should not be the slightest hesitation to press vigorously in all political arenas for support of the enterprise system. Nor should there be reluctance to penalize politically those who oppose it. (Powell)

Hard cut: *The Filth and the Fury*—Julien Temple's 2000 film about the Sex Pistols—depicts British life in the interregnum between Powell's memo and the coronation of neoliberalism in London and D.C. We watch a rapid succession of images: A young White man rushes an older White man (the racial identifications are crucial to the scenes) and rips a Union Jack from his hands, proceeding to beat him with the flag pole. A Black woman, her face torqued with anger, delivers a looping right hand to the left ear of a White, helmeted English policeman, sending him reeling.[1] A bearded White man in glasses brandishes a piece of lumber as photographers document the arc of his terrified swings. Finally, the film's camera zooms in on three White teenagers on a tower block balcony. The edit gives the appearance that they are looking down on this pandemonium, laughing and smoking. Behind these scenes some vaguely regal classical music provides flurries of descending and ascending violins, pimped by momentous tympani. The words of Johnny Rotten frame (and are framed by) these scenes and this music: "I don't think you can explain how things happen other than sometimes they just should. And the Sex Pistols should have happened and did" (Temple).

While you can't exactly claim that Punk rock emerged as a response to Thatcherism and Reaganism, the "Powell Memorandum" makes it plain that the conditions of possibility for both neoliberalism and Punk's rejections were firmly in place by 1976. As the welfare state receded, faith in private enterprise and a meritocracy (based on White male merits) came to justify the dog-eat-dogism of life in the self-proclaimed beacons of freedom, democracy, and social mobility. Powell's future smashed headlong into Johnny Rotten's "no future." (They were really the same thing.) The result, described in situ by Caroline Coon in 1977, was a whole generation backed into a corner.

As Johnny, and his punk fans grew up, the good life was crumbling around them—literally. Hastily-erected tower blocks, which replaced the decaying but

---

[1]   These first two images are taken from footage of the so-called "Battle of Lewisham," a conflict in south London instigated by the racist National Front marching in majority-Black Lewisham on August 13, 1977.

tight-knit slum communities, cost local councils thousands of pounds to repair; and when these blocks didn't fall into disrepair through shoddy workmanship, so alienating was the environment that, as sociologists had warned, the teenagers themselves tore them apart. Vandalism was rife.

On the high-rise estate where Johnny lived there were no official play areas. To amuse themselves, gangs would throw bricks from the protection of the fifth floor at passing cars. (Coon, "The Sex Pistols," 1977)

Let's call it a crux. Hal Foster has used the word to describe the position occupied by minimalism in the firmament of postwar American art. Minimalism is not only the rational conclusion of modernism but also its subversion, its culmination, its pinnacle, and its end. We might think of the crux of minimalism as a pivot, or a tipping, point. The crux is neither before nor after this fulcrum. It is the fulcrum's very apex. Within a given circumstance, "crux" designates the most important point. It is also a point of difficulty. And of course, it is the Latin word for cross—Jesus's no doubt, but, for our purposes, Robert Johnson's too: the crossroads. We'll reuse the word with all these connotations purposely intact. We will use it to describe the 1970s, a decade of difficult importance; a cross(road) upon which deals are made with devils.

So it was, that when the British monarch arrived at her twenty-fifth year on the throne, one segment of the nation planned a grand display of pride and prestige, while another smelled a rat. Those who enjoyed no spoils of the Empire's preeminence could only understand the Silver Jubilee as a massive thumbing of the aristocracy's collective nose; a garish exhibition of hypocrisy, attended by the highbred nonchalance of those who had never had to consider how their behavior played for the great unwashed. And so it was that a handful of the unwashed took it upon themselves to throw their own kind of party—the party of anti-piety and antipathy, henceforth known as Punk.

Richard Branson spent 500 pounds to rent the Queen Elizabeth (the boat) to float the Sex Pistols down the Thames during the Silver Jubilee of Queen Elizabeth (the Queen).[2] As the boat sallied past the Houses of Parliament, amidst squealing cadenzas of feedback approximating what it might sound like if Merzbow were a Klezmer band, the Pistols performed a handful of songs (Sex Pistols "Live on Boat Trip . . ."). As the Pistols' great chronicler, Jon Savage, wrote in *Sounds* at the time, the band is "playing for their/our lives" (Savage). The event was staged by manager Malcolm McLaren to promote the new single,

---

[2] As a point of comparison, in 2021, Branson spent 450,000 dollars to float himself into space.

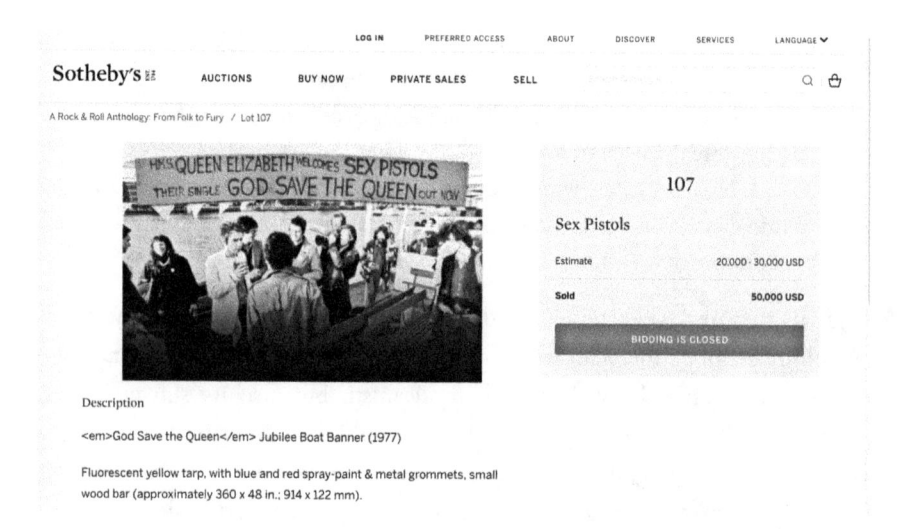

**Figure 9.1** Sotheby's auction page for the banner used during the Sex Pistols' Thames Boat Cruise (1977). [Note sale price.]

"God Save the Queen." Despite a press, radio, and retail ban, the single claimed the number-one spot that week. The charts, barred from printing the name of either the band or the song, featured a blank at the top. Police boarded the Queen Elizabeth and arrested McLaren, putting an abrupt end to the Pistols' Thames joyride (Figure 9.1).

But the bigger, more consequential joyride that the Pistols were leading charged onward in a carjacked London off-license minicab, across the byways of Britain, bevies of bands in the backseat, a torrent of Tories in pursuit like Keystone Cops on the trail of a fishtailing fire truck. Everyone involved knew that it would end badly. Whether by stalling on the tracks in the path of the last of the steam-powered trains or by plowing into a primary school during morning lessons, nobody, however, knew. The Pistols played their part of the boys on the tower block balcony, laughing, smoking, hurling bricks at passing cars. Good and decent English society played their part of passersby, appalled for the most part, by the punks' uncivilized response to the privileges of their very own civilization. On the Queen Elizabeth skiffing the Thames, dredging the streets later that night, trolling from pub jubilee soiree to bail desk at the Metropolitan Police station, Jon Savage could feel in his bones what was at stake.

> To a certain extent the barriers are down a bit more. That means if you look anything like a Sex Pistol, or a "punk-rocker," you're likely to get pulled in. Right:

that means—No martyrs, No victims, No heroes, No stereotypes. No games on this score, No provocation. Things have gotten more serious. No escalation . . .? (Savage)

That closing question mark denotes not a question but a decision point: a crux.

Remember, though, that the crux, the crossroad, does not dictate a direction. One might just as easily go left as right, down or up, right or wrong. Case in point: Scritti Politti—formed, as did so many bands in England, after seeing the Sex Pistols, The Clash, The Damned, and Johnny Thunders on the infamous "Anarchy in the UK" Tour. The tour stopped at Leeds Polytechnic University on December 6, 1976. After the gig, Gartside, then a student at nearby Leeds College of Art and Design, conscripted fellow art student, Tom Morley, to play drums and persuaded his childhood friend, Nial Jinks, to move to Leeds to play bass. They adopted the name Scritti Politti, a bastardized transcription of the Italian for "political writing," meant to simultaneously conjure the Italian Marxist Antonio Gramsci, while also tapping the joyous nonsense of Little Richard's "Tutti Frutti."

If you were an art student in 1977, 1978, or 1979 in either the United States or the United Kingdom—you were just as likely to form a band as you were to rent a studio and invest in canvas stretchers. Art colleges were viral breeding grounds for Punk. Incorporating elements of Dada, performance, and Fluxus, bands formed, played first gigs, and folded in the blink of an ear. At art school, conceptual art was all the rage. And bands sought ways to square the circle of conceptual rigor and Punk impetuousness. As Simon Reynolds tells, "conceptualist approaches were in the ascendant" at Leeds College of Art and Design,

> this brand of conceptualism was starkly different from the playful process-oriented art school sensibility that informed Wire and Talking Heads. Influenced, like his Leeds contemporaries Gang of Four and the Mekons, by Art and Language's hard-core critical sensibility, Green would come to think of that style of post-Eno art punk [*that of Wire and Talking Heads*] as "formalism," decadent and disengaged, arty for artinesses' sake. Scritti had *political* motivations for messing with musical structures. They wanted to create revolutionary consciousness through the radicalization of form as much as through their politically radical lyrical content. (Reynolds, 181)

If you were an art student in 1972, 1973, or 1974, you probably arrived thinking that your ability to draw your family's golden retriever or your Aunt Clara would get you through. What a headfuck—your professors would call it a "paradigm shift"—when you were confronted with Duchamp's urinal, with Manzoni's tinned shit, with Art & Language's *Index 01*: eight gray office-grade filing cabinets installed in the august halls of Documenta '72—the international art exhibition held every five years in Kassel, Germany. The filing cabinets contain texts published and distributed by the collective over the previous few years, exhaustively cross-referenced to facilitate varying paths through myriad political, philosophical, and aesthetic themes and topics. The idea that an artwork was a simple or singular thing exploded. Lost was the idea that you could put a frame around it, point at it during a critique and say, "this is my work." *Index 01* challenges this most commonsensical idea of the aesthetic object. It also challenges the self-containment or self-sufficiency of such objects. The only way to make sense of *Index 01*—and one *had* to make sense of it, by dint alone of the fact that it was in Documenta—was to follow its trails and tributaries, all the leaks and seepages that allowed the world into the work and the work into the world. There was no clean way to frame it. It was everywhere and nowhere. Not a thing but an idea; a collection of ideas, attributed not to a singular author, but to a collective.

Art & Language formed in 1967 in Coventry, England, positioning themselves as the most rigorous, linguistic, Marxist conceptualists of them all. Tellingly, their early energies were directed not toward the production of images or objects for exhibition, but into a journal, *Art-Language*, which began in 1969. Art & Language have survived to this day, riding out the comings and goings of scores of members and a bi-continental split—when the English and New York contingents came to intellectual blows during the 1970s. Art & Language acted as the vanguard of a philosophical and political revolution in the art world, challenging prevailing notions of formalism, aesthetic autonomy, the market, the cult of genius, and nearly anything else, emitting even a faint odor of the modernist paradigms propping up everything from Manet to Motherwell. Their activities in the 1960s and 1970s were motivated by a Marxian rejection of market capitalism in general, but more specifically of the market takeover of artistic production and reception and of the co-optation of the critical values that obtain at both ends of this exchange. Art & Language embraced the so-called "linguistic turn" in philosophy as a justification for turning their backs on the exchangeable art object. What they retained in their collective practice was language: the discourse, traditionally thought of as supplemental or subsequent to the proper work of art. This strategy situates Art & Language as central in the "conceptual turn" of the visual arts in the late 1960s. More profoundly than any of their contemporaries, Art & Language map the conceptual turn in the visual arts to the linguistic turn in philosophy. A work of art, in their cosmology, needn't be a discrete thing. *Index 01* is not the kind of thing that you hang on the wall and get a light on it. Art & Language make work that is not bounded by space— as with a frame around a painting—or by time—the moment of encounter when we stand in the presence of the work. Instead, Art & Language begins from the presumption that the work of art not only *can*, but necessarily *does*, merge with things and meanings beyond what we might conventionally call its "self." The work leaps; it keeps tripping switches: a chain reaction tumbling both forward and backward in time to engage history and art history, experience, and reference: the woven nature of what the theorists of the 1970s were fond of calling "intertextuality," the back and forth of any construct of meaning with dozens or hundreds of other adjacent constructs. Conceptuality, in the ways that Art and Language employed it, was akin to—practically synonymous with—textuality.

At art college in Britain in the 1970s, Art & Language was the measure of one's intellectual sophistication and political rigor. Scritti Politti's main songwriter and de facto leader, Green Gartside, honed his critical sensibilities in such an environment, tested by the example of Art & Language and their sardonic attitude toward "things just as they are." Scritti Politti relocated from Leeds to the Camden Town area of London, where they occupied a squat with like-minded punks. While only Gartside, Morley, and Jinks played instruments, the band operated as an extended collective. A gang of up to twenty friends and co-squatters functioning as the philosophical and political arm of Scritti Politti, debating the band's musical, economic, and promotional strategies. "Rehearsals" were often closer in spirit and letter to meetings of the Young Communists League that Gartside had founded at the age of fourteen in his hometown of Cwmbran, Wales.

Scritti Politti's early songs are the very definition of shambolic, all stops and starts, loose ends and lapses. None of the formulae of rock and roll—never mind the nascent Punk movement—are taken for granted. For Gartside, Morley, and Jinks, there was no convincing reason that a song must cohere, that a pulse must be consistent, that a band must play "together," that a melody must ride the contours of the chord changes and rhythms that function as its foundation. Nowhere was it written that a band was simply the people with the instruments in their hands. The modus operandi of the moment was DIY and that included devising the rules and how the game was to be played.

In 1978, Scritti Politti released their first single on their own St. Pancras label. The song's title, "Skank Bloc Bologna," conflates the skanking dance style of Jamaican ska, with Gramsci's notion of the "historic bloc." The title also references Max Jaggi's book, *Red Bologna*, published the previous year, which provides an account of Bologna's social reforms as the seat of the Italian Communist Party. Clearly, Gartside is eager to rise to Art & Language's challenge. The following year, 1979, Scritti Politti recorded the second of three sessions for legendary BBC DJ, John Peel, and by the end of the year, they'd released these four songs, again on their St. Pancras label, but this time in conjunction with the fast-growing indie label, Rough Trade. The Peel Session EP delivers Scritti Politti's aesthetic manifesto in the form of a one-minute and forty-eight-second song entitled "Messthetics." They offer their political manifesto in a two-minute and ten-second song, "Hegemony."

Somewhat surprisingly, Art & Language was trying their hand at music too. In 1976, they released an LP of their own, entitled *Corrected Slogans*. It also carries a sub- or alternate-title: *Music-Language*, as if the journal *Art-Language* has mutated into an audio format. The record is a collaboration with the Red Krayola, a wayward psych band from Houston, Texas. To call this meeting of the minds "unlikely" would be a vast underestimation of the distance separating British conceptual art from underground American rock and roll. And yet... The Red Krayola formed in 1966, as part of a small, underground scene that included the 13th Floor Elevators. Their first two albums—1967's *The Parable of Arable Land* and 1968's *God Bless the Red Krayola and All Who Sail With It*—received what we'll call "modest" attention. Throughout their five-decade run, the band's one consistent member has been Mayo Thompson. And it was Thompson who, in 1972, handed a cassette tape of his music to Michael Baldwin and Philip Pilkington of Art & Language's UK branch. Over the next few years, Thompson was drawn increasingly into the Art & Language orbit, leading eventually to their collaboration.

According to the album's liner notes, the album was written and rehearsed in various locations, including Oxfordshire, New York, and Captiva Island, Florida, where Mayo Thompson worked as an assistant to Robert Rauschenberg. Rauschenberg's foundation, Change, Inc. helped finance the album. The same year as *Corrected Slogans*, the Red Krayola and Art & Language also produced a video entitled *Nine Gross and Conspicuous Errors*, which captures the collaborators at 112 Greene Street in New York, performing, in a rather unrehearsed mode, for the camera of eventual Oscar-winning director, Kathryn Bigelow, an early Art & Language co-conspirator.

(I warned you that "unlikely" would be inadequate.)

Both the LP and the video are experiments in context, setting Art & Language's anti-capitalist texts to minimal guitar and piano arrangements of ersatz music hall folk melodies. The project scans like a middling, if ambitious, 1920s Moscow community theater attempting to make a Leninist musical review. Song titles like "Penny Capitalists," "Plekhanov," and "The Mistakes of Trotsky" (a waltz!) give away the game. But they can hardly communicate the cack-handed, slapped-together mash-up of form and content that unfolds awkwardly across the album's twenty-one songs. The only track that fully embraces the sounds and spirit of the period's rock and roll is "An Harangue," which pairs unaccompanied, chunky, distorted electric guitar chords with a spoken text of boilerplate Marxspeak delivered in an upper-class English accent; it begins:

> The insecurity of crystalline political superstructures as a consequence of economic crisis and social conflict is not in itself a new form of social organization making deep changes in the social project. Unless a conscious socialist transformatory alternative develops the result of crisis must be a further entrenchment of reaction and the growth of mass repression in lieu of solutions to society's problems.

Probably not the most popular Karaoke choice down at the pub.

In 1979, the Red Krayola and Scritti Politti toured together in the UK. The two outfits shared an interest in politics, philosophy, and conceptualism. Influenced by the French thought then disseminating in Anglophone academia, both questioned the seeming naturalness of the common sense and the conventional. That which is taken for granted soon starts to assume the status of given, immutable, universal. And this taking-for-granted allows things as they are to stay as they are. Scritti Politti's "Hegemony" leverages Gramsci's analysis of the social and political mechanisms that encourage blind acceptance of prevailing values and judgments. Like their mentors-in-absentia, Art & Language, the early Scritti Politti take none of the conventions of their field for granted. As listeners, we are welcome—encouraged, even—to understand aesthetic naturalness and social common sense as symptoms of the same underlying danger: that of not knowing or noticing that one's taste; one's reading of works of art; one's making of value judgments and categorizations; one's very *desires* are a product of history, class, gender, and acculturation. Likely, it was this shared skepticism, along with each group's connection to Art & Language—direct in the case of the

Red Krayola, and indirect, in the case of Scritti Politti—that led to them touring together.

Scritti Politti emerged, along with a throng of other bands, as part of a multifarious expansion of the initial Punk impulse. Bands formed, intent on remaining difficult by expanding on Punk's disobedient example. Inspired by a de-skilled approach to composition and performance, by DIY convictions about making and promoting records, these Post-Punk bands, aimed to extend Punk's rejection of the mainstream, without embracing its back-to-basics musical formula. But by the early 1980s, this music was experiencing its own backlash. New bands and fans began to question the decidedly underground status of post-punk. If one of Punk's radical subversions had been to reimagine who gets to be in a band, then what use is that subversion if the "new" musicians solely populate underground bands, leaving the "old" image of the musician unperturbed in the mainstream? Post-Punk bands who, like the early Scritti Politti, suffered for their art and their independence began to question if squat living, dumpster diving, bad health, bad drugs, and bad sex were worth it.

Likewise, the term and the form of rock came under scrutiny. The insularity of Post-Punk's White Myddle-class boys' club seemed to merely repeat the sins of the past. Worse yet, more fans and critics started to reckon with the fact that rock and roll had been appropriated by White Myddle-class boys without credit or compensation to their Black forbears. With Jamaican music part of Punk from the early days, with the new popularity of disco, with the re-discovery of American soul music, a new ethic and a new aesthetic began to emerge as an alternative to the notion of "rockism," a mindset associated with race, class, gender, and a claim to authenticity that pop as a genre never had and probably never wanted. The bands who rejected rockism in favor of what was known in Britain as "New Pop"—bands like The Art of Noise, ABC, and Human League, but also their managers and the press—invented their own " -ism" to describe the object of their ambitions. Maybe more precisely, they invented the term "entryism" to distance their ambitions from the very rockist accusation of "selling out." Rather than suggesting, as the phrase "selling out" does, a retreat from the underground and a surrender of rock's authenticity, "entryism" suggests an insistence on inclusion, on being accepted into the club from which this Post-Punk generation had previously been excluded. We might think of entryism as selling out, but with its poles reversed; something like "selling in." In an interview from 1981, we can see Gartside already grappling with these issues.

Marginal music has never transcended its own history or invaded the mainstream. As a consequence it ends up asserting little other than its own marginality, its difference from the majority. But mere difference is not enough, especially when it soon created a tradition as stale as that of the mainstream, as stale and as self-enclosed. (Gartside, quoted in Cooper)

Gartside organized his newfound doubts and ambitions into a plan of action, and some months later, delivered it to his band mates, Morley and Jinks. Gartside argued that, in order to mean something, Scritti Politti would have to sell in. In order for their politics and their aesthetics to have any effect in the world, it would have to reach the world. Their songs would need to land on the radio and on the TV. The band would have to become pop stars. Morley and Jinks were apparently, and understandably, dubious. But after reading Gartside's screed—by some accounts it exceeds 100 pages—and after some long, late-night conversations, they agreed.

Scritti Politti were hardly the only British band in the early 1980s wanting to sell in. But none of the other entryist bands had the political and philosophical pedigree of Scritti Politti. What's more, none of them had such a pedigree as learned at art college. The early Scritti Politti's Marxist convictions and their Derridean/Wittgensteinian/Gramscian reading of the mechanisms of culture and language had been transmitted by Art & Language, and by conceptual art more generally, and received by art students as communiqués from headquarters, as both motives and tactics for an anti-Thatcherite aesthetic militancy. (Recall, that while Thatcher only became prime minister in 1979, she had been the leader of the Conservative Party since 1975 and, from 1970 to 1974, had been education secretary putting her very much in the minds of those at the university.) By the early 1980s, when Scritti Politti directed their collective energies at entryism, their relationship to the charts, to mass media, and to capital was necessarily different from that of their contemporary entryists.

Now it's one thing to decide to become pop stars. It is another thing entirely to manage it. But so it was that, on April 12, 1984—just five years after the Peel Session EP of 1979—a new version of Scritti Politti, now without Morley or Jinks, appeared on *Top of the Pops*, the BBC TV show featuring performances of songs that have landed in the top 40 of the British pop charts. Bearing little resemblance to his former self, Gartside, along with his new bandmates, performed the song "Wood Beez (Pray Like Aretha Franklin)."

Flaunting a new appreciation for African American music, the single jettisons all of the band's clanky amateurism, replacing it with slick, technologically facilitated grooves. Employing drum machines and sequencers, programed by new member, David Gamson, "Wood Beez" and the rest of the album, *Cupid and Psyche 85*, on which it appears, is propelled by a funky synthesized bass line and crisp electronic drums. Gartside's vocals are packed in a soft-edged cloud of harmonies and reverb, functioning as a vehicle for the song's melody rather than an enunciation of a message. His voice is sweet, vaguely androgynous. The reference to Aretha Franklin announces the traditions to which Scritti Politti were now attaching themselves. But clearly, it is not the swampy Muscle Shoals soul of 1960s Aretha that they take as their model, so much as the contemporary, mid-1980s production of New York dance pop and R&B. The song slides through its three–and-a-half-minute duration, leaving only a hint of form. It is mostly punctuation, draped in sashes of then up-to-date techno-whiz. The song is meant to work subliminally, registering as confection, demanding a sympathetic sway, eschewing anything we might call a "reading." And yet, if we've been paying attention, tracking the path that Scritti Politti have traveled to this unlikely moment, a reading is available.

Performances on *Top of the Pops* are mimed. The band pretends to play along to the recorded track while the singer lips synchs. Gartside doesn't even have a microphone. He is dressed in a knee-length white tunic with white trousers beneath. A broad black leather belt holds it tight at the waist. Between its epaulets, an iron cross medallion dangles from the closure of the tunic's mock turtleneck. Gartside's hair is long and bleached blonde. He is the epitome of the New Romantic movement, which included bands such as Visage, Spandau Ballet, and Classix Nouveaux. Despite the fact that the sounds are decidedly electronic, the band plays conventional instruments including a bass guitar and an acoustic drum kit. Gartside himself is playing a hollow-body, archtop Gretsch guitar, the kind preferred by jazz guitarists such as Wes Montgomery. He strums away when no such guitar is audible in the mix and stops—with no apparent effect on the song—in order to pose with his arms folded across the top of the guitar. Scritti Politti is very much playing along with *Top of the Pop's* shallow conceit that what the audience is witnessing is the band performing their song. It's a winking conceit—a tacit we-know-you-know pact between the audience, the performer, and the program. The deceit to which everyone consents is that the band's performance is that of a band pretending to perform, a performance of a performance. This performance is staged strictly for the camera and the frame of its mise-en-scène. Scritti Politti perform tidily, acquiescently within the frame, while what we hear and see is further framed—or, one might say, formed—by *parerga* both spatially and temporally beyond the broadcast.

Many of the camera angles emanate from below the band, from the perspective of the audience gazing up at the stage. This reveals the lighting rigs and disco balls above. Obviously, it is unnecessary that the shots include this apparatus of performance. But the shots are engineered to maintain the illusion. There is an audience present in the studio, all facing the band and swaying back and forth to the music. A smaller handful of dancers are arrayed across the stage, behind and interspersed within the band members. The status of the dancers is unclear—audience? performers?—but for the fact that the jig's been up from the start. Everyone here is a performer. The only audience is the one at home gathered around the boob tube. Throughout the broadcast—as this type of performance is also known—a large screen is positioned directly behind the band, projecting a head and shoulders shot of Gartside. It's a screen within the projected image on TV screens across Britain. When the main shot shows us Gartside straight on, the screen behind him shows him from a slightly divergent angle, perhaps ten degrees to the left, depicting him in quarter profile. There is no need for this screen. There are no cheap seats in this venue from which the punters would need an enhanced, enlarged Gartside to get their money's worth. The screen merely confirms and reinforces the televisuality of the event; frames and lights framed and lit for the illuminated boxes in living rooms in Brighton, Birmingham, and Blackpool.

By the time they appeared on *Top of the Pops*, Scritti Politti were eight years clear of the "Anarchy in the UK" tour. They were seven years from the Sex Pistols' Thames joyride and "God Save the Queen" landing at number one on the UK charts, despite being banned from airplay on the BBC and being pulled from the shelves of many national retailers. In the intervening years, major labels had descended to the desert floor to pick at the carcass of Punk. They signed bands in swathes, while also branding and selling a kind of defanged version of Punk known as "New Wave." Scritti Politti had mutated from an overt manifestation of Punk's politics of form, into an unabashed example of pop as the saccharine narcotic of the masses.

To fully track the musical, political, and philosophical meanings of Scritti Politti's trajectory, you have to shake the easy effects of a song like "Wood Beez." You have to listen beyond the music and lyrics. The supplements of their practice—the fashion, the haircuts, the technology, the interviews, and liner notes—are, in many cases, more telling than what lies in the grooves of their records. Cross-referencing the Scritti Politti of 1984 and "Wood Beez" with that of 1979 and the Peel Session EP allows us to hear each through the filter of the other. The sweet pop yearning is already there in the early recordings, buried beneath philosophical defenses and political skepticism. Likewise, there is a self-awareness in the later version of the band; an allergy to willful naïveté even in songs as apparently lovestruck as "Wood Beez" or "Absolute," also from *Cupid and Psyche 85* and also performed on *Top of the Pops,* a few months later in 1984.

Even as we watch Scritti Politti perform on *Top of the Pops,* assenting in approach and appearance to the conventions of the program, we can detect another layer of meaning. This layer depends on some of the archaeology we've already engaged with. Gleaning its import requires an even deeper dive. Granted it's an effort most viewers or casual listeners won't even realize they can make. Making it, however, transforms 1980s Scritti Politti into something altogether more complicated than the *Top of the Pops* broadcast is equipped to convey. We can start by looking back at the inner sleeve for the Peel Session EP. We encounter a gatefold collage suggesting items scattered on a tabletop in Scritti Politti's squalid, if erudite, Camden Town squat. Arranged across this tableau, set atop the scattered items on the table, is what appears to be a book, open to pages 179 and 180. At the top of each page, in italics, the running heads supply the title: *Scritto's Republic.* Recalling Plato's treatise on individual and collective justice, but attributed to a kind of philosophical avatar for the band—"Scritto"—this text suggests both a deep intellectual rationale and an acknowledgment of the legitimacy of that rationale within the sphere of philosophical discourse (Figure 9.2).

In making sense of "Scritto's Republic," it's helpful to remember the lessons Gartside would have learned from Art & Language: that the object does not stand alone. It is supported by its discursive supplements. Gartside would have learned that the relationship of the object—the painting, the sculpture, the movie, the song—to its supporting supplements is not simple, unidirectional, or hierarchical. As Jacques Derrida suggests, the supplements construct the object via the play of *différance.* Discourse constructs the object by establishing its limits. In so doing, the supplements mark the ontology of the object. What it *is*—its very constitution—is a product of the "trace" of various other adjacent forces: other music, history, critical writing, past and present cultural currents, indeed: liner notes. Derrida would argue that the object is less a singular and self-contained entity than a construct of myriad influences being brought to bear on something in a particular place at a particular time. Adopting Greek terms that Immanuel Kant used in his

**Figure 9.2** Scritti Politti, Peel Session EP, St. Pancras Records, 1979.

1790 aesthetic treatise, the *Critique of Judgement*, Derrida calls these influences "parerga," in relation to the "ergon," the work itself. And, listen, I know that many pop theorists make the mistake of imposing complicated intellectual motivations on simple entertainments, like forcing Derridean deconstruction onto the music of a band like Scritti Politti. But in this case it's no imposition. In 1982, Scritti Politti released the Rough Trade single, "Jacques Derrida." Apparently, some of Derrida's students heard the song and alerted their professor to the fact that a British pop group was singing his praises. Derrida invited Gartside to Paris where, according to notes in each of their diaries, the two had dinner together in the Beaubourg.

Working in the medium of songs also allows the opportunity for a kind of internal discourse in the form of lyrics. In the early Scritti Politti recordings—songs like "Messthetics" and "Hegemony"—Gartside leverages that discourse, while also performing his anti-aesthetic, anti-hegemonic convictions musically. But it's easy to see why he couldn't leave it at that. Under the sway of Art & Language, persuaded by their rigor and militancy and persuaded by Derridean ideas of differance, the trace, and the parergon, Gartside felt obliged to supply his own supplements: his pre-production rationale, his post-production account of the process.

And when I use the word "account," I do so in both the narrative and budgetary senses. On the back of the outer sleeve of the Peel Session EP, the band includes the costs of the various stages of the manufacturing process: the cutting of the masters, the pressing of the vinyl copies, the printing of labels and sleeves, and so on, while also supplying the addresses and phone numbers of the companies who provided these services so that other bands could also seize the means of production.

The text available to us on pages 179 and 180 begins with a critique of the truth claims of theory in general and of scientific Marxism in particular:

> "Theory" could not ultimately justify a particular political theory/ideology above any other, and there could be no theory, no body of ideas, which had a, or *the*, claim to being "concrete reality" reflected or apprehended in thought.

> The axioms of Marxism were not objects of science but those of discourse and were developed, established and used according to specific conditions.

Nevertheless, the songs on the EP still seem to wear their theory and their Marxism figuratively on their sleeves, offering a short but astute summary of Gramscian critique, while refusing to coalesce into a seamless commodity form. Yet the literal record sleeve allows this "outside" message, seemingly from a source external or adjacent to the band, to interfere with the song's ideological/aesthetic consistency. The songs behave "theoretically" at the same time that the liner notes are repudiating theory. We might try to resolve this contradiction by accepting it as a kind of dialectical performance meant to produce a productive reconciliation. From where we sit now, thinking of the later performance of "Wood Beez" on *Top of the Pops*, we're entitled to wonder if the "New Pop" Scritti Politti was this reconciliation? Or if what we are witnessing, as the divide between music and text, indicates the beginning of a renunciation—conscious or not—of Gartside's political and philosophical convictions?

By the end of the portion of "Scritto's Republic" that is visible on the EP sleeve, the analysis takes a Lacanian turn. Language is identified as the culprit (or perhaps as merely culpable), obscuring, in the pronoun "I," the individuality of the subject to whom it refers, while also trapping speakers and writers and readers in narrow channels of experience and expression.

> Language pre-exists our entry into it and defines what is normal and represses that which will not or cannot be covered or developed by its framework. . . . To leave speech and language uninterrupted is to submit to the cultural order by which sexuality, thought etc. is regulated.

The text ends abruptly and tantalizingly, in mid-sentence, just as it begins to suggest a rapprochement between language's carceral impulses and rock and roll's extra-linguicity:

> There is a difficulty for productive language in beat music where semiotic instability is a norm, is style, but . . . and it was a big but

We might understand this merely as the end of this page (p. 180) with the sentence continuing on the next, inaccessible page. But, of course, this is not an image of an actual book. There is no reason to believe that there is, in fact, a page 181. What we are presented with is an artifact in its entirety. There is no before or after of this text, only what is printed on the EP sleeve. The mid-sentence breaking of the text is a performance of the kind of interruption that constitutes what the text refers to as the refusal to "submit to the cultural order by which sexuality, thought etc. is regulated." Gartside already has doubts about systems of thought and their tendency to regulate. In a sense we can begin to hear Scritti Politti moving past a music that states and performs its anti-hegemonic positions and toward a music that leverages the potency of pop forms to engage experiences beyond the reach of language and theory. We can, in a sense, already see them performing "Wood Beez" on *Top of the Pops* five years later. We can also see and hear "Wood Beez" retrospectively, as filtered through the past, inflected by the text of the Peel Session EP, the trace of each in the other. This is how time functions in our reception of works of art. Each moment of encounter is not insulated from those which precede it. Nor are such moments insulated from those which follow. What we think of as perception is continually updated and reformulated based on subsequent experience.

So what we read and hear in the difference between 1979 and 1984 Scritti Politti is not just a movement from the fringes to the mainstream. In the ensuing years, Gartside has come to doubt the signifying efficacy of words, theoretical positions, and formal, musical gestures. By 1984, Gartside is placing his faith in the ability of musical expression to circumvent linguistic regulation. What Gartside seems to believe is that the explicit declarations and explanations of songs like "Messthetics" and "Hegemony" and of texts like *Scritto's Republic* annul themselves to a significant extent in their own exposition.

At the moment that Scritto's text breaks off, we are confronted by what at first seems like a random, incidental, or extraneous imposition of unrelated information. The bottom of page 180 includes a table, breaking down the words of two related sentences into their parts of speech, demonstrating substitutions along the paradigmatic axis. The sentences include references to "these boys," or the substitutions, "some men," "this boy," and "a man." These subjects then either walk home, away, or out (Figure 9.3).

We might be tempted to read this as an announcement of Gartside's intentions as he begins to walk away from the squat and his principled isolation. Still, this

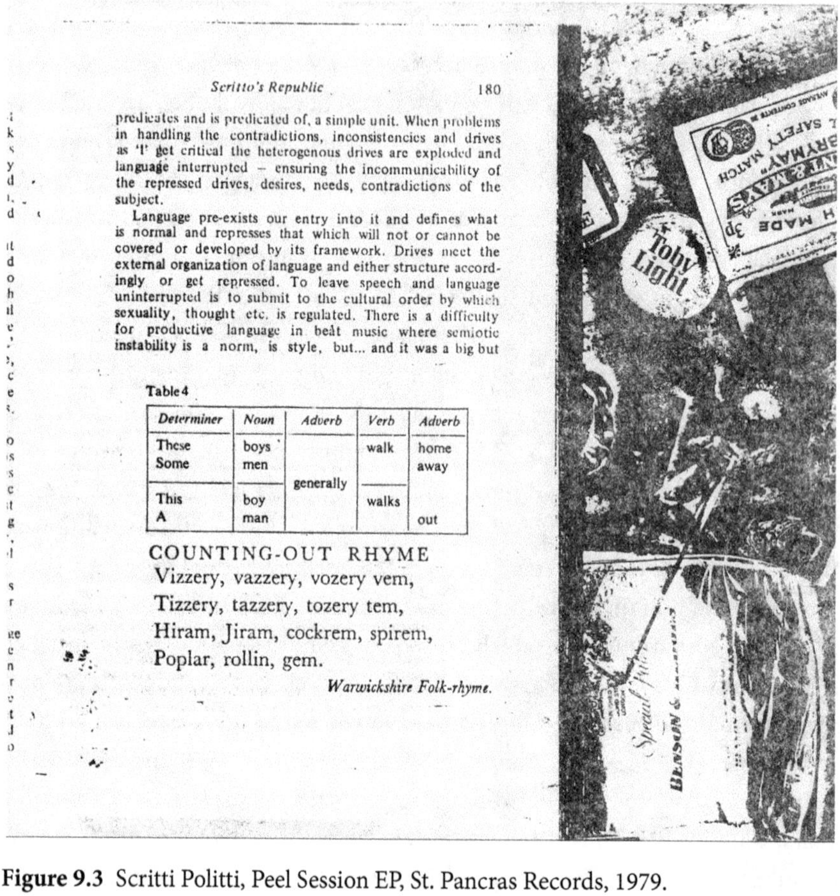

*Scritto's Republic* 180

predicates and is predicated of, a simple unit. When problems in handling the contradictions, inconsistencies and drives as 'I' get critical the heterogenous drives are exploded and language interrupted – ensuring the incommunicability of the repressed drives, desires, needs, contradictions of the subject.

Language pre-exists our entry into it and defines what is normal and represses that which will not or cannot be covered or developed by its framework. Drives meet the external organization of language and either structure accordingly or get repressed. To leave speech and language uninterrupted is to submit to the cultural order by which sexuality, thought etc. is regulated. There is a difficulty for productive language in beàt music where semiotic instability is a norm, is style, but... and it was a big but

**Table 4**

| *Determiner* | *Noun* | *Adverb* | *Verb* | *Adverb* |
|---|---|---|---|---|
| These<br>Some | boys<br>men | generally | walk | home<br>away |
| This<br>A | boy<br>man | | walks | out |

COUNTING-OUT RHYME
Vizzery, vazzery, vozery vem,
Tizzery, tazzery, tozery tem,
Hiram, Jiram, cockrem, spirem,
Poplar, rollin, gem.

*Warwickshire Folk-rhyme.*



**Figure 9.3** Scritti Politti, Peel Session EP, St. Pancras Records, 1979.

impulse is subjected to the violence of language as a structuring restraint. The table performs the linguistic anxiety that plagues Gartside. Below the table is a "Counting Out Rhyme," identified as a Warwickshire Folk-rhyme. If the table demonstrates the straightjacketing restrictions of language, the "Counting Out Rhyme" giddily performs the freedom of nonsense. Remember that Gartside conceived of the name of the band itself as a collision of Gramscian signification and Little Richard-ian musical glossolalia such as "Tutti Frutti" which, as you will recall, begins: "A-wop-bom-a-loo-mop-a-lomp-bom-bom!" The table represents the rudiments of language as a semantic code. The rhyme represents the rudiments of language as a *non*-semantic code, but as nonetheless patterned and sonic: something like music. In the liner notes to the Peel Session EP, if not yet in the musical and lyrical construction of its songs, Gartside is no longer simply subverting the dual languages of music and lyric from within, as Scritti had done to this point. Instead he is looking for a way to circumvent language entirely, leveraging the non-semantic codes of nonsense, rhyme, and what he calls "beat music" to simultaneously subvert the cultural order imposed by language, to engage with a joy that Gartside has decided is external to language.

Whether we're talking about narrative structures, camera angles, harmonic systems, or brush strokes, artistic choices always relate to the history from which they emerge and respond to the events and conditions—artistic and otherwise— of their time of production. Those who see artistic practice as inexorably tied to contemporary social, political, and economic practices, tend to connect the codes of artistic production to the allowances and restrictions of the culture in which they are produced. By this account, we *learn*—how to see the paintings, how to read the novels, and how to hear the music of our time. This learning process involves the assimilation of the prevailing codes of our artistic moment. As Pierre Bourdieu notes, this doesn't mean we are necessarily aware of either the code or our decoding activity:

> Lovers of classical music may have neither awareness nor knowledge of the laws obeyed by the sound-making art to which they are accustomed, but their auditive education is such that, having heard a dominant chord, they are induced urgently to await the tonic which seems to him the "natural" resolution of this chord, and they have difficulty in apprehending the internal coherence of music founded on other principles. (Bourdieu 227–8)

Bourdieu is actually under-reporting the extent of the coding at play. Describing the listener who, having heard a dominant chord, urgently awaits the tonic which seems the "natural" resolution of this chord, Bourdieu omits crucial information. What are we listening to? Would this be as true for Schoenberg as it is for Black Sabbath? When we hear (or think we hear) a dominant chord in Nancarrow or Merzbow, is the tonic the *last* thing we urgently await? I don't point this out in order to provincialize Bourdieu's observation, but on the contrary, to expand it.

The code is not limited to the formal arrangement of units within the work. This arrangement could be said to be one code among many at play in the composition and reception of the work of art. But as we quickly see when testing Bourdieu's example against particular music, there is a second code that is just as crucial. This code extends beyond the work at hand. It consists of the tendencies of other works by the same artist, by the relation of this artist's work to tendencies in the work of other artists. But even these codes are subject to another overlaid code: that of the acceptance, rejection, or adaptation of gestures; quotations; adoptions of structures and styles. All music partakes of these practices. As Carl Sagan once said, "If you wish to make an apple pie from scratch, you must first invent the universe." No songwriter invented the idea of "song" from whole cloth. The act of borrowing forms and approaches encodes a relationship to the appropriated "original." This, too, must be decoded in order to thoroughly "read" the work. Green Gartside was well aware of the origami-like nature of coding and decoding a song. As he told the New Music Express in 1982:

> In terms of readings or writings then a song is as closed or as exploded as you or I wish to make them, which isn't to reduce it to some horrible, anarchic, endless relativism. (Gartside, quoted in Bohn NME 1982)

What's often mistaken for relativism is actually this deeply complicated overlay of codes. We do not listen simply to the sound, we do not listen simply with our ears. Instead, we listen to the overlay of codes and contexts that license and legitimate the sound to function in certain ways and to mean certain things to certain audiences in certain places at certain times.

Probably, the most productive way to hear Scritti Politti's work in the 1980s, despite Green Gartside's avowed intentions, is as something still in thrall to the examples of Art & Language. We can listen to Scritti Politti in the 1980s as "conceptual," in a particular sense of that term. The songs work best when we are mindful—or earful—of their supplements. As an integrated construct— songs, images, record sleeves, interviews, the band's history—Scritti Politti communicates intentions and formulates meanings that are not apparent at first listen. As slick as Scritti Politti's music gets, it is never slippery enough to fully evade the grasp of its intertextuality and its *parerga*. The most interesting meanings generated, or acquired, by the music, arrive via this dispersed interaction with context. While Gartside may have turned his back on the lessons of Art & Language and of conceptual art more broadly, the extrinsic construction of meaning is not something the artist can accept or reject. All aesthetics is messthetics. So, you see, we're back where we, and Scritti Politti, started.

But if this dispersed, contextual, *parergonal* network of factors remains dispersed, then it remains elusive, too diffuse to be assigned an ontology such as "song." In order for us to recognize it, to analyze it, to talk about it, it must coalesce somewhere. It must organize itself around an absence that designates the common ground of the network. And that's why the "song" exists: to initiate the conversation. The simple noun doesn't frame a simple thing that holds still for the illumination of the spotlight. Instead, it leaks into the shallows, dispersed, and incoherent. We are still the cameras, the microphones. We need to "pick it up," record it. In multiple senses of the word, we must "produce" it or *co-produce* it with the times and places in which it is made and received, with all its adjacencies, histories, gifts given and received. In an interview, in 1985, Gartside speaks about another song on *Cupid and Psyche 85*, conceding that the song must accomplish its work, generate its meaning, as a co-production.

> Obviously, I couldn't make that point in a three minute pop song. All I could do was allude to it and hope that someone like you would happen along me and say that's a stupid fucking lyric. (Martin)

# 10

# Video Killed the Radio Star

"We're using up primetime." These are the first words uttered by Ronald Reagan after being officially nominated in 1980, as the Republican Party candidate for president of the United States. They come a full minute before the primetime-stealing applause dies down enough for Reagan to begin his scripted remarks: "Well, the first thrill tonight, was to find myself, for the first time in a long time, in a movie on primetime" ("Ronald Reagan's Acceptance Speech"). Had there been any doubt that for Reagan and his handlers his campaign was predicated on Reagan's familiarity with the camera and the screen—on viewers' familiarity with him on their screens—these words openly dispel such doubt. By 1980, the screen had accumulated a kind of critical mass of meaningfulness and gravity in the American psyche. So much so that a face could make the easy transition from movies and TV to the presidency without having to make any effort to conceal the basis of the transition. Reagan could play the role of the man playing the role of the presidential candidate and then the president, donning the role before our very eyes, narrating the dissemblance as it was constructed before and for the cameras.

And while Reagan is commonly remembered as the "movie star President," the truth is that he ingratiated himself to those who would later vote for him on the small screens in their living rooms. In 1954, Reagan became the "program supervisor," host, and occasional actor for *General Electric Television Theater*, an established but under-performing anthology series on CBS" (Raphael 120). For eight years he appeared weekly as a combination of fatherly host, pitchman, and spirit guide to the ease of modern living with the assistance of General Electric's array of labor-saving devices for the home. Reagan undoubtedly served the interests of the GE brand by demonstrating the benefits of what became known in real estate patois as "all mod cons": the dishwasher, the electric range, flexible domestic lighting, washer, dryer, and, implicitly, the very television upon which Reagan's face appeared. But there is little doubt that GE served Reagan's interests just as powerfully. It's unlikely at the time that either party understood how, or even that, this was happening. But as Reagan became an affable weekly presence in homes throughout America, as he established his trustworthiness and likeability, as he built an association between himself and the advantages of modern living, technology, comfort, and domestic harmony, he cultivated a relationship between himself, the camera, and the viewer that would not only serve but generate his political ambitions.

In 1984, his re-nomination a foregone conclusion, Reagan made his first convention appearance on a giant screen, looming above both the proceedings and his wife, Nancy, as she stood on the convention stage, waving adoringly at her husband. President Reagan appeared not to have a care in the world, leaning back in a casual white shirt, unbuttoned at the collar. He would deliver his acceptance speech in person later that evening. But this first glimpse of the man was staged to convey him as relaxed and thoroughly in control; Nancy's adoration clearly intended as a synecdochic stand-in for the adoration of a besotted party.

Statistics paint a telling picture of the role of television in American life. It is estimated that in 1947, there were approximately 14,000 TV sets in the United States. But in 1952,

> after the FCC lifted its four-year freeze on licensing new stations stores selling televisions began opening at the rate of a thousand a month. By 1954, the year Reagan began as host, the number of televisions had more than doubled to almost 32 million. By the time Reagan left the show in 1962, television was in 90 percent of American homes, the average American watched five hours of television per day. (Raphael 127)

Meanwhile, a more qualitative picture is painted by the trajectory of Ronald Reagan from afterthought movie actor to steadfast confidant of American domestic life. Four years after leaving the GE TV Theater in 1962, he parlayed his television-honed image into a successful run for governor of California. By 1980 he had learned to run a political campaign like a brand campaign. As Tim Raphael puts it, "Reagan's performance was a product launch designed to dazzle the gathered delegates and the consumers watching on TV with the new media campaign for the revamped product line that would be marketed through the Reagan brand" (Raphael 114). Reagan's handlers, too, understood how to play to the camera.

According to Donald Regan, Secretary of the Treasury and subsequently [Michael] Deaver's successor as [Reagan's] Chief of Staff, Deaver "designed each presidential action as a one-minute or two-minute spot on the evening news" and "conceived every presidential appearance in terms of camera angles." (quoted in Raphael, 118)

Contemporaneously, with Reagan's ascension in the 1980s, the TV screen became an even more ubiquitous and multifaceted element in modern life. No longer was television merely the home of thirty-minute sitcoms, news programs, sportscasts, and game shows. The 1980s ushered in the era of infotainment: advertising masquerading as entertainment programming, entertainment used to smuggle advertising (product placement) or ideological content into American leisure time. In 1983, for instance, one could tune in to anti-drug messaging on *Diff'rent Strokes* ("The Reporter" episode) and a nuclear war cautionary tale in the form of the made-for-TV-movie, *The Day After.*

Two years prior, in 1981, popular music's relation to television—indeed to the moving image writ large—changed radically and irrevocably. MTV (Music Television) launched that August as a 24-hour infotainment network for the product known as rock and roll. The ever-present MTV theme song was a bash of tightly compressed power chords and hyper-paced flams and drum fills touting nothing so much as a kind of erector set version of rock and roll, clumsy and rigid, built of the genre's conventional materials, bearing a clear resemblance to the real thing, but reduced to boilerplate geometries, fret squeals, and tom rolls straight out of an Aaron Spelling casting call for the part, "Rock Band." The theme song set the stage, but also the style, of MTV, announcing a format equal parts advertisement for music and music itself. The product functioned simultaneously as the thing being sold and the thing doing the selling. In this respect, it followed in the footsteps of Ronald Reagan building his brand by being his brand on *GE TV Theater.* As quickly as MTV rippled inward through the music industry, it rippled outward into other industries, becoming one of the brands that marked the 1980s, writing the playbook for how to build and be a brand.

Images of brands were ubiquitous in the 1980s. Brand logos emerged from the inside of clothing to advertise the wearer's status and the company's image. Corporate sponsorship branded the built environment from cityscapes to sports stadiums, cultural venues to schools. In the music industry, concert tours were opportunities for what the somnipractors termed "live-action advertising," and MTV became the paradigm for fully branded media integration. (Raphael 114)

The term "sominpractor" is borrowed from Gary Willis, who uses it to characterize Reagan as a figure capable of arranging and directing other people's dreams. The music videos of the 1980s also engage the unconscious. By cutting rapidly among images appropriated from fine and pop sources, playing a game of cultural free association without regard to history, context, or juxtaposition, videos drop little packages of collective memory like breadcrumbs meant to lead us to the witch's house. As *New York Times* music critic Jon Pareles observed at the end of the decade,

> music video directors have riffled through and parodied a huge stock of old movies, paintings, television series, advertisements and even other music videos. To academic observers, music video is quintessentially postmodern, drawing indiscriminately from high and low culture and past and present styles to create an all-encompassing, dizzyingly self-conscious pastiche. Ever-trendy MTV now calls its underground rock show "'Postmodern MTV'" (Pareles)

When signifiers are detached from their signifieds they can be reassigned at random by subsequent usage. *Birth of a Nation* or *Triumph of the Will* can be reappropriated as markers of style, stripped of their original intentions and their abhorrent history. MTV and Reagan are twinned not only as somnipractors of the 1980s but also in their relation to signs. Both raid the past to rescue, not so much artifacts of the actual, but staged impressions of how things were, and why. Equipping their cameras with rose-colored lenses, both MTV and Reagan cast their gazes backward at memories and montages constructed on the back lot or in the editing suite to convince us of some tragically lost idyll to which we once had access. As James W. Carey describes him, Reagan "is always waking up the past in order to sing it back to sleep."

> He is our first postmodern president—all surface and no depth. For all his championing of the rugged individualist and the traditional middle class, he is the archetype of the new middle class: the class that not only manipulates words, images, statistics, financial reports but believes there is nothing behind the symbols manipulated. Reagan is like the "bubble baby" that lived throughout his life in a clear, contained but totally artificial environment, never to rub up against the real world. (Carey)

MTV, of course, conjured a different past and different values. Reagan etched lapidary images of a 1940s bursting with national pride and domestic propriety (magically emptied of their equally paradigmatic Nazi terror, domestic racism, and atomic bombs). MTV projected pictures of the groovy afterglow of rock and roll liberation, tenderized by the ethical superiority of sympathy with the Civil Rights Movement and what would emerge as smug, Clintonian liberalism. "Watching MTV," writes Simon Reynolds, "it sometimes feels like you're living in a ghastly pastiche of the Sixties: a world where rock has won, has become the new mainstream, and thereby lost all meaning" (Reynolds). Reagan and MTV understand that a mythical past is a powerful nostrum. It heals, no matter what ails you. It heals even if nothing, in fact, ails you. The phrase "Make America Great Again"—uttered by Reagan in his time and weaponized by Trumpism in ours—relies on precisely this placebic delusion. Its aim is coalescence: to pull disparate elements and identities together into a comforting whole known as "us"; to put a frame around this fictional entity in order to clearly mark where it begins and ends.

> MTV . . . depends on outmoded figments and mythical unities like "youth," "rock," "the kids": the illusion that everybody's gathered in the same spot, looking to figurehead artists who will somehow "explain" them. (Reynolds)

Just as the frame gathers and contains, it also excludes. By definition, the frame initiates an equal and opposite disaggregation of "us" from a similarly unnatural and constructed "them."

This disaggregation is as old as evolution. The survival of the fittest depends on organisms pitting their own needs against the needs of others. The means of both parasite and predator are predicated on their separation from host and prey. But the particular forms of framing that concern us here are considerably more recent. One can begin to date them—and indeed many have—from the Quattrocento (the fifteenth century) in Italy. The discovery (or invention) of Renaissance perspective organizes continuous perceptual space and experience as a construct of discrete frames. Such organization works on both subject and object, on thing and sensation, that which is and that which is apprehended. It makes claims both ontological and epistemological. As Christopher Wood points out, "Perspective encourages a strange kind of identification of the art-object and the world-object. It is perspective, after all, that makes possible the metaphor of *Weltanschauung*, a worldview, in the first place" (Wood, in Panofsky 13). Perspective permits us to conceptualize the image—whether painting, screen, or simply vision—as a central projection mediating the relation between the object and the subject. The image is a floating screen of sorts from which perspectival lines draw back toward the object, culminating in the contours and surfaces of the thing, whether face, landscape, or fruit-filled bowl. On the other side of the image, receding in the opposite direction—verso to the object's recto—practically identical lines race toward convergence in the subject's eye (curiously modeled as singularly monocular).

The carving out of the "thing," safely framed as a monadic entity, is accomplished in multiple directions and in multiple ways. The grid that emerges through Alberti's veil divides continuous experience into framed units capable of being isolated from the holistic perception. The world can now be understood as a whole made of parts. More radically, sensation too, can be atomized; time and space emerge as constructs of individuated components, each separable and quantifiable. What's more, both object and subject are isolated as culminations of lines, which model an invisible, structuring force. Everything starts with the object and ends with the subject. Or it could be the other way around—it hardly matters. The point is that this is the very circuit of teleology; of alpha and omega, origin and destination, each dependent on, and foretold in, the other.

This schematic imposes objectivity on what is experienced, and often explained away, as subjective. There is an order to the universe, whether divine or natural. In this order, the beholder occupies one of two crucial positions. The thing beheld occupies the other. And via the image the relation between beholder and beheld is sanctified. As Martin Jay summarizes,

> Growing out of the late medieval fascination with the metaphysical implications of light—light as divine lux rather than perceived lumen—linear perspective came to symbolize a harmony between the mathematical regularities in optics and God's will. Even after the religious underpinnings of this equation were eroded, the favorable connotations surrounding the allegedly objective optical order remained powerfully in place. (Jay 6)

From these Albertian understandings, it is but a hop, skip, and a jump to Kant's disinterested subject whose judgment has the right to assume the assent of others based, as it is, on what Kant calls "universal subjective validity." This Enlightenment worldview—sometimes referred to as Cartesian perspectivalism—situates the subject as the intended receiver of the data of the world, the entity for whom such data exists and within whom it establishes the truth of its being. In *Perspective as Symbolic Form*, Erwin Panofsky notes that, under the regime of Cartesian perspectivalism, the organization of images serves the central figure of the beholding subject. This centrality determines not only how the image is constructed nor how it represents the "real thing" being depicted; it also provides the axis of the Weltanschauung, the worldview, that is both implicit and necessary to these acts of depiction and the relations generated between artist and object, audience and object, artist and audience. These relations are extrapolations and illustrations of existing hierarchies and circuits of interconnection available in the early stages of what we are identifying as modern life.

> Perspective subjects the artistic phenomenon to stable and even mathematically exact rules, but on the other hand, makes that phenomenon contingent upon human beings, indeed upon the individual: for these rules refer to the psychological and physical conditions of the visual impression, and the way they take effect is determined by the freely chosen position of a subjective "point of view." Thus the history of perspective may be understood with equal justice as a triumph of the distancing and objectifying sense of the real, and as a triumph of the distance-denying human struggle for control; it is as much a consolidation and systematization of the external world, as an extension of the domain of the self. (Panofsky, 67–8)

Once the Enlightenment subject is so situated, legal, political, and economic systems develop in response. For Adam Smith, when individual agents pursue their own self-interests—each imbricated in the vast network of others' interests—the result is the warp and woof of the fabric of society. Smith describes the collective push and pull of all this self-interest as an "invisible hand" turning the crankshafts of industry and commerce. The system is driven not by charity or cooperation but by the collisions, collusions, and compromises of multifarious self-interest.

> It is not from the benevolence of the butcher, the brewer, or the baker, that we expect our dinner, but from their regard to their own self-interest. We address ourselves, not to their humanity but to their self-love, and never talk to them of our own necessities but of their advantages. (Smith, Adam 1937)

It is hardly a coincidence that the House of Medici emerges in the same century, in the same city as many of the painters whose work depended on Cartesian perspectivalism for both their production and reception. This "way of seeing," to adopt John Berger's phrase, frames a fifteenth-century European conception of subject and object within which capitalism also emerges in nascent form. Both Smith's capitalism and Alberti's perspective revolve around the sovereign subject, arraying the world and all its objects as planets about a moon. The

Kantian notion of the ergon and its parerga—the work and its supplements—models itself on this self/other distinction; the segregation of the thing from its accessories and adjuncts, *everyotherthing* that accompanies the thing, reinforces its thingness, serves its self-serving demands, confirms the relation of the one to the many. Synchronous developments including Gutenberg's printing press and double-entry bookkeeping usher in the modern culture of the self. The word is privatized. Actuarial quantification of previously ephemeral experience transforms everything in its purview into a commodity-in-waiting. Thus, for Berger, the image as screen or window can be imagined in other ways.

> It is usually said that the oil painting in its frame is like an imaginary window open on to the world. This is roughly the tradition's own image of itself [. . .] if one studies the culture of the European oil painting as a whole, and if one leaves aside its own claims for itself, its model is not so much a framed window open on to the world as a safe let into the wall, a safe in which the visible has been deposited. (Berger 109)

If you're strictly here for the rock and roll, you're likely getting a little antsy at this point. So let me reassure you that we're still talking about rock and roll. Ultimately, I'm trying to make a case that I haven't seen made before about rock and roll as a counter-modernist project. This requires establishing what is meant here by "modernist," or in the less technical form I've been using, "modern life." I've strategically saved the heavier theorizing for this last chapter, after touching down on a series of case studies that trace the outline of my argument. The hope is that the significant claims have emerged from the particulars of the preceding chapters.

Rock and roll does not engage with theory in the same way that literature or painting does. Nobody digs the professor trying to prove that he "gets" Zeppelin or explaining a Thurston Moore feedback freak-out with Schenkerian pitch analysis. Rock and roll as a practice has not evolved in dialogue with theory. Instead, the first generation of rock journalists bent to the will of practice, forging a critical method that echoed the visceral, reason-evading workings of the form itself. Both rock and roll and the writing that analyzes and translates it often defy simple explanations, outplaying both syllogistic logic and what Roland Barthes famously called "the paradigm." Nevertheless, I am not so romantic as to contend that gut responses live exclusively and entirely in the gut. As we now know about the reality that informs this metaphor, our guts are home to myriad "outside" influences, so much so that to call them "outside"—or, for that matter, to call our insides "inside"—is to misfigure the relation of the thing to itself. Indeed, it belies a mistake in our thinking of "the thing" (it misthinks the things we call our bellies). It misunderstands anything we might take to be discrete and self-sufficient in its identity. This fantasy is my target. I aim to dismantle the stubborn insistence that we can put a frame around a thing, call it "it," and be done with it. Across the landscape of postwar modern life, this fantasy pervades: on supermarket shelves; in planned housing developments; in the conception of suburbia itself; in national, gender, and racial identities; in notions of the self (self-improvement, self-help, self-service); in demographics, charts, genres; in our understandings of the singular work of art, the film, the song.

Rock and roll is understood in these pages as an instrumental factor in a resistance mounted against this ontological fantasy of the "it." Ultimately, I'm forced to concede, not only did rock and roll fail to overthrow the regime of the self-identical, but—after a period of guerilla opposition—it capitulated, ultimately collaborating with the enemy. To the extent that we can understand rock and roll as participating for a time in a motley countercultural effort to revitalize experience as something alive, processual, and time-based, we can also understand television as both instrument of, and metaphor for, societal norms trapping experience in technological and ontological frames for easy identification and consumption. This is why so many of the stories told in the preceding chapters focus on rock and roll presented on or for television. In pointing a finger at the camera and the screen, it is not my intention to join the chorus of critics who see the "spectacle" (Guy Debord) or the "simulacrum" (Jean Baudrillard) as the controlling allegories of our time. My concerns about framing are not about the potential of the image to tragically replace the real. The real is no less constructed than any image of it. Rather, the question is whether experience (real or not) can be lived without reifying strictures, wrangling it into a discernible ontological form. This is not a critique of ocularcentrism, per se, or a "scopic regime" as we find in the work of various art historians, philosophers, and, more recently, theorists of sound.[1] Nor am I partaking of the 100-year-old debate around the over-identification or alienation of the viewer of the image as engaged by—among others—Viktor Shklovsky and Bertolt Brecht, Walter Benjamin, Christian Metz, and Jacques Rancière. There should certainly be no confusing this jeremiad with a psychoanalytic critique of the castration inherent to the image. Last, on the list of what-this-is-nots: a critique

---

[1] See, for example, a survey of such critiques in Martin Jay. *Downcast Eyes: The Denigration of Vision in Twentieth-Century French Thought*, University of California Press, 1993.

of Cartesian perspectivalism. What is at stake in the preceding pages and the few that follow is not about the conventions of perspective within a picture. Rather, what I offer is an ontological argument, focused on the worldview of which Renaissance perspective is product and exemplar. It is an argument about the framing of the image as a discrete thing. It makes no difference if the image is figurative or abstract, photographic or fabulist. The frame is what bestows upon its contents a certain thingness and a thingly certainty. There is no doubt that any characterization of an object has consequences for the subject who beholds it. How a "thing" is defined (which things qualify as "things") has significant implications for both individual and collective identities. The reader is certainly encouraged to unreservedly consider such consequences. In the end, this is an argument about the formation of a modern (if not properly "modernist") ontology of "the thing" that undergirds—especially in America, but also in American influence elsewhere—postwar consumer culture, conceptions of housing and autonomous lives lived therein, formalisms, and subjectivities.

It is also, throughout, an argument about rock and roll. But in order to be about rock and roll, it must first/also be about everything else. Perhaps to truly be about rock and roll, it must not be about rock and roll. Looking back over the preceding pages we're entitled to entertain such a thought: maybe it's not.

The first song aired on MTV was not commissioned by the network. Yet it's hard to imagine a better anthem for MTV, for music videos in general, indeed for the dawn of the 1980s. The Buggles' "Video Killed the Radio Star" is a succinct encomium to the triumph of the image. The song was written by Bruce Woolley and the two Buggles, Trevor Horn, and Geoff Downes. It's instructive to learn that a few months prior to the release of the Buggles' version, the song was released by Woolley's band, whose name—the Camera Club—is almost too good to be true. The effect is magnified when one also considers that Horn and Downes improbably joined the prog rock band, Yes, in 1980, producing the album *Drama*, which included the song "Into the Lens"—the refrain of which, "I am a camera," is sung no fewer than eighteen times —and that when Horn left the band in 1981, the remaining members regrouped, with Horn now in the producer's chair, under the name Cinema. (Commercial forces pressured them to drop this name and re-adopt the Yes moniker for the album that yielded the number one hit "Owner of a Lonely Heart.")

But it was the Buggles who made "Video Killed the Radio Star" famous and established it as the bearer of the video music standard. The song garnered the top chart position in sixteen countries including the UK, Australia, and Japan and landed in the top 10 in a handful more. The video for the song begins with a shot of a silent movie moon reminiscent of the Lumiere Brothers. The camera zooms out to reveal a mylar sheet rippling like ocean waves below the moon. The camera then tilts down to show a young girl, perhaps five or six, tuning the Bakelite knobs of a 1940s RCA radio. A high-contrast black-and-white image of singer Trevor Horn is superimposed over the scene. Horn leans in from the left in glasses and a tuxedo. To signify the past and invoke a nostalgia that may (or may not) be ironic, Horn holds a Sure 55S microphone, famously used by Elvis and countless 1940s and 1950s crooners. The song bubbles with pop ebullience while also adopting a machinic rigidity in its rhythms and staccato chords. Horn's vocal delivery minimizes any overtly emotive humanness, artificially emphasizing each syllable as he sings, "They took the credit for your second symph-oh-ny, rewritten by machine on new tech-nol-oh-gy." The vocals are severely compressed and equalized to emphasize midrange frequencies while removing the warmth of lower frequencies, mimicking the sound of a telephonic voice or one recorded or broadcast in some never-quite-actual technological past.

The song makes a timid effort at "man-machine" music as introduced by artists including Kraftwerk, Giorgio Moroder, Tangerine Dream, Herbie Hancock, and the Belleville Three (Juan Atkins, Kevin Saunderson, and Derrick May). But, unwilling to fully discard their musical humanity in favor of robot sensibilities, The Buggles retain a pop sweetness that allowed the song to succeed as it did. In addition to announcing the music video era and the ascendancy of MTV, the lyrics can also be understood as responding to the picturization of modern life. As Horn sings, this is not a phenomenon that is limited to advertising or television. The song's bridge locates it "in my mind and in my car." The world is filtered through a pictorial sensibility, invading human consciousness and our most prevalent technologies. This transformation is not a fad or a phase. The genie won't consent to return to the bottle.

> We can't rewind, we've gone too far
> Pictures came and broke your heart
> Put the blame on VCR
> (The Buggles)

Let's talk about gobbing. In the mid-1970s in London, audiences spat on performers. This was not an act of rejection, exactly. Rather it was a kind of rejection-solidarity. Gobbing was a way of acknowledging that the performers were part of Punk's countercultural rejection of the mainstream and that they—the gobbers, the audience—were part of it too. In a sense gobbing is a very real, very embodied way to interact with someone else, as you extract a bit of something from inside of you and cast it upon them. Sharing is caring. You're sharing your condition—societal, biological, emotional. Of course, if you've got a cold (or something worse), you're sharing that too. Gobbing was an expression of frustration with the frames that kids felt so palpably. The "fourth wall," dividing performer and audience, was exposed as nothing more than a convention, an artificial definition of roles based on one particular worldview. The division can be breached from either side: Iggy wading into the crowd, or the crowd dousing the Sex Pistols in spit. Both the proscenium arch and the TV screen prove to be flawed vehicles of conveyance for the corporeal, temporal, situational experience of the best rock and roll.

In 1978, manager Malcolm McLaren arranged a Sex Pistols' tour of the United States. Rather than parlaying the Pistols' notoriety and notoriousness into big, established venues in major cities, McLaren booked off-the-beaten-path honkytonks and ballrooms across the South: Atlanta, Memphis, San Antonio, Baton Rouge, Dallas, and Tulsa. While the audience-culture they confronted on the US tour was very different from the UK Punk scene, these rooms would not have been completely alien to the Sex Pistols. They were compact and sweaty, with low stages that allowed eye-to-eye contact with the audience. But when the tour closed at Winterland in San Francisco in January 1978, things were different. This was by far the largest venue and San Francisco was the biggest, most cosmopolitan city on the itinerary. At Winterland, the stage lifted the band above the audience. The venue had been one of the epicenters of the Bay Area flower power culture, hosting concerts by the Jefferson Airplane, Quicksilver Messenger Service, the Grateful Dead, Big Brother and the Holding Company, Moby Grape, the Chambers Brothers, and the Byrds. They also hosted out-of-town bands expanding the parameters of psychedelic rock: Pink Floyd, Procul Harum, the Mothers of Invention, the Doors, the Who, Cream, and Traffic. By the time of the Sex Pistols' gig, rock and touring were clearly established as industries and Winterland was one of the cogs of the North American machine. It catered not to a particular scene or style but to the booming business of rock and roll. The three shows that followed the Sex Pistols' appearance were headlined by Styx, Charlie Daniels, and Mahogany Rush.

The Pistols would have been out of their element at Winterland. Butterflies in pack ice. There would have been the kinds of mismatches that a good band can sometimes overcome: an audience unfamiliar with their sound and swagger, skeptical of what the band represents. They would have found themselves in a city whose identity was still in the thrall of the very failed utopian idealism against which the Pistols, as a proposition, as an ideology, stood. It would be another twenty years—1998, when Larry Page and Sergey Brin founded Google in Menlo Park—before the phrase "no future" would acquire similar resonance in the Bay Area. But the Pistols also faced tangible material obstacles. Perched in rock star position, sophisticated lighting rigs trained upon their pockmarked skin, a sweeping balcony spanning the entirety of the horseshoe room. Just fourteen months prior, the Band had held their farewell bacchanal, The Last Waltz, at Winterland with illustrious guests including Muddy Waters, Joni Mitchell, Neil Young, and Bob Dylan. This was not the level playing field in which the Pistols made their reputation. It was not the kind of room in which gobbing would or should happen. Johnny Rotten could not look straight ahead on even footing into a sea of eyes, each pair just as alienated, disturbed, angry, and desperate as his. The Winterland stage was not a mirror in which the audience could see themselves. This was a stage where rock concerts—not Punk shows—happened. So when a fan climbs up onto the stage after the second song, "I Wanna Be Me," he makes no effort to approach—never mind confront—anyone in the band. He raises his hands in apparent victory, like a fan rushing onto the field at a baseball game. The goal is merely to make it to the sanctified space, not to do anything once there. A pair of security personnel escort him gently off to the wings as if he were an elderly customer who'd accidentally wandered through an "Employees Only" door. Later, just before they start "EMI," putting a fine point on the whole spectacle, Rotten complains about the nature of the items being hurled on stage. Paul Cook shouts, "give us a hundred dollar bill, you cocksuckers!" Rotten suggests an alternative, "cameras? Can we have a couple of cameras?" All of this concocted, it would seem, for the lucre and the lens (Sex Pistols, "The Sex Pistols - Full Concert . . ").

This, of course, is the same infamous show in which the Sex Pistols imploded. During the encore, a cover of the Stooges' "No Fun," Rotten turns the lyrics inward directing the refrain, like little detonations, at the interior walls of the cage/penthouse/asylum they'd fashioned for themselves. (Although we must agree—otherwise we've both wasted our time traveling this far together in the confines of this book—that they didn't really construct it for themselves. Nor did McLaren set them up in this luxury condo in the collective consciousness. It was in fact the collective that summoned them, demanded them, housed them/trapped them—however briefly—in their gilded rubber room. It was the particular place and the particular time that necessitated a response and to which the Pistols responded.) "This is no fun," bellows Lydon in a voice that distances itself from the shrieking caterwaul that Rotten had injected forcibly into the mind's ear of every Briton from prepubescent punks in Preston to Parliamentarians in Plymouth. This is the show that ends with Rotten crouched on the stage, bemused, and disinterested, laughing at himself and at everything he's been party to, "a-ha-ha! Ever get the feeling you've been cheated?" he asks, rhetorically, I guess. This is the show during which Rotten realizes there really was no future for the Sex Pistols. From there on out it would have been bigger stages, bigger audiences, press and punters inured to the Pistols' lashings, until they became mere schtick; camp and cant; canned and stocked like soup, like soap. This is the night that Johnny Rotten quit.

Two-and-a-half years later, in May of 1980, this same Johnny—now Lydon (his given name)—would appear on American TV screens from coast to coast with his band Public Image Ltd. ABC's *American Bandstand* was unlike the BBC's *Top of the Pops*. An artist didn't necessarily need a hit to appear. No doubt, it was Lydon's lingering Sex Pistols notoriety that earned PiL their invitation. The album they were promoting, 1979's *Metal Box*, is their musical pinnacle (although the next one, 1981's *Flowers of Romance*, has its own distinct merits). The appearance on *American Bandstand*, however, may better encapsulate Lydon's position in the cultural firmament of the early 1980s than anything else. Here, we witness—through the lens of the camera, the network, the broadcast, the screens of our metal boxes—Lydon embracing the very rock star trappings he'd rejected from the stage of Winterland. At the same time, we see him undermining the format and conventions of the program so severely that for the viewer in 1980 and even for us now, it is difficult to come to grips precisely with how we are supposed to consume this transmitted product, this product of transmission. Like *Top of the Pops*, bands on the show mimed and lip synched to recordings. In the interests of the frames that segment the temporal flow of network TV, *American Bandstand*'s producers took the liberty of editing the two songs that the band would play, "Poptones" and "Careering." Lydon felt that the edits had altered the cues that would have allowed him to anticipate his points of entry into the song, leaving him unable to successfully maintain the illusion of performance. One suspects that for Lydon there may have been other things that attracted him to the notion of disregarding the pretense altogether.

In either case, the broadcast stands as a singularly perverse moment of televised music. After Dick Clark's generous introduction, the song starts, as it does on the album, with the sound of audio tape engaging mid-performance.

Needless to say, this is not how the start of an actual performance would sound. From the get-go the veil is already pulled aside. The first shot is of the band—Keith Levene on guitar, Jah Wobble on bass, and Martin Atkins on drums—looking as if, perhaps, despite the tapehead tell, they might in fact be making the dubby, off-kilter racket. Next, we see Lydon, née Rotten, sitting on the glossy white steps of *Bandstand's* stage, glitzy, showtime lights, slightly out of focus, behind him. The pose is similar to the one he assumes at the close of the Winterland show: low to the ground, bemused, perusing the scene as if barely part of it. He is no longer festooned in the Punk regalia of rent linen and safety pins. Instead he wears a white suit and colorful shirt open at the collar. He rises and immediately waves his arm in a "come on" gesture, encouraging the audience toward him, toward the stage. He walks to the front row of seats and, palm up, entreats the assembled to rise. They oblige. The singing has begun on the pre-recorded track, but Lydon has yet to mouth a syllable, nor even to bring the microphone in the direction of his lips (Figure 10.1).

He walks into the audience, moving toward the back/top of the bleachered seating. Like Iggy Pop in Cincinnati, Lydon enters his audience, loses himself among them. But because this situation has been carefully designed for the benefit of the cameras—of which there are many—the loss is only partial. Wherever Lydon goes, there's a camera waiting. Handheld cameras follow him as he skips and dances through the field of flowers. From the back of the audience he begins to push. Audience members respond by taking a few steps down closer to the stage. They part as Lydon moves through them. When he reaches the bottom, he grabs the hand of one woman in a red and white striped,

**Figure 10.1** John Lydon, of Public Image Ltd., on *American Bandstand*, May 17, 1980.

"Where's Waldo?" sweater and pulls her up onto the stage. He returns to the crowd and grabs two more—a woman in a bright yellow sweater and a small woman wearing, inexplicably, a St. Louis Cardinals' baseball uniform: hat, jersey, stirrup pants, and high baseball socks. (Why did someone wear this to a taping of *American Bandstand*? The Cards finished fourth in the NL East that year.) The audience is catching on. All Lydon has to do with the next pair of punters is take their hands and guide them past him toward the stage like a child hand-paddling a small raft. He starts directing people toward the stage, encouraging them with gentle shoves. The stage now filled by the audience, Lydon merely paces among them, only occasionally singing along. Impassively, the band plays it straight. Lydon leads a couple up the stairs to a raised dance platform. He leans back against the railing, watching them dance, reversing the roles and the relationship that they and the show always take for granted.

For stretches of the second song, "Careering," the cameras lose momentary sight of Lydon as he gallops among the throng now occupying the stage. It's a top-down coup. When the camera can find Lydon, he's often partially obscured by someone dancing in the foreground. On a few occasions the broadcast cuts to a wideshot showing the whole scene and then zooms in on Lydon, picking him out cinematically from amidst the pulsating mass. By this time, members of the band have traded instruments and Jah Wobble is bashing the drums spasmodically, out of time with the still-rolling song. The handheld camera catches up with Lydon dancing casually toward the rear of the stage. He leans in and the camera suddenly rotates away from him, coming to a stop with a dancer centered in the frame. Lydon has apparently pushed the camera, redirecting its gaze onto someone else. With a minute and a half left in "Careering," Lydon hands his microphone to a member of the audience and points at him. The man holds the mic to his mouth and does what Lydon has steadfastly refused to do: he sings along, using his face and body to express investment in the music and words. Briefly, on the camera that is our visual surrogate, we catch a glimpse of the monitor of another camera, a frame within our frame. The device is momentarily bared. But the director calls out for another camera and dissimulation is restored.

The gasoline that burned beneath the Sex Pistols leaked not from Malcolm McLaren's imagination nor from what we might think of as a properly "political" motivation. It bubbled up from the sand tars of class resentment and from the stultifications of the postwar order. As frames went up around everything important—from detergents to politicians, refrigerators to rock stars—certain things were left out. Certain people, designated by class, education, gender, color, ethnicity, and sexual orientation, were left unframed, unrecognized, unincorporated. When he was Rotten, John Lydon understood that the citations of his work, his sources, the references upon which it was built had to represent this unframedness.

> In a weird way that whole persona of, say, Richard III helped when I joined the Sex Pistols—deformed, hilarious, grotesque. The Hunchback of Notre Dame is in there. And just bizarre characters that somehow or other, through all of their deformities, manage to achieve something. [. . .] I'd have to just pull things out from deep down inside. "Seventy six trombones to the hit parade." There's Arthur Askey in there. There's Ken Dodd—"we are the diddymen, we come from Knotty Ash." (Lydon in Temple)

Lydon looked nothing like, acted nothing like, the rock stars with whom we were familiar. He occupied the spotlight, held the microphone, not by divine right, but by accident, by lark. His position was temporary (no future) and transferable. And, of course, a dozen, a hundred, bands accepted the transfer avariciously.

By the time he was Lydon again, the means had changed. Estrangement doesn't remain strange for long. With Public Image Ltd., the music itself was strange: dark, dubby, and repetitive, lacking discernible chord structures and hooks; the vocals caterwauling aimlessly against the dislodged, unsettled racket. Declaring PiL "a company, simple, nothing to do with rock and roll, doo dah" ("Public Image Limited (John Lydon) on Tom Snyder 1980 Part 1"), Lydon leveraged his position on the platform to loosen the bolts of the platform, destabilize it, allow the rest of us outside the frame to see it for what it was: a platform stabilized with bolts. There is nothing natural about the frames with which we are presented, about the order they establish and preserve. The exposure of the artifice cannot be accomplished by the star within the frame. He must relinquish his frame and play the fool, speaking truth to his own power. Thus, on *American Bandstand*, Lydon relinquishes the bandstand, surrenders it to the punters.

Early on in this book, we find Lester Bangs asking "Who's the fool?" The answers scattered across these pages suggest that, now and then, rock and roll puts forward a fool who confounds the frame, who, in the words of Roland Barthes, "outplays the paradigm." In Cincinnati, Iggy Pop submerges himself in the crowd, making experience, rather than a show. He denies the cameras their quarry, confounding the media apparatus of modern life and leaving Jack Lescoulie no option but to cut to a "message." On *American Bandstand*, John Lydon refuses to participate in the puppet show, cutting the strings, granting life to the other puppets. The cameras give chase, pursuing the star in the white suit down the rabbit hole. As the-show-which-must-go-on goes on, the viewers are presented with something they didn't bargain for: a centerless spectacle, a non-performance, an exposé of the mechanics of televisual deceit. In the cases of both Pop and Lydon, we are confronted by the fool, the figure who is granted the exclusive right to speak truth to power, who under cover of foolishness escapes the consequences of leveling with the king.

In the estimation of Bangs, the figure of the fool is both what rock and roll needs and what makes it a curative for the sicknesses of the early 1970s. Hearkening back to the birth of hip culture described by Norman Mailer, Bangs sees the Stooges as offering a kind of attenuated vaccine, in which the disease is introduced in small doses in order to boost the culture's immunity.

> A lot of changes have gone down since Hip first hit the heartland. There's a new culture shaping up, and while it's certainly an improvement on the repressive society now nervously aging, there is a strong element of sickness in our new, amorphous institutions. The cure bears viruses of its own. The Stooges also carry a strong element of sickness in their music, a crazed quaking uncertainty, an errant foolishness that effectively mirrors the absurdity and desperation of the times, but I believe that they also carry a strong element of cure, a post-derangement sanity. (Bangs, 1987, 32)

The fool reflects the foolishness of the society back upon itself, initiating realization and response. By exposing the constructedness of its condition, the fool subverts the rationale that licenses the inevitability of modern life. The scales fall from the camera's eye. It casts its renewed electronic iris with incipient fervor upon the set, the stage, the marks to be hit, the direction (explicit and implicit), establishing the m.o. and the meaning of modern life.

> It takes courage to make a fool of yourself, to say, "See, this is all a sham, this whole show and all its floodlit drug-jacked realer-than-life trappings, and the fact that you are out there and I am up here means not the slightest thing." (Bangs, 1987, 36)

Ultimately, the fool doesn't fit in, doesn't figure into the schematic that guides the placement of the pieces that compose the machine; the pixels that comprise the picture. The fool is that speck, that smudge, that trace, which inhabits the frame without being assimilated by it. It cannot be assimilated because it does not submit to the prevailing order. Not that it necessarily or overtly resists, simply that there is no proper place for it.

Roland Barthes calls such a misfit "the Neutral." He capitalizes it. As Anca Parvulescu explains,

> The neutral is a "thing" (no qualifying adjective) that outplays, baffles, or dodges the "implacable binarism" of language as seen through Saussurian linguistics: in order to produce meaning, one is in the same breath choosing A and refusing B. The search here is for a "thing" that might suspend, thwart, or elude the paradigm, what Barthes calls its arrogance. (Parvulescu 32–3)

Barthes introduces the term in lectures he delivered at the College de France in the academic year 1977–8. He pursues a concept that he has flirted with throughout his immensely influential career. Elsewhere he has called it (or something like it): "degree zero," "the third meaning," "the obtuse," "the punctum." Once a leading proponent of semiotics and structuralism in the study of literature and culture, Barthes was vexed by the fleeting conviction that there were often (if not always) elements of the text that would not submit to systematic analysis; facets that could not be easily incorporated into the apparatus.

Against the overarching vision of thingness, in which the frame defines the contours of the thing, and everything within the frame contributes equally and seamlessly to the thing's identity, the Neutral is errant. It slips out of alignment; won't be subdued, won't click into place. The tricky thing is that you can't put your finger on it. The Neutral is not a thing. It refuses to be an it. Yet Barthes comes to see the Neutral not as an offshoot or a by-product of little consequence. "The Neutral doesn't refer to 'impressions' of grayness, or 'neutrality,' of indifference." For Barthes, the Neutral exists in "intense, strong, unprecedented states. 'To outplay the paradigm' is an ardent, burning activity" (Barthes, 7). The Neutral is that (not-)thing that we assume accountants don't get. Against the smugness of capitalist property, of accumulation for accumulation's sake, the Neutral is (or contains, or sparks) an opposing set of stakes: not smug, not self-justifying, not pompous, imperious, or proud. The Neutral reconciles. The Neutral confesses. The Neutral wears its inassimilability on its sleeve, like blood, like dirt from the graveside. In the Neutral (and perhaps nowhere else) we find

> the difference that separates the will-to-live from the will-to-possess: the will-to-live being then recognized as what transcends the will-to-possess, as the drifting far from arrogance. (Barthes, 14)

Barthes gives a name to the certitude of the frame. It is arrogance.

To oppose that certitude is an act of humility: humility as an act of protest. Rock and roll, for all its brashness, its cockiness, its braggadocio, can be humble. It can play the fool. In the best instances—the kind that this book has tried to capture—rock and roll infects the frame, like a computer virus, like termites. It undermines the frame and its arrogance. It leaves nothing (no thing) over which to obsess, to fetishize, to sell, or to sanctify. Granted, in nearly every example, there is a later stage in which the subversion is recuperated and reified; reinstated in the calcified order. Iggy in a Royal Caribbean Cruise Line commercial. The Velvet Underground as public radio bumper music. James Brown on the supermarket P. A. The Ramones taught to ten-year-olds at the School of Rock™. The Neutral has a short half-life and a shorter shelf-life. But it leaves a marker, a twinge of code in the runscript of modern life. It remains as a disturbance, or perhaps more precisely, as the condition of possibility for disturbance. It is a bump in the road. A red light amidst a string of greens. It is a "no" delivered just when we had every reason to expect a "yes."

> In the end, its essential form is a protestation; it consists of saying: it matters little to me to know if God exists or not; but what I know and will know to the end is that He shouldn't have simultaneously created love and death. The Neutral is this irreducible No: a No so to speak suspended in front of the hardenings of both faith and certitude and incorruptible by either one. (Barthes, 14)

It's inevitable. This account threatens to slip into romanticism. It practically must. In the end, this argument on behalf of rock and roll's place in postwar culture, positioning it as the site (or device) of the Neutral, refuser of the frame and its insistence on the thingness of both matter and ideas, is bound to slide back into the swamp of rockist self-assurance: a mysticism born of arrogance. I realize and am resigned. But if, in glimpses and pilfered impressions, tiny incessant scratchings against the doors we've been taught to keep shut, a familiar sensation rises along the ridges of your knuckles, in the crackly echo of a dusted-off memory, in the pang of a yearning that has yet to arrive; if you recognize the effects described herein, if you've felt them brush your cheek just before melting, then I've paid my debt to rock and roll.

There's little I can offer by way of conclusion. The refusal of the frame is equally the refusal of conclusion. Barthes saw this too. He knows he cannot capture the Neutral, stuff and mount it. No skin. Not a frame, but a skeleton, around and within which—over, under, and through—the organs, the nerves, the viscera are woven impermanently, fragilely. Escape and capture play to a draw. We build the skeleton from terms "in which the Neutral tinkles." So too here. Constructed with a selection of Barthes's terms: rock and roll as I have experienced it, as I understand it:

Benevolence
Weariness
Silence
Tact
Sleep
Affirmation
Anger
Consciousness
Rites
Conflict
Oscillation
Retreat
Intensities

And lastly, one of my own:

Not-death, for now.

# Acknowledgments

It is an acknowledgments commonplace to testify that no one writes a book alone. But that's a lie. Writing a book is a profoundly solitary task. The hours spent Tetrising words and ideas into complementary, adjacent shapes happen in the vacuum of space and time. Until it is finished, the book takes the form of a dream. And we all know that no one else is interested in the accounts of our dreams. Still, it is understood what authors mean when they claim that they didn't write their books alone. Writing unfolds according to a series of laws that the author did not write; forces social, genetic, and intellectual. As Roland Barthes put it:

> We know that a text does not consist of a line of words, releasing a single "theological" meaning (the "message" of the Author-God), but is a space of many dimensions, in which are wedded and contested various kinds of writing, no one of which is original: the text is a tissue of citations, resulting from the thousand sources of culture.

This book suffered through an extraordinarily long period of gestation. I could claim that it all began at the little book and record store in the Arcadian Shopping Center in Ossining, New York, when at age twelve I purchased—at the same time—my first two LPs: The Captain and Tenille's *Love Will Keep Us Together*, and Black Sabbath's *Sabbath Bloody Sabbath*. But this book truly began to coalesce—as a book—in 2011 when I taught a class about rock and roll, art, and culture at the School of the Museum of Fine Arts in Boston. The class has mutated a number of times, but is still taught, now at the School of the Art Institute of Chicago. Anyone who has taught will tell you that you don't really learn a subject until you teach it. And teaching this course has honed my relationship to the materials and ideas that now take book form. I was waiting for the right version of this book to emerge from thinking and teaching. Thus, I am indebted to the decade of students who have engaged, encouraged, and contested my take on rock and roll. If any of them is reading this now: hello! and thanks.

Listening is a craft. I took up the craft, as is the custom, in my teens when Brad Larrabee and I imbibed everything from the James Gang to the Grateful Dead; Alvin Lee, Pat Metheny, and the Cure, before eventually discovering Mission of Burma and realizing that there was indeed a world for us out there: smart, sardonic, angry, arty, and unlikely to end up on Don Kirshner's Rock Concert. I wouldn't be the listener nor indeed the person, I am without Brad's brilliant, critical, punny, camaraderie.

In college, my friend Joseph Chaves introduced me to a universe bordered by Television, Miles Davis, and Olivier Messiaen. I sold my Chicago and Steely Dan records and never looked back. The expansions that followed—of mind, of worldview, of courage, and of thought—have defined the concept of "taste" for me ever since.

As a musician, I could not have dreamed up a better collaborator than Michael Lenzi, who has pushed, pulled, understood, and trusted me through our myriad false starts, noble failures, and occasionally miraculous fumblings. Michael and I have spent countless hours making music together at the Plastic Skull, and even more talking about music at tables with glasses of beer in various states of depletion. The doing and the talking have always been inextricably intertwined for me. And Michael's twinned enthusiasm and skepticism about all things music have kept me more honest than I would have been without him. During the pandemic, starved for bonhomie and stimulation, Michael and I got together out of doors with bluetooth speakers (and more beer) to listen to music together and talk about how we hear it. We've been joined in this ritual by Seth Brodsky whose utterly brilliant and idiosyncratic takes on music amounted to an Einsteinian revolution for Michael and me. Until Brodsky, it was as if we'd been listening in mono. Brodsky is the most exacting and generous listener I know. That he balances these two qualities with such seeming effortlessness is a highwire act worthy of Philippe Petit. This book—or at least the best parts of it—have been tempered and tenderized by these prized, pandemic sessions with the incisive ears of Messrs. Lenzi and Brodsky. Thank you, my friends.

I lost my mother while writing this book. It is a loss from which I know I cannot recover. I count myself immensely fortunate to have shared not just my mother's life but also her death with my amazing siblings, Matthew and Rebecca. We have pulled more tightly together in her absence. A fact that would have made our mom very, very happy. Aside from the obvious—that I would not exist without her—I also know that I could never have written this book without my mother's love, her support, her parenting, her pride. More importantly, without her, I would never have become the kind of person who cares about the kinds of things that constitute this book. Without her now, I am diminished; the world is diminished. I miss her every single day.

Still, there is Jules and there is Noa. Whatever is beautiful and true in this world, whatever creates the palpable texture of worth, of knowing, of love and respect, it starts and ends with you. Nothing else matters. And now that the sequestering that this book required is done, I will prove this to be more than platitude. My loves, my alpha and omega, this book belongs to you, because I do and everything in me.

# Works Cited

Advisory Panel on White House Tapes, The. *The EOB Tape of June 20, 1972: Report on a Technical Investigation*, 1974.

Aitken, Jonathan. *Nixon: A Life*. Regnery Publishing, 1996.

Arrighi, Giovanni. *The Long Twentieth Century: Money, Power and the Origins of Our Times*. London: Verso, 2010.

Assayas, Olivier (director). *Carlos* (DVD). Criterion Collection, 2011.

Baldwin, James. "The Black Boy Looks at the White Boy" [1961]. In , edited by Toni Morrison. The Library of America, 1998, pp. 269–85.

Baldwin, James. Take This Hammer, KQED, 1963. https://diva.sfsu.edu/bundles/187041.

Bangs, Lester. "Astral Weeks: Van Morrison." In *Stranded: Rock and Roll for a Desert Island*, edited by Greil Marcus. Da Capo Press, 1979, pp. 178–87.

Bangs, Lester. "MC5: Kick Out The Jams." Rolling Stone, April 5, 1969. http://www.rocksbackpages.com.proxy.artic.edu/Library/Article/mc5-kick-out-the-jamsi (accessed February 9, 2021).

Bangs, Lester. "Of Pop and Pies and Fun: A Program for Mass Liberation in the Form of a Stooges Review, or, Who's the Fool?" [1970]. In *Psychotic Reactions and Carburetor Dung*, edited by Greil Marcus. Anchor Press, 1987, pp. 31–52.

Bangs, Lester. "Patti Smith's Top 40 Insurrection." *Phonograph Record Magazine*, May 1978. http://www.oceanstar.com/patti/crit/7805bang.htm

Bangs, Lester. "The Shaggs: Better Than the Beatles (and DNA, Too)." *Village Voice, The*, 1981. The Shaggs. Rock's Backpages. http://www.rocksbackpages.com.proxy.artic.edu/Library/Article/the-shaggs-better-than-the-beatles-and-dna-too (accessed January 20, 2021).

Barthes, Roland. *The Neutral: Lecture Course at the College de France (1977–1978)*. Translated by Rosalind Krauss and Denis Holier. Columbia University Press, 2007.

Barry, Robert. "MoMA Web Page for Inert Gas Series/Helium, Neon, Argon, Krypton, Xenon/From a Measured Volume to Indefinite Expansion." 1969. https://www.moma.org/collection/works/109710 (accessed February 4, 2021).

BBC. "Obituary: Hunter S. Thompson." February 21, 2005. http://news.bbc.co.uk/2/hi/entertainment/4283349.stm

Berryman, John. *The Dream Songs*. Farrar Straus and Giroux, 1991.

"Bob Dylan San Francisco Press Conference 1965." YouTube, https://www.youtube.com/watch?v=wPIS257TVoA (accessed March 1, 2021).

Bourdieu, Pierre. "A Sociological Theory of Art Perception." In *The Field of Cultural Production*. New York: Columbia University Press, 1993.

Broven, John. *Rhythm and Blues in New Orleans*. Pelican Publishing, 2016.

Brown, James. "Mother Popcorn." Music Scene [1969]. https://www.youtube.com/watch ?v=5eoSXpNZD9o (accessed March 3, 2021).

Bryson, Norman. *Vision and Painting: The Logic of the Gaze*. Yale University Press, 1983.

Buchloh, Benjamin. "From Gadget Video to Agit Video: Some Notes on Four Recent Video Works." *Art Journal* 45, no. 3 (Fall 1985): 217–27.

Burden, Chris. *Documentation of Selected Works 1971–74*. 1971–75, 34:38 min, color and b&w, sound.

Burke, Patrick. "Rock, Race, and Radicalism in the 1960s: The Rolling Stones, Black Power, and Godard's *One Plus One*." *Journal of Musicological Research* 29 (2010): 275–94.

Bustillos, Maria. "Lester Bangs: Truth Teller." The New Yorker, August 21, 2012. https:// www.newyorker.com/books/page-turner/lester-bangs-truth-teller

Butler, Judith, interviewed by Masha Gessen. The New Yorker, February 9, 2020. https:// www.newyorker.com/culture/the-new-yorker-interview/judith-butler-wants-us-to -reshape-our-rage

Carey, James W. "The Demagogue as Rabblesoother." *Illinois Issues*, 23, July 1987. https://www.lib.niu.edu/1987/ii870721.html

Cleaver, Eldridge. "Convalescence." In *Soul on Ice*. Ramparts Press, 1968.

Coon, Caroline. "Patti Smith: Punk Queen of Sheba." Melody Maker, 1977. http://www .rocksbackpages.com/Library/Article/patti-smith-punk-queen-of-sheba

Coon, Caroline Coon, Caroline and uncredited writer. "The Sex Pistols: Lou Reed Joins Pistols Furore." Melody Maker, 1977. http://www.rocksbackpages.com/Library/ Article/the-sex-pistols-lou-reed-joins-pistols-furore.

Cooper, Mark. "Scritti Politti: Suspicious Minds." Record Mirror, 1981. Scritti Politti. Rock's Backpages. http://www.rocksbackpages.com/Library/Article/scritti-politti -suspicious-minds.

Dargis, Manohla. "The Days, Nights and Years of the Jackal: The Tale of a Terrorist." The New York Times, October 14, 2010. https://www.nytimes.com/2010/10/15/movies /15carlos.html?ref=movies

Derrida, *Of Grammatology*. Trans. Gayatry Chakravorty Spivak. Johns Hopkins University Press, 1997 [originally published in French in 1967].

Dezeuze, Anna. "Meat Joy." *Art Monthly*, 257, June, 2002.

Didion, Joan. "Slouching Towards Bethlehem." Saturday Evening Post, September 23, 1967.

Du Bois, W.E.B. *Black Reconstruction in America*. Oxford University Press 2014 [originally published 1935].

Dunn, Christopher. *Brutality Garden: Tropicalia and the Emergence of a Brazilian Counterculture*. University of North Carolina Press, 2001.

Elshaw, Gary. "The Depiction of Late 1960's Counter Culture in Jean-Luc Godard's *One Plus One/Sympathy for the Devil*." 1998. http://elshaw.tripod.com/jlg/ OnePlusOne.htm

Eshun, Kodwo. *Dan Graham: Rock My Religion*. Afterall Books, 2012.

Foster, Hal. "Dan Graham: Whitney Museum of American Art." *Artforum*, October, 2009.

Franklin, Aretha. "Aretha Says She'll Go Angela's Bond If Permitted." *Jet*, December 3, 1970.

Fricke, David. *The Velvet Underground: Peel Slowly and See*, liner notes. Polydor, 1995.

Fried, Michael. "Art and Objecthood." *Artforum*, Summer 1967.

Godard, Jean-Luc (director), *One Plus One* (DVD). ABKCO Films, 1968.

Graham, Dan. *Rock My Religion*, Electronic Arts Intermix, 55:27 min, b&w and color, sound, 1983–84.

Graham, Dan. *Rock My Religion: Writings and Projects 1965–1980*. Edited by Brian Wallis. MIT Press, 1994.

Graham, Dan. "Sound is Material: Dan Graham in Conversation with Eric de Bruyn." *Grey Room* 17 (2004): 108–117.

Greenberg, Clement. "Modernist Painting" [1960]. In Francis Fascina and Charles Harrison (eds.), *Modern Art and Modernism: A Critical Anthology*. Harper and Row, 1982, pp. 5–10.

Harron, Mary. "The Lost History of the Velvet Underground: An interview with Sterling Morrison." *New Musical Express*, 1981. Velvet Underground. Rock's Backpages. http://www.rocksbackpages.com/Library/Article/the-lost-history-of-the-velvet-underground-an-interview-with-sterling-morrison.

Hinckle, Warren III and Sidney E. Zion. "Editorial." *Scanlan's Review* 1, no. 1 (March 1970): unpaginated.

Hobson, Laura Z. "As I Listened to Archie Say 'Hebe'. . ." The New York Times, September 12, 1971. https://www.nytimes.com/1971/09/12/archives/as-i-listened-to-archie-say-hebe-as-i-listened-to-archie-as-i.html (accessed March 10, 2021).

Hoffman, Abbie. *The Best of Abbie Hoffman*. Four Walls Eight Windows, 1989.

Hoffman, Abbie. *Soon to be a Major Motion Picture*. Perigee, 1980.

Jay, Martin. "Scopic Regimes of Modernity." In *Vision and Visuality: Dia Art Foundation Discussions in Contemporary Culture, Number 2*, edited by Hal Foster. Bay Press, 1988, pp. 3–23.

Jones, Amelia. "'Presence' in Absentia: Experiencing Performance as Documentation." *Art Journal* 56, no. 4 (1997): 11–18.

Jones, LeRoi. "The Changing Same." In *Black Music*. New York: Da Capo Press, 1998. [Originally published: 1967.]

Kant, Immanuel. *Critique of the Power of Judgment (The Cambridge Edition of the Works of Immanuel Kant)*, Edited by Paul Guyer, translated by Paul Guyer and Eric Matthews. Cambridge: Cambridge University Press, 2000.

Kendrick, Monica. "This Wreckage Was No Accident: The Complete *Fun House* Sessions." *The Chicago Reader*, July 13, 2000.

Kerner Commission, The. *Report Of The National Advisory Commission On Civil Disorders*. 1968.

King, Martin Luther Jr. "The Burning Truth In The South." *The Martin Luther King Jr. Papers Project* [originally published in *The Progressive*, May 1960].

Kimizuka, Masanori. "Historical Development of Magnetic Recording and Tape Recorder." *National Museum of Nature and Science* [Japan] *Survey Reports on the Systemization of Technologies*; Vol. 17, August, 2012.

Kramer, Hilton. "Art: Xeroxophilia Rages Out of Control." The New York Times, April 11, 1970.

Lethem, Jonathan. "The Genius of James Brown." *The Ecstasy of Influence: Nonfictions, etc.* Vintage, 2012.

Lyotard, Jean-François. "The Sublime and the Avant-Garde." In *The Lyotard Reader*, edited by Andrew Benjamin. Blackwell, 1989, pp. 196–211.

Mailer, Norman. "The White Negro." In *White Riot: Punk Rock and the Politics of Race*, edited by Stephen Duncombe and Maxwell Tremblay. Verso, 2011, pp. 18–23.

Marcus, Greil. *"Carlos:* What The Film Wanted." *Carlos* DVD booklet, 2010.

Marcus, Greil. *The Old Weird America: The World of Bob Dylan's Basement Tapes.* Picador, 2011. [Originally published in 1997 as *Invisible Republic.*]

Marcus, Greil. "Introduction to *The Stammering Century* by Gilbert Seldes." New York Review Books, 2012. https://greilmarcus.net/2014/11/21/introduction-to-gilbert -seldes-the-stammering-century-2012/

Marsh, Dave. "Patti Smith: Her Horses Got Wings, They Can Fly." Rolling Stone, 1976. Rock's Backpages. http://www.rocksbackpages.com/Library/Article/patti-smith-her -horses-got-wings-they-can-fly.

Martin, Gavin. "Scritti Politti: Psyched Out." *New Musical Express*, 1985. Rock's Backpages. http://www.rocksbackpages.com/Library/Article/scritti-politti-psyched-out

Marx, Karl. *Capital A Critique of Political Economy, Volume I Book One: The Process of Production of Capital.* Translated by Samuel Moore and Edward Aveling, edited by Friedrich Engels. German 1867, English 1887, Progress Publishers, Moscow, USSR.

Meltzer, Eve. "The Dream of the Information World." *Oxford Art Journal* 29, no. 1 (2006): 115–35.

Meltzer, Richard. "Lester Bangs Recollected in Tranquility." The San Diego Reader, December 6, 1984. https://www.sandiegoreader.com/news/1984/dec/06/lester -recollected-tranquility/

Midsummer Rock, https://www.youtube.com/watch?v=Pf-sDjS8YR8, (accessed January 4, 2021).

Minkema, Kenneth P. "Jonathan Edwards Defence of Slavery." *Massachusetts Historical Review* 4, "Race & Slavery." 2002.

*Mr. Soul!*, Melissa Haizlip, dir. 2020. https://www.pbs.org/independentlens/videos/mr -soul/ (accessed March 10, 2021).

New York Times. "Chris Burden, a Conceptualist with Scars, Dies at 69." https://www .nytimes.com/2015/05/12/arts/chris-burden-a-conceptualist-with-scars-dies-at-69 .html (accessed March 2, 2021).

New York Times. "U.S. Judge William L. Lynch; Was Former Daley Law Partner." Obituary, August 10, 1976. https://www.nytimes.com/1976/08/10/archives/us-judge -william-l-lynch-was-former-daley-law-partner.html (accessed February 1, 2021).

Panofsky, Erwin. *Perspective as Symbolic Form.* Translated by Christopher S. Wood. Zone Books, 1991. [Originally published as "Die Perspektive als Symbolische Form." 1927.]

Pareles, Jon. "After Music Videos, All the World Has Become a Screen." *The New York Times,* December 10, 1989.

Paraino, Judith A. "I'll Be Your Mixtape: Lou Reed, Andy Warhol, and the Queer Intimacies of Cassettes." *The Journal of Musicology* 36, no. 4 (2019): 401–36.

Parvulescu, Anca. "The Professor's Desire." *diacritics* 37, no. 1 (Spring 2007): 32–9.

Piper, Adrian. *Out of Order, Out of Sight, Vol. I: Selected Writings in Meta-Art 1968–1992.* The MIT Press, 1996.

Piper, Adrian. Funk Lessons (video documentation), 1983. http://www.adrianpiper.com /vs/videofl.shtml (accessed March 12, 2021).

Piper, Adrian. Funk Lessons Meta-Performance (video documentation), 1987. (video documentation), 1983. http://www.adrianpiper.com/vs/videoflmp.shtml (accessed March 12, 2021).

Pollitt, Daniel H. "Dime Store Demonstrations: Events and Legal Problems of First Sixty Days." *Duke Law Journal* 3 (Summer, 1960): 315–65.

Powell, Lewis. The Powell Memorandum, August 23, 1971. https://reclaimdemocracy .org/powell_memo_lewis/

Public Image Ltd. "Public Image Ltd.- Poptones & Careering (American Bandstand 1980)." https://www.youtube.com/watch?v=hZLhqTzjpUM

Public Image Ltd. "Public Image Limited (John Lydon) on Tom Snyder 1980 Part 1." https://www.youtube.com/watch?v=OirTyITUJ1Y

Raphael, Tim. "The Body Electric: GE, TV, and the Reagan Brand." *TDR* 53, no. 2 (2009): 113–38.

Reagan Library. "Ronald Reagan's Acceptance Speech at Republican National Convention." July 17, 1980, https://www.youtube.com/watch?v=SBP2gvZTnwM

Red Bull Music Academy. *The Note,* episode 4, "Disco Demolition: Riot to Rebirth." https://www.youtube.com/watch?v=AiDYGlSJY1E (accessed March 15, 2021).

Reynolds, Simon. *Rip It Up and Start Again: Postpunk 1978–1984.* London: Penguin, 2006.

"Rip Torn vs Norman Mailer - The Infamous "Maidstone" Brawl - UNCUT!." https:// www.youtube.com/watch?v=6AzmhorISf4 (accessed January 13, 2021).

Robinson, Cedric. *Black Marxism: The Making of the Black Radical Tradition.* University of North Carolina Press, 2000. [Originally published, 1983.]

Savage, Jon. "What Did You Do On The Jubilee? The Pistols on the Thames." *Sounds,* June 18, 1977.

Sex Pistols. "Live on Boat Trip Queens Jubilee 1977." https://www.youtube.com/watch?v =Mxmj6ahQfNk

Sex Pistols. "The Sex Pistols - Full Concert – 01/14/78 – Winterland (OFFICIAL)." https://www.youtube.com/watch?v=QBVDSz5Qd6g

Scott-Heron, Gil. "The Revolution Will Not Be Televised." *Pieces of a Man*. Flying Dutchman Records, 1971.

Scott-Heron, Gil. Interview, 1990. https://www.openculture.com/2020/06/gil-scott-heron-spells-out-why-the-revolution-will-not-be-televised.html (accessed March 9, 2021).

Shahan, Cyrus. "The Sounds of Terror: Punk, Post-Punk and the RAF after 1977." *Popular Music and Society* 34, no. 3 (July 2011): 369–86.

Slobodian, Quinn. *Globalists: The End of Empire and the Birth of Neoliberalism*. Cambridge: Harvard University Press, 2018.

Smigel, Eric. "'To Behold with Wonder': Theory, Theater, and the Collaboration of James Tenney and Carolee Schneemann." *Journal of the Society for American Music* 11, no. 1 (2017): 1–24.

Smith, Adam. *An Inquiry into the Nature and Causes of the Wealth of Nations*, Book One, Chapter Two. The Modern Library, 1937. https://www.marxists.org/reference/archive/smith-adam/works/wealth-of-nations/, unpaginated.

Smith, Patti. "Gloria." Saturday Night Live, April 17, 1976. https://vimeo.com/155133943

Smith, Tony. "Talking with Tony Smith." Samuel J. Wagstaff. *Artforum*, December, 1966. Quoted in Robert Storr's essay. "A Man of Parts." in MoMA's catalogue of the Tony Smith exhibition (unpaginated).

Stadler, Gustavus. "'My Wife': The Tape Recorder and Warhol's Queer Ways of Listening." *Criticism* 56, no. 3 (Summer 2014): 425–56.

Sterne, Jonathan. *The Audible Past: Cultural Origins of Sound Reproduction*. Duke University Press, 2003.

Temple, Julien. *The Filth and the Fury* (DVD). Film Four, 2000.

Thomas, David C. (director). *MC5: A True Testimonial*, 2002 [unreleased].

Thomas, Samuel. "Yours in Revolution: Retrofitting Carlos the Jackal." *Culture Unbound: Journal of Current Cultural Research* 5 (2013): 451–78.

Thompson, Hunter S. "The Kentucky Derby is Decadent and Depraved." *Scanlan's Monthly* 1, no. 4 (June 1970): unpaginated.

Thompson, Hunter S. *Fear and Loathing in Las Vegas: A Savage Journey to the Heart of the American Dream*. Random House, 1971.

Thompson, Hunter S. "Fear and Loathing at the Super Bowl." *The Great Shark Hunt*, Simon and Schuster 1979. [Originally published in *Rolling Stone*, February 15, 1973.]

Thompson, Hunter S. "Fear and Loathing in the Bunker." The New York Times, January 1, 1978, section L, page 19. https://www.nytimes.com/1974/01/01/archives/fear-and-loathing-in-the-bunker-no-questions-asked-the-cheap-dream.html

Trotsky, Leon. "Art and Politics in Our Epoch." Letters to *Partisan Review* [1938]. https://www.marxists.org/archive/trotsky/1938/06/artpol.htm (accessed February 12, 2021).

U.S. Dept. of Commerce, Bureau of the Census. *Historical statistics of the United States, colonial times to 1970*. Kraus International Publications, 1989.

Veal, Michael. "Starship Africa." In *The Sound Studies Reader*, edited by Jonathan Sterne. Routledge, 2012, pp. 454–67.

Veloso, Caetano. "Speech at 1967 Festival Internacional de Canção." http://tropicalia .com.br/en/identifisignificados/e-proibido-proibir/discurso-de-caetano (accessed March 17, 2021).

Velvet Underground, The. "Beginning to See the Light." *The Velvet Underground*, MGM Records, 1969.

Wald, Gayle. *It's Been Beautiful: Soul! and Black Power Television*. Duke University Press, 2015.

Walker, Daniel. *Rights in Conflict: The Violent Confrontation of Demonstrators and Police in the Parks and Streets of Chicago During the Week of the Democratic National Convention of 1968 (Also Known as "The Walker Report")*, 1968. http://chicago68 .com/ricsumm.html (accessed February 2, 2021).

Warhol, Andy. *The Philosophy of Andy Warhol (From A to B & Back Again)*. Harcourt Brace Jovanovich, 1975.

Willis, Ellen. "Dylan." In *The Essential Ellen Willis*, edited by Nona Willis Aronowitz. University of Minnesota Press, 2014.

Yeginsu, Ceylan. "BBC to Resurrect Full "Rivers of Blood" Speech, Spurring Outrage." *The New York Times*, April 13, 2018. https://www.nytimes.com/2018/04/13/world/ europe/bbc-rivers-of-blood-enoch-powell.html.

# Index

13th Floor Elevators, The (band)   160

ABC (band)   162
ABC (TV network)   40, 69, 188
Abstract Expressionism   8, 15, 41, 43, 49, 50, 52, 145
AC/DC (band)   100
Adorno, Theodor (Teddy)   91
Advisory Panel on the White House Tapes, The   126, 127
Alberti, Leon Battista   180, 181
Alexander, Dave   5
All In The Family (TV show)   42, 77, 78
Altamont (music festival)   143
American Bandstand (TV show)   188–91
Anarchy in the UK Tour, The   157, 165
Anka, Paul   24
Anti-Vietnam War Movement, The   5, 36, 43, 47, 107
Antonioni, Michelangelo   104
Antropófagia   86
Arm of the Arab Revolution, The   93, 97
Arrighi, Giovanni   94
Art & Language (aka Art and Language)   157–61, 163, 166, 168, 172, 173
"Art and Objecthood" (Michael Fried essay)   5, 42, 133, 150
Artaud, Antonin   14, 41, 62
Art of Noise, The (band)   162
Asheton, Ron   2, 5
Asheton, Scott   5
Askey, Arthur   191
Assayas, Olivier   95, 98–100, 108, 109
Atkins, Juan   185
Atkins, Martin   189
Atomic Bomb   21, 67, 179
Attali, Jacques   98

Baader Meinhof Gang, The   107
Baez, Joan   13, 59
Baker, James   137

Baker, Susan   137
Baldwin, James   20–2, 26, 27, 32, 60, 68, 72, 73, 145, 147, 148
Baldwin, Michael   160
Bangs, Lester   10–14, 16, 17, 25, 39, 40, 46, 124, 125, 135, 141, 144, 145, 149–51, 191, 192
Baraka, Amiri (LeRoi Jones)   101–3
Barreto, Luís Carlos   86
Barry, Robert   45, 46
Barthes, Roland   122, 182, 191, 193–5
Basement Tapes, The   125, 126
Battle of Lewisham, The   154
Battle of Michigan Avenue, The   36, 40
Baudelaire, Charles   151
Beach Boys, The   24
Beatles, The   5, 24, 47, 51, 52, 86, 87, 101, 135
Becker, Cacilda   89
Beckett, Samuel   62
Bell, Daniel   21
Belleville Three, The   185
Benjamin, Walter   183
Berger, John   181, 182
Berry, Chuck   24, 102, 146
Berryman, John   66
Big Brother and the Holding Company   56, 186
Bigelow, Kathryn   160
Big Pink   134
Billboard Charts   24, 58, 99
Bin Hassan, Umar   77
Black Flag (band)   136
Black Panther Party, The   5, 29, 37, 103, 107
Black Power Movement, The   37, 107
Black Sabbath   172
Blair, Ezell, Jr.   28
Blankfein, Lloyd   95
Blood, Sweat, and Tears (band)   37
Bloom, Allan   137–9
Blue Cheer (band)   39

Bochner, Mel　45
Booker, James　143, 144
boredom　10, 66, 67
Bossa Nova (music genre)　86
Bourdieu, Pierre　171, 172
Brando, Marlon　23
Branson, Richard　155
Brecht, Bertolt　96, 183
Brin, Sergey　187
British Broadcasting Corporation, The
　　　(BBC)　99, 131, 160, 163,
　　　165, 188
Brown, James　57, 69–73, 81, 90, 92, 194
Brown *vs.* Board of Education　28,
　　　32, 143
Buchloh, Benjamin　140, 141, 146
Buggles, The　184, 185
Burden, Chris　66–8, 73, 125, 126
Burke, Patrick　102–4
Burroughs, William S.　135
Bustillos, Maria　144
Butler, Judith　96, 97
Byrd, Joseph　37
Byrds, The　24, 59, 186

Café Bizarre　115
Cage, John　45, 117
Cale, John　115, 121, 124
camera　1–5, 8, 10, 11, 17, 20, 21, 23, 31,
　　　36, 38–42, 44, 45, 51, 56, 58–60,
　　　62, 64, 69, 75–9, 82, 83, 87, 90,
　　　101, 102, 104, 105, 112, 114,
　　　116, 125, 126, 141, 142, 149,
　　　154, 160, 164, 165, 171, 173,
　　　175–8, 183–5, 187–92
Camera Club, The (band)　184
capitalism　9, 10, 17, 25, 30, 36, 43, 46,
　　　52, 53, 86, 87, 93, 94, 99, 100,
　　　106, 107, 109, 120, 143, 144,
　　　146, 149, 153, 158, 161, 163,
　　　181, 193
Caray, Harry　84
Carey, James W.　178
Carlos (Ilich Ramírez Sánchez)　93, 95,
　　　97, 99, 100, 107–9
Cartesianism　180, 181, 184
Cash, Johnny　24
Castro, Fidel　60

CBS (TV network)　40, 77, 175
Chambers Brothers, The　186
Chaney, James　77
Chaplin, Charlie　60, 65
Charts (Record Sales). *See* Billboard
　　　Charts
Checker, Chubby　29, 30, 51
Chess, Leonard　25
Chess, Phil　25
Chess Records　24, 25, 102
Chicago　24, 25, 35–8, 40, 81–5, 90, 102,
　　　106, 129, 137, 143, 153
Chicago, Judy　47
Chicago House (music genre)　83, 84
Chicago White Sox　82, 83
Cincinnati Pop Festival (1970)　2, 4,
　　　9–12, 119, 123, 189, 191
Civil Rights Movement, The　5, 29, 47,
　　　74, 106, 107, 179
Clark, Dick　188
Clark, Petula　24
Clash, The (band)　99, 136, 157
Classix Nouveaux (band)　164
Cleaver, Eldridge　13, 29–33, 101–3, 106
Clinton, George　81
Coca-Cola　57, 58, 98
Cold War, The　36, 100, 107
Coleman, Ornette　60
Collins, Bootsy　72
Collins, Catfish　72
Colonization　11, 27, 28, 35, 47, 52, 53,
　　　66, 86, 93, 94, 96, 97, 100, 103,
　　　106, 107, 149
Comiskey Park　82–4
Community Reinvestment Act of 1977,
　　　The　80
Conceptual Art　45, 46, 51, 66, 79–81,
　　　117, 118, 134, 135, 150, 157–61,
　　　163, 172, 173
Cook, Paul　187
Coon, Caroline　141, 154, 155
Cooper, Al　37
Cooper, Alice　10–14, 40
Coppola, Francis Ford　104, 108
Cosell, Howard　151
Costa, Gal　88
Country Joe and the Fish　37
Crass (band)　99

Cream (band) 186
Creem Magazine 12
Cronkite, Walter 5, 74

Dada 157
Dahl, Steve 83–5
Daley, Richard J. 35, 36, 83
Damned, The (band) 157
Daniels, Charlie 186
Danko, Rick 125
Dargis, Manohla 99, 100
Dave Clark Five, The 24
Davis, Angela 148
Dead Boys, The 95, 96
de Andrade, Oswald 86
de Assis, Chico 89
Deaver, Michael 177
Debord, Guy 1, 183
Declaration of New International
    Economic Order, The
    (1974) 94, 100
de Kooning, Willem 49
Deleuze, Gilles 122
Dellinger, Dave 36
Democratic National Convention, The
    (1968) 35, 143
Derrida, Jacques 91, 99, 123, 166, 167
Detroit 2, 38, 40, 73, 143, 148, 153
Detroit Tigers 82
Dezeuze, Anna 52
Diddley, Bo 24, 102
Didion, Joan 55, 56, 61, 68, 129
Diggers, The 41
Dimon, Jamie 95
Disco (music genre) 82–5, 90, 92, 162
"Disco Demolition" 83–5, 90, 92
D.O.A. (film) 23, 24
Dobson, James 137
Documenta '72 (exhibition) 158
Dodd, Ken 191
Doors, The (band) 108, 186
Downes, Geoff 184
Dubček, Alexander 85
Du Bois, W.E. B. 147
Duchamp, Marcel 158
Dunn, Christopher 86–8
Dunson, Frederick 83, 85
Durgnat, Raymond 104

Dylan, Bob 5, 24, 56, 57, 59–66, 73, 86,
    90, 125, 134, 147, 187

Edwards, Jonathan 7, 8, 53, 133–6, 138,
    139, 141, 142, 144
Eisenhower, Dwight 130
electricity 25, 26, 37, 59, 88, 123, 138,
    148, 175
Elektra Records 40
Ellsberg, Daniel 119, 132
Elshaw, Gary 105
Enlightenment, The 3, 5, 6, 9, 30, 31, 49,
    142, 180, 181
Entryism 162, 163
Épater la Bourgeoisie 14, 139
Eshun, Kodwo 136, 145, 146
Evers, Medgar 77
Exploding Plastic Inevitable, The
    (EPI) 113, 115

Factory, The (Warhol studio) 114, 115
Fall, The (band) 136
Falwell, Jerry 137
Faubus, Orval 143
Federal Communication Commission,
    The (FCC) 153, 176
Federal Home Loan Bank Board, The 80
Feelies, The 95–8, 100, 108
Festival Internacional de Canção
    (1968) 88, 89, 91
Festival of Life, The 36–8
Flavin, Dan 135
Fluxus 43, 46, 47, 157
Foster, Hal 139–42, 155
Four Tops, The 24
Frankie Knuckles Foundation, The 83
Franklin, Aretha 147–9, 163, 164
Freedom 22, 24, 27, 28, 42, 58, 72, 87,
    94, 120, 129, 145–8, 154, 171
Fried, Michael 5–10, 13, 15, 17, 22, 26,
    27, 31, 32, 37, 39–43, 45, 46, 48,
    50, 58, 65, 66, 133, 134, 137–9,
    141, 142, 145, 150
Friedman, Milton 95
Fugs, The 44

Gaedel, Eddie 82
Gamson, David 164

Gang of Four (band)   98, 99, 157
Garbo, Greta   65
Gartside, Green   99, 157, 159, 160, 162–73
Gary Lewis and The Playboys   24
Geithner, Timothy   95
General Electric Television Theater   175–7
Genovese, Kitty   68
Gil, Gilberto   86, 88–90
Gilberto, João   86
Ginn, Greg   136
Ginsberg, Allen   60
Gleason, Jean   63
Gleason, Ralph   62
Gobbing   185–7
Godard, Jean-Luc   57, 98, 100–8
Gold Standard, The   106
Goldstein, Patrick   150
Gore, Al   137
Gore, Lesley   52
Gore, Tipper   137
Graham, Dan   45, 135–42, 145, 146
Gramsci, Antonio   99, 157, 160, 161, 163, 168, 171
Grateful Dead, The   56, 186
Greenberg, Clement   5, 6, 8, 15, 48–50
Greensboro Four, The   28
Greenspan, Alan   95
Guess Who, The (band)   120
Gutenberg (printing press)   182
Guthrie, Arlo   37
Guthrie, Woody   60

Haight-Ashbury   55–7, 61
Haizlip, Ellis   74–6, 90
Haldeman, H.R.   127
Hancock, Herbie   185
Hank Ballard and the Midnighters   29
happeningness   66
happenings   13, 42, 43, 45, 46, 48, 65, 66, 70, 71
Harron, Mary   120, 121
Hayek, Friedrich   95
Hell, Richard   68
Helm, Levon   125
Hendrix, Jimi   47, 86, 146
Henry Moore Institute, The   118

Hentoff, Nat   151
Herman's Hermits   24
Hesse, Eva   45
hijacking   97, 125, 126
Hinckle, Warren   132
Hippies   4, 55–7, 100–2
Hobson, Laura Z.   77, 78
Hoffman, Abbie   36–8, 40–6, 48, 51, 58, 62, 66, 72, 90
Hollywood   23, 39
Home Mortgage Disclosure Act of 1975, The   80
Horn, Trevor   184, 185
Hot Dog Stand   37
House, Son   25
Howlin' Wolf   102
Hudson, Garth   125
Human League   162
Hunchback of Notre Dame, The   191
Hutton, Bobby   77

Ian, Janis   37
International Monetary Fund, The (IMF)   96
Isley Brothers, The   120

Jagger, Mick   103
Jaggi, Max   160
Jay, Martin   180, 183
jazz   22–4, 26, 30, 70, 121, 150, 164
Jefferson Airplane, The   47, 186
Jensen, Jerry   65
Jinks, Nial   157, 159, 163
Johns, Jasper   47
Johnson, Lyndon B.   35, 73, 106
Johnson, Robert   25, 101, 134, 155
Jones, Amelia   52, 53
Joplin, Janis   146
Jovem Guarda   86
Joy Division   96
Judd, Donald   6, 43, 45, 57

Kahn, Douglas   117, 118
Kain, Gylan   76
Kalakuta Republic, The   85
Kant, Immanuel   5, 30–2, 49, 91, 92, 122, 139, 150, 166, 180, 182
Kaprow, Allan   42, 43, 45, 48

Kaye, Lenny   142
Kellgran, Gary   120
Kelly, Mary   47
Kennedy, John F. (JFK)   35, 47, 60, 102,
      130, 131
Kennedy, Robert F. (Bobby)   35, 45, 47,
      102, 106, 117, 118
Kerouac, Jack   26
Keynesianism   98
Kiesinger, Kurt-Georg   107
King, Martin Luther, Jr.   28, 29, 47, 106
Kingsmen, The   39, 120
Kinks, The (band)   135
Kiss (band)   40
Kosuth, Joseph   45
Kozlov, Christine   45, 117–19, 127
KQED (TV station)   62–4, 90
Kraftwerk   185
Král, Ivan   142
Kramer, Hilton   118
Kramer, Wayne   38, 39
Kristeva, Julia   122
Kristofferson, Kris   146, 147
Kuti, Fela   85

Lacan, Jacques   168
land art   46
LaRue, Ray   23
Last Poets, The   75–8
Lawrence, Vince   83–5
Lear, Norman   78
Led Zeppelin   47, 100, 182
Lee, Ann   136, 140, 141
Legendary Guitar Amp Tape,
      The   124, 125
Lescoulie, Jack   2–4, 9, 15, 31, 32, 191
Lethem, Jonathan   70–2
Levene, Keith   189
Lewis, Jerry Lee   24, 146
LeWitt, Sol   45, 79, 80, 135
Linich, Billy (aka Billy Name)   115
literalism   6, 9, 48, 66
Little Richard   24, 52, 99, 157, 171
Long, Loretta   76
Lumiere Brothers, The   185
Lutjeans, Phyllis   125
Lydon, John (aka Johnny Rotten)   154,
      187–92

Lyotard, Jean-François   46, 122, 125, 142

McCain, Franklin   28
Macomba Lounge   25
McLaren, Malcolm   155, 156, 186,
      187, 190
McLuhan, Marshall   40, 41
McNeil, Joseph   28
McShine, Kynaston   116
Magnetic Tape   45, 91, 102–4, 106,
      111–13, 116–19, 121, 124–7, 129
Mahogany Rush (band)   186
Maidstone (film)   19–21
Mailer, Norman   19–24, 26, 27, 30, 32,
      37, 42, 58, 66, 68, 72, 192
Malcolm X   47, 60
Manet, Édouard   158
Mangold, Robert   45
Mann, Claude   63
Manuel, Richard   125
Manzoni, Piero   91, 158
Maoism   101–3
March on the Pentagon (1967)   43–6
Marcus, Greil   61, 95–7, 100, 106,
      108, 109, 134, 135, 137, 139,
      142, 145
Marcuse, Herbert   154
Marx, Karl   7
Marxism   82, 98, 101, 107, 157, 158, 161,
      163, 168
May, Derrick   185
May '68 (France)   47, 106, 123, 154
MC5, The   37–40
Mekons, The   157
Melody Maker, The   99
Meltzer, Eve   116, 118
Meltzer, Richard   150, 151
Melvin, Jo   118
Memphis   24, 186
Merkel, Angela   95
Merzbow   155, 172
Metz, Christian   183
microphone   9, 14, 25, 62, 64, 89, 101,
      103–5, 111–14, 124, 126, 148,
      149, 164, 173, 185, 189–91
Midsummer Rock   2, 4, 10, 14
Miller, Perry   7, 8
Miller, Roger   146

minimalism 6, 8, 42, 43, 45, 46, 48, 90, 133, 135, 155
Minor Threat (band) 135
Mises, Ludwig von 95
Mitchell, Joni 187
Moby Grape 186
modern 1–3, 6, 10, 11, 17, 26, 42, 46, 48, 58, 87, 119, 125, 133, 138, 175, 176, 182, 184
modernism 2–10, 13–15, 22, 43, 46–50, 52, 53, 65, 66, 86, 90, 98, 120, 122, 133, 134, 140, 150, 155, 158, 182, 184
modernity 2, 3, 5, 36, 82, 87
Modern Life 4, 24, 27, 46, 47, 91, 121, 142, 143, 177, 181–3, 185, 191, 192, 194
Monet, Claude 140
Montgomery, Wes 164
Moore, Thurston 182
Morley, Tom 157, 159, 163
Moroder, Giorgio 185
Morris, Robert 6, 8, 43, 65, 140
Morrison, Sterling 115, 120, 121
Morrison, Van 144, 151
Morrissey, Paul 114
Mothers of Invention, The (band) 186
Motherwell, Robert 140, 158
Motown Records 24
Mountain (band) 4
MTV 177–9, 184, 185
Museum of Modern Art, The (New York) 13, 116
Música Popular Brasileira (MPB) 86–8
Musique Concrete 112

Nader, Ralph 154
Nancarrow, Conlon 172
National Advisory Commission on Civil Disorders, The (Kerner Commission) 73, 74
National Guard, The 47, 143
National Mobilization Committee to End the War in Vietnam (MOBE) 36, 43
NBC (TV network) 40
Nelson, David 75–7
Neoliberalism 17, 95–8, 108, 154

Neutral, The (Barthes) 122, 193–5
New Jersey Turnpike 6, 32, 50
Newman, Barnett 9, 49
New Musical Express, The (NME) 99, 172
New Order (band) 95, 96, 99, 100
Newport Folk Festival, The 57
New York Stock Exchange 41, 43, 44
New York Times, The 36, 66, 77, 78, 118, 130, 178
Nilija 76
Nixon, Richard 68, 93, 98, 106, 119, 125–7, 129–32, 143–5, 153
Nobel Prize for Literature, The 57, 59
Nolen, Jimmy 71

O'Brien, Edmund 23
Ochs, Phil 37, 63
Oiticica, Hélio 86
Olitski, Jules 8
Organization of Petroleum Exporting Countries, The (OPEC) 93, 94, 97, 99, 107
Os Mutantes 88, 89
Oswald, Lee Harvey 102
Oyewole, Abiodun 76, 77

Page, Larry 187
Palestine Liberation Organization, The (PLO) 107
Palmer, Robert 71
Panofsky, Erwin 179–81
Paraino, Judith 112
Pareles, Jon 178
Parents Music Resource Center, The (PMRC) 137
Parker, Charlie 112
Parker, Maceo 70, 71, 73
Parliament-Funkadelic 72, 81
Partisan Review, The 49
Parvulescu, Anca 193
Peanut Butter 15
Peel, John 160, 163, 166–71
Pentagon Papers, The 119, 132
Pere Ubu (band) 96
Perkins, Carl 24
Perlman, Sandy 135
Pessoa, Fernando 89
Peter, Paul, and Mary 59

Photocopier Machine   45, 118, 119
Pie (in the face)   12, 13, 16
Pigasus   37
Pilkington, Philip   160
Pink Floyd   186
Piper, Adrian   47, 79, 84, 90, 92
Pitchford, Russell   76
Plastic People of the Universe, The   85
Plato   166
Pollock, Jackson   41, 45, 48, 49, 52, 65
Pontius Pilate   102
Pop, Iggy   2–5, 9–11, 14–16, 27, 31, 42,
          43, 47, 90, 114, 119, 123, 124,
          186, 189, 191, 192, 194
Post, Rollin   64
Post-Punk (music genre)   95–100, 106,
          108, 109, 135, 162
Poststructuralism   142
Pound, Ezra   65, 98
Powell, Enoch   103
Powell, Lewis   153, 154
Prague Spring, The   36, 47, 85, 106, 153
Presley, Elvis   24, 30, 52, 114, 138
"Press Conference Bob Dylan"   62–5, 90
Primitives, The   105
Procul Harum   186
Public Image Ltd. (PiL)   188, 190, 191
Punk (music genre)   68, 96–100, 106,
          109, 154–7, 159, 162, 165, 185–9
Pyś, Pavel   118

Quarrier, Iain   102, 105
Queen Elizabeth (boat)   155, 156
Queen Elizabeth (monarch)   155
Question Mark and the Mysterians   39
Quicksilver Messenger Service   56, 186

radio   6, 24, 25, 47, 59, 109, 114, 115,
          156, 163, 184, 185, 194
Ramones, The   194
Rancière, Jacques   183
Randolph Street Gallery   81
Ransome-Kuti, Funmilayo   85
Raphael, Tim   175–8
Rauschenberg, Robert   47, 160
Reagan, Nancy   176
Reagan, Ronald   95, 100, 108, 137, 153,
          154, 175–9

Red Army, The   107
Red Army Faction, The (RAF)   99, 107
Red Brigades, The   107
Red Krayola, The (band)   160–2
Redding, Otis   149
Reed, Lou   115, 120, 124, 125, 150
Regan, Donald   177
Reich, Steve   60
Renaissance Perspective   3, 149,
          179–81, 184
Reynolds, Simon   98, 157, 179
Richard III   191
Richmond, David   28
Ricks, Christopher   59
Righteous Brothers, The   24
Rimbaud, Arthur   57, 136
Robertson, Robbie   125
Robinson, Cedric   82
Rock and Roll   3, 9, 10, 12, 16, 17, 22–7,
          30, 39, 40, 43, 46, 52, 53, 57–9,
          82, 83, 86, 90, 91, 96, 97, 102,
          103, 108, 111, 113, 121, 123,
          134, 135, 137, 139, 140, 144–6,
          149–51, 159–62, 169, 177, 179,
          182–4, 186, 191, 192, 194, 195
Rocket from the Tombs   96
rockism   162, 194
Rodgers, Jimmie   24
Rodríguez, Carlos Andrés Pérez   107
Rogers, Kenny   146
Rolling Stone (magazine)   39, 62, 70, 131
Rolling Stones. The (band)   24, 25,
          100–2, 106, 107, 115
Rollins, Henry   136
Rothko, Mark   8
Rough Trade Records   160, 167

Sagan, Carl   172
Sanders, Ed   44
San Francisco Mime Troupe   41
Sarkozy, Nicolas   95
Saunderson, Kevin   185
Savage, Jon   155–7
Schaeffer, Pierre   112
Schleyer, Hanns-Martin   107
Schneemann, Carolee   47, 50–3, 57, 73
Schoenberg, Arnold   65, 172
Scorsese, Martin   108

Scott-Heron, Gil   75
screen(s)   1, 2, 4, 9, 13, 42, 68, 74, 90, 92, 102, 105, 112, 116, 129, 136, 165, 175–7, 179, 182, 183, 186, 188
Scritti Politti   99, 157, 159–73
Scritto's Republic   166, 168, 170
Seeds, The   39, 88
Seldes, Gilbert   134, 135
Sex Pistols, The   154–7, 165, 186–8, 190, 191
Shaggs, The (band)   16, 149
Sherrell, "Sweet" Charles   71
Shklovsky, Viktor   139, 183
Siegelaub, Seth   45, 46
Silver Jubilee   155
Simulacra   1, 183
Sinclair, John   37, 39, 40
Sinclair, Leni   39
Sirhan, Sirhan   102
Situationists, The   104
Slobodian, Quinn   94, 95
Smith, Adam   181
Smith, David   49
Smith, Mark E.   136
Smith, Patti   135, 139–42
Smith, Tony   6, 7, 32
Smithson, Robert   45, 135
Sonic Youth (band)   136
Sonny and Cher   24, 59
Sotheby's   156
Soul! (TV program)   74–8, 90
Spandau Ballet (band)   164
Spectacle   1, 10, 88, 183, 187, 192
Stadler, Gustavus   114–16
Staple Singers, The   59
Starks, John "Jabo"   69, 71–3
Steadman, Ralph   132
Stein, Gertrude   7, 65
Steinberg, David   69
Sterne, Jonathan   111, 117, 118
Stooges, Iggy and the   2, 3, 5, 10, 11, 13, 14, 16, 22, 43, 47, 48, 89, 124, 187, 192
Streeter, James   23
structuralism   142, 193
Strummer, Joe   99, 136
Stubblefield, Clyde   69, 71–3

Students for a Democratic Society (SDS)   36
Studio 54   120
Styx (band)   186
Summer of Love   55, 106, 143, 144
Summers, Lawrence   95
Sun Records   24
Supremes, The   24, 52

Talking Heads (band)   98, 157
Tangerine Dream   185
tape recorder   102–4, 111–13, 116, 119, 127
Teenagers   24, 40, 53, 99, 101, 139, 141, 154, 155
Teer, Barbara Ann   75
television (TV)   1–4, 10, 35, 57, 62, 69, 73–8, 83, 87, 88, 90, 91, 95, 109, 116, 119, 125, 126, 129, 142, 153, 163, 165, 175–8, 183, 185, 186, 188
Temple, Julien   154, 191
Temptations, The   24
Terrell, Tami   120
terrorism   93, 95–7, 99, 106–9, 125, 126
Thatcher, Margaret   95, 100, 108, 153, 154, 163
Thompson, Hunter S.   129–33, 143, 144
Thompson, Mayo   160
Thunders, Johnny   157
Till, Emmett   77
Top of the Pops   163–6, 168, 169, 188
Torn, Rip   19, 20
Traffic (band)   4, 186
Tropicália   86–8, 90
Trotsky, Leon   49, 50, 161
Tucker, Maureen "Mo"   121, 124
TV Eye (Stooges song)   2, 3, 10
Twist, The (Chubby Checker song)   29, 30, 33, 51
Tyner, Rob   40

Ukeles, Mierle Laderman   47
United States of America, The (band)   37
United States Supreme Court, The   28, 32, 33, 153
Up Against The Wall Motherfuckers, The   41
U.S Chamber of Commerce, The   153

Veal, Michael 72
Veeck, Bill 82
Veloso, Caetano 86–91, 123
Velvet Underground, The 47, 60, 67, 105, 113, 115, 120–4, 194
Vietnam War, The 5, 35, 36, 68, 94, 107, 133, 144
Visage (band) 164

Wald, Gayle 74, 75, 77
Walker Report, The 36
Wallace, George 143
Warhol, Andy 45, 57, 112–20, 139
War on Terror, The 100
Warwick, Dionne 120
Watergate 125, 153
Waters, Muddy 24, 25, 65, 101, 123, 187
Weather Underground, The 107
Weber, Max 96
Weill, Eric 62, 63
Wesley, Fred 71, 73
West, Leslie 4
White House, The 33, 119, 127, 129, 132, 143
"White Negro, The" (Norman Mailer essay) 20, 21, 26, 68
White Panther Party, The 37
Who, The (band) 186
"The Whole World Is Watching" 35, 36, 129

Wiazemsky, Anne 101, 105
Wichard, Al "Cake" 23
Wild One, The (film) 23
Williams, Marion 75
Willis, Ellen 57, 58, 60, 63
Willis, Gary 178
Winwood, Stevie 4
Wire (band) 95–8, 100, 108, 109, 157
WLWT (TV station) 2–4, 10, 90, 119
Wobble, Jah 189, 190
Wood, Christopher 179
Woods, Rose Mary 127
Woodstock (music festival) 143
Woolley, Bruce 184
Working drawings and other visible things on paper not necessarily meant to be viewed as art (exhibition) 45
World Trade Organization, The (WTO) 96

Yes (band) 184
Young, Neil 187
Young, Whitney 78
Youth International Party, The (Yippie!) 36, 37, 43, 44
YouTube 2, 3, 12, 19, 63, 69, 70

Zé, Tom 88
Zion, Sidney E. 132

Printed in the USA
CPSIA information can be obtained
at www.ICGtesting.com
LVHW051228300723
753743LV00005B/219

9 798765 101315